What People Believe When They Say That People Believe

What People Believe When They Say That People Believe

Folk Sociology and the Nature of Group Intentions

Todd Jones

LEXINGTON BOOKS
A division of
ROWMAN & LITTLEFIELD PUBLISHERS, INC.
Lanham • Boulder • New York • Toronto • Plymouth, UK

Published by Lexington Books
A division of Rowman & Littlefield Publishers, Inc.
A wholly owned subsidary of The Rowman & Littlefield Publishing Group, Inc.
4501 Forbes Boulevard, Suite 200, Lanham, Maryland 20706
www.lexingtonbooks.com

Estover Road, Plymouth PL6 7PY, United Kingdom

British Library Cataloguing in Publication Information Available

Library of Congress Cataloging-in-Publication Data

Jones, Todd E.
  What people believe when they say that people believe : folk sociology and the nature
of group intentions / Todd Jones.
    p. cm.
  ISBN 978-0-7391-4820-4 (cloth : alk. paper) — ISBN 978-0-7391-4822-8 (electronic)
  1. Public opinion. 2. Social groups—Public opinion. 3. Belief and doubt. 4. Social
science—Research—Evaluation. I. Title.
  HM1236.J66 2010
  303.3'8—dc22   2010028154

Printed in the United States of America

Contents

v

Acknowledgements

This book has been a long time coming. I can truly say that I have been confused by people saying things like "What the American people really want is . . ." since I was a little kid. This book is my attempt to find answers to the questions about what people mean by such phrases. I began working on the book in earnest during a sabbatical from the University of Nevada, Las Vegas in 1997–1998. It's only now, a dozen years later that I am satisfied that I've found answers that I am somewhat happy with.

Far more people have helped me with the book than I can ever begin to thank here. But some people's help is impossible not to mention. I'll begin, where I should begin, with my parents, William and Elaine Jones. They taught me that being confused and curious was not a bad state to be in, and that the most common answers people suggest to me are not necessarily the right ones. While I'm thanking my family, I shouldn't neglect to mention the invaluable contributions from my brother Chad and my sister Marni. Indeed, this book can be looked at as part of an extended argument I've been having with them for decades about what it is and isn't proper to generalize about. I hope this book will provide fuel for discussion with them for decades to come. My sons Liam and Donovan have also been helpful. Despite their youth, they never cease surprising me with quick possible counterexamples to my hypotheses.

In much of this book, I discuss peoples' ideas and intuitions about what is and isn't acceptable to say about groups. This means that often it was often relatives (who have little choice but to put up with me) who were first pestered for their views on these matters. My uncle Edwin Lynch and my aunt Gail Stoudt have graced me with their considered opinion about what is and isn't acceptable to say, and other philosophical matters for several decades now. My wife's family, too, has been very helpful—with sisters Carolyn and Sally and brother Terry providing useful ideas and support. I especially benefitted from extended discussions with my wife's parents, Jack and Rosemary Maloy, about what people consider to be a "norm" or "custom."

Various friends, over the years, have also told me when they've considered my views be right or wrong, and have given me many insightful suggestions about what does and doesn't seem permissible to say, in their circles. Especially noteworthy were the contributions of Kenn Seward, Bruce Goldstone, and Steve Tager.

In the end, however, this book is a work of analytic philosophy, and I certainly benefited from the comments and criticisms of numerous philosophers. I gave talks on the topics discussed in the book for audiences of mostly academic philosophers at places like Gettysburg College, Union College, Hampton-Sydney College, Reed College, City University of New York Graduate Center, the University of Nevada, Reno, the University of Oregon, and the University of Idaho where attendees gave me many useful suggestions. My colleagues at the University of Nevada, Las Vegas have given me a good amount of feedback over the years. Others at UNLV have been supportive as well. Students Shannon Gould and Adam Kennedy were especially helpful, proofreading the entire manuscript, and making many useful suggestions about how to make the prose clearer. Marie Torres, the philosophy department's administrative assistant, has done all kinds of things to make the UNLV Philosophy Department a productive place to work. The people most helpful to me at UNLV, however, have been the numerous students I've had over the years, whom I've tried out ideas on, and who have helped set me right when I seemed to be going astray.

I would also like to thank Rowman and Littlefield editors John Sisk and Jana Wilson for the encouragement they've given me throughout this project. The final version of this book also benefited from the advice of an anonymous referee who provided a number of useful ideas about how to make the book a better one.

Some portions of this book are further developments of essays that first appeared in various journals. Chapter 2 evolved from "How many New Yorkers must like bagels before 'New Yorkers like bagels'? Analyzing collective ascription," which appeared in *Philosophical Forum* 34:3. Chapter 3 evolved from "What CBS wants. How groups can have (difficult to uncover) intentions," which appeared in *Philosophical Forum* 32:3, and from "FIC descriptions and interpretive social science: Should philosophers roll their eyes?" which appeared in *Journal for the Theory of Social Behavior* 29: 4. Chapter 4 evolved from "'We always have a beer after the meeting.' How norms, customs, conventions, and the like explain behavior," which appeared in *Phi-*

losophy of the Social Sciences 36:3. Part of chapter 5 evolved from "Norms and customs can't cause anything," which appeared in the *International Journal of the Social Sciences* 3:6. I'd like to thank the editors of those journals for their comments and suggestions about earlier forms of the arguments that eventually made their way into this book.

Finally I'd like to thank my wife Jacqueline Margaret Mary Maloy for the combination of constructive criticism and unflagging support she's given me for a long, long time. Her keen mind is one I've always wanted to emulate. I've spent a lot of time working on this book and trying to figure out what others believe when they say certain things. But when I really want to know what I should believe and what the right thing to say is, it's been to her I've turned since the moment we met.

Introduction

Statements about Groups: The Problem

"The world is governed, especially in the democratic age, not by the accumulation of money, or even goods, but by the accumulation of opinions. History is formed by, and politics dependent upon, how and what large masses of people are thinking and desiring, fearing and hating."

—John Lukacs, *Democracy and Populism: Fear and Hatred*

Nearly every day I have a peculiar experience. Glancing at a magazine, I will come across a phrase such as this one: "The real goal of the Republicans is to try to get working people to vote based on their prejudices, rather than their economic interests."

For a moment, I will read on, feeling that perhaps I understand American politics a little better than before. But invariably I do a sort of double take. Wait a minute. What was meant by the phrase "the real goal of the Republicans"? There are over fifty million registered Republicans in America; surely they don't all have the same goal. Perhaps the writer wasn't speaking of all or most Republicans, but only party leaders. But if so, why didn't he say so? And how likely is it that the *leaders* all have the same goal? Perhaps the writer wasn't speaking about the feelings of any individual. Maybe he was talking about a general custom held by the group. Or maybe he was saying something more exotic. Perhaps the group Republicans, *as a whole,* has this goal. But can a group (rather than the people in it) really have goals or beliefs? If so, how? I soon find myself feeling like I know less than before I read the sentence, and put down the magazine in frustration.

We read and hear such phrases about the beliefs of groups all the time. During election season their frequency increases dramatically. Over and over we hear phrases like:

"The American people believe that the money they earn is theirs to keep."
"The American people know that we can do better than this."
"The American people think it's time for a change."
"The American people want to do all they can to reduce poverty."
"It's what America wants, not what France or Germany wants, that we should be interested in."

The politicians uttering these phrases seem to be saying something about the beliefs, desires, and actions of some kind of *group of people*. They are not speaking of Bill, Hector, or Jean's desire for change, but the desire of some amorphous entity they call "the American people."

And journalists and pundits too, as in my magazine, are forever talking about "what Americans really want," "what Russia's interest is," or "what the Syrians believe." Throughout their day-to-day lives, people in different professions talk about what the *government* does, or what the *people in Biglerville* think of the new high school. (Notice, I just did it myself in the last sentence—talking about what is said by the group "people in different professions.") Even people trying to do careful social scientific work often speak in this way. It is not uncommon for anthropologists to say things like "Jamaicans rarely eat vegetables other than starchy 'foods'. . ." (Sobo 1993); or for a political scientist to say "Japan has relied much more than the United States on informal mechanisms of social control . . ." (Lipset 1996).

CONFUSION ABOUT GROUP STATEMENTS

People clearly talk about the features of groups all the time. But statements like "The university thinks the state doesn't really care if it loses money," immediately present us with a number of difficulties. The casualness and commonality of these sorts of statements belie their complexity. We say things like "corporate executives have a custom of having drinks with lunch" or "avoiding reading is part of teenage culture," without clearly understanding what kind of thing a custom or a culture is, or how such things can causally interact with individuals. We talk about Japan wanting to avoid a tariff war, without a good picture of what it means for a *country* to want something. Understanding the social situations described by these statements is much more difficult than one might initially think. And along with the problems we have in understanding what *external* social situations people are describing with such statements, we also have difficulties understanding what *speakers believe* when they make these statements. In English, statements that an X group of some kind believes or does some Y are not only vague (how many X members are there?), but they are systematically ambiguous. I think it's useful to divide what "the X do Y" statements describe into three (overlapping) families of situations. When a doctor says something like "Canada loves to find more ways to treat its citizens paternalistically," she might be saying merely that *many* Canadians act this way. She might be saying that Canada acts as some kind of unitary intentional agent, with a desire to treat its citizens as children. Or she might be saying that there is a cultural norm of paternalistic government in Canada.

The first interpretation points to a common family of meaning for X-do-Y statements in which the claim is about a number of *individuals within* the X group. In ordinary discourse, we constantly say things like "New Yorkers feel less secure after 9/11," to talk about the attributes of individuals within a group. When we say things like "the French prefer wine to beer," we are usually saying that individuals in France are disposed to prefer wine. Surprisingly few scholars have looked at the *different* things that can (and can't) be meant by various statements about the individuals in groups, or how such statements differ from other statements about groups. Our default linguistic rule regarding things we refer to as *"the* X," rather than "some X" or "twelve X," is that we are saying something about *all* or most of the people in the group. Yet we quite often use such phrases when far fewer than most members of the group engage in a certain practice. In chapter 2 of this book, I'll discuss claims about groups that are really about the individuals in it, the five main *exceptions* to the rule that "the X" means *all* the X, and how these exceptions develop on the basis of both cognitive processes and social practices.

A second way we interpret X-do-Y statements is quite different. We make statements like "Mattburgers are repairing their windows this week," to describe situations in which we think that each adult who lives in Mattburg, Florida is engaged in repairing his or her windows after a severe storm. But we can also use this locution to make a different kind of claim. Sometimes we talk about what groups do, not because each of their members behaves in a *similar* way, but because each group member's actions, together, tend to produce *a unitary net effect.* When we say "Mattburgers are rebuilding their town hall after the storm," we are talking about a situation in which some Mattburgers are manning drill bits, others are pounding nails, and still others are driving for supplies, while others are pouring lemonade for workers. Then we are talking about the activities of the group, not to say anything about what each of the individuals in the group is doing, but to talk about a collection of people (as a whole) producing a unitary net effect.

In my view, there are two main types of claims about groups as a whole. The stronger claims talk about groups as full-blown intentional agents, entities that act and have beliefs and desires in their own right. The weaker claims talk about groups that have unitary effects without necessarily being things with their own goals. In chapter 3 of this work, I will give a theory of what criteria have to be met before an entity can be said to have intentional states like beliefs and desires (where the stronger kinds of claim can be true). I will explain how certain types of groups could meet these criteria for intentionality (e.g., how the Starbucks corporation could have goals.) If they do, then speakers could be saying something literally true when they say something like "CBS is worried that . . ." I will discuss the advantages of talking about groups in intentional terms, and the epistemic difficulties involved in assessing what a group's real intentions are.

A third way we use this "the X-do-Y" locution is to talk about a family of attitudes and activities that are simultaneously *both* individualistic and collectivist. We can use expressions like "Chicagoans wear green on St. Patrick's Day" to talk about the presence of *a custom or a norm*. We can talk about norms or customs without using those terms at all, as in the previous sentence; we can explicitly use these terms; or we can use related terms such as "convention," "tradition," "rule," and "culture." A norm or custom is a collective phenomena, in that it is something that can be possessed only by a group (Bill or the mayor usually can't have a norm). And we mainly speak of a norm when we have a behavior that is caused by group pressure in various ways. At the same time, norms or customs are non-collective in that we don't usually use these terms to talk about a group, as a whole, acting in harmony to do something. When we describe a norm, we describe a situation in which *individual* group members tend to behave in a similar manner. And we typically think of norm-following as one of the main causes of individual behavior.

The study of norms and cultural practices is at the center of the social sciences. They form the basis of what philosopher John Searle (1995) calls "social facts." But exactly what these entities are is surprisingly unclear. In chapter 4 of this book, I will look at the principles underlying all of these terms in what I call the "what's done" family. I will also look at the differences between these terms.

The fact that ambiguous X do Y phrases can be used in English to describe any of the different situations means that when we hear such statements, we don't always automatically know what a speaker is trying to tell us, or what he believes. He might be making any of these three different kinds of claims (or any of their subtypes). Or he might not have any of these particular claims in mind. He may merely have a vague notion that Y-doing is being practiced by a certain number of X group members. Having a language where vague and ambiguous social terms are frequently employed does not encourage people to make sharp distinctions before they speak. The situation is further confused by the fact that different social arrangements might actually be present *simultaneously*. Suppose that during a political revolution, a popular practice begins whereby mobs regularly gather outside of prisons and free the prisoners inside. Here, the mob *as a whole* may be acting as a unitary agent, using multiple means to try to reach a goal. At the same time, *each member* of the mob is trying to free prisoners inside. And if any group member tries to stop the break-in, he or she might be scorned by the others, indicating that the group has developed a *norm* of prison breaking. Being told that the X do Y, then, may not tell us much about what a speaker believes or what social situations are there, unless we make a careful effort to decipher the statements. And social scientific statements can often be in as much need of decipherment as ordinary statements. Social scientists often use the same vocabulary for talking about groups that people in everyday life do, such as when anthropologist Evans Prichard says things like "The Nuer believe that twins are birds," or when historian Paul Johnson says things like "Russia wanted to make sure Germany would never rise again." Terms like "customs," "norms," and "culture" are also used in both scholarly and everyday vocabulary.

The fact that such statements are vague and ambiguous has led many to be suspicious and dismissive of statements about groups. But I don't believe we can afford to wait for a utopian future in which our language has been reformed so that only the clearest of terms remain. These statements are made very often and are used by people to think about and plan social actions. Rather than just dismissing such statements, we need to make an effort to really understand what people mean when they make them. One of the aims of this book is to differentiate the kinds of things people might be saying about the social world while describing it with similar phrases. This should help us start avoiding the confusions that can come from not clearly understanding what is being claimed about the social world. Studying such statements can also help clarify what they can and cannot tell us about the external social situations that the statements purport to describe.

PROFESSIONAL FAILURES TO
UNDERSTAND WHAT PEOPLE MEAN

Over the years there's been much discussion in the scholarly literature concerning claims about groups. Not infrequently, a social scientist will define her terms in the beginning of an article, specifying what she will mean by "norm" or "convention." Sometimes a social scientist will devote an entire article to theoretical questions like those concerning what culture really is. And there has been interesting recent work discussing the different ways people can operate cooperatively by philosophers such as Christina Bicchieri, Margaret Gilbert, Michael Bratman, Raimo Tuomela, Seaumus Miller, and Christopher Kutz. But there has not been much focus on the problem of what ordinary people *believe* when they make statements about the social world. There is often failure to note the ambiguity of X-do-Y statements. A good understanding of social claims must begin by differentiating between claims made about groups as a whole, claims made about individuals in the group, and claims that simultaneously refer to both—and this is something that has not, to my knowledge, been given a lot of attention by philosophers. As we have been discussing, the difference between these various sorts of claims is not a distinction noted in ordinary language. Perhaps the failure of philosophers to commonly note this distinction is an example of what Wittgenstein described as being "bewitched" by the surface form of a language: thinking that the way things are said reveals deep metaphysical principles that are not really there. The surface form of English, indeed, often does not make distinctions between very different ways of thinking about groups. A sentence like "Serbia regrets ever having let Albanians settle in Kosovo," for example, looks as though it expresses a single proposition. But this same sentence is one that is acceptable for expressing three very different propositions. The speaker might be saying something about the country, Serbia, as a unitary agent; about the customs and practices of Serbs; or about the feelings of most individual Serbs. Even specific terms like "norm" can refer both to situations where there is routine behavior with little social pressure (e.g., a norm of putting salt on spaghetti), and where there is social pressure without corresponding routine behavior (e.g., handwriting thank-you notes for gifts).

One result of not distinguishing between these classes is that the important category of group ascription claims that refers to the attributes of *individuals in the group* are barely discussed at all in any of the works described above. Philosopher Raimo Tuomela, for example, is typical in not recognizing this as an important category for social theorizing. Writes Tuomela: "A mere aggregate of facts about people having the same attitude (say fear) is not fully social, because it lacks an appropriate doxastic connection between the participants" (2002, 24). This dismissal is unfortunate. It is especially important to understand how such individualistic group ascription claims function as: a) they use the same terminology as other types of group claims and it is important to understand exactly how they differ from them, and b) a *majority* of claims about groups are probably in this category. This book will hopefully improve our understanding of the underlying nature of different types of collective ascription claims, and how such claims do and do not overlap.

If one problem with contemporary discussions of claims about groups is that philosophers mirror ordinary language use in glossing over important distinctions among social phenomena, another is that they often do the opposite. Philosophers frequently give narrow technical definitions, without enough regard for how ordinary speakers (or social scientists) use social terms. Much of the most prominent recent philosophical work in the area talks about how the social world works, not using familiar terms from ordinary language and in the social sciences but using special new terms-of-art coined by philosophers such as "plural subject," "joint action," "social action," and "institutional facts" (see, for example, Gilbert 1989; Searle 1995; Miller 2001; Tuomela 2002). And when philosophers do look at more familiar social concepts, they often look past what ordinary speakers and social scientists typically mean by these concepts and focus on the actual underlying *ontology* of the entities described. When someone asks, "What is a custom?" there are at least three different ways one might try to answer the question. One might try to specify what most *experts* have in mind when they use the term (the definition or meaning of "custom"). One could try to describe how the term is *used most often* in ordinary discourse. Or one might try to precisely specify what kinds of *conditions in the world are being referred to* when people use that term (the ontology of customs). Many of these philosophers looking at social phenomena tend to gravitate toward the third project. This is unsurprising. The underlying ontology of customs or conventions (or joint action) is not well understood in the way that the underlying ontology of dishwashers or suburbs is. So there is much important philosophical clarification to be done there. The result is that philosophers often speak about customs or conventions defined in a more clear and consistent *reformed* manner, than the way these terms are ordinarily used.

There is definitely something worthwhile in these sorts of projects. We certainly want to get the most accurate and clear picture of the social world that we can. But the sorts of reforming projects that philosophers of social science are enamored of can create confusion as well. Anytime scholars use terms in different ways, it can cause confusion. And the more a term diverges from ordinary or social scientific usage (even if the divergence is in the service of more consistency), the more difficult it is for readers to initially know what is being referred to. There are also many reasons we want to know about the meanings of these terms as they are actually used, however unclearly or inconsistently. We not only want to know how norm-like structures directly affect behavior, we want to know what people *believe* about norms. These beliefs not only affect the way people understand and explain the social world, they also affect how people behave. In focusing largely on underlying ontology, philosophers can miss important facets of how these notions are used by people to make sense of the social world.

In general, the commitment of many philosophers to giving a *reforming and clarifying* account of the mechanics of the social world (perhaps in response to the lack of clarity of many traditional social scientific terms) can prevent them from being more helpful in enabling us to understand how people commonly try to describe and explain behavior using more familiar concepts and terminology. These philosophical works on the social world, then, leave problematic social explanations still mysterious. Despite the numerous attempts in various disciplines to define and clarify norms, conventions, culture, and other social terms and claims, we still don't understand them very well.

In this book, I hope to help improve this situation. I want to spend much more time looking at how people use social concepts to understand their world, both in ordinary discourse and in the social sciences. I approach this project of understanding what people mean when they make statements about the social world from my position as a professor of philosophy. The central way in which I've worked on this project harkens back to a manner of doing philosophy that was very common from the 1940s to the 1970s but has been much less in fashion since then. "Ordinary language philosophy," as it was called, looked carefully at the way "regular people" use certain terms, often in contrast to how philosophers or other scholars used them (see Ebersole 1979; Cook 1980). Ordinary language philosophers often looked at their own term usages in everyday contexts and at their intuitions about how a term ought to be used, according to the rules of English. They believed that much could be learned by looking at everyday word usage this way, in contrast to thinking about the meaning that academics give such terms. As I discuss in the next chapter, I utilize many of the techniques of ordinary language philosophy to look at how people actually use terms about groups. But I've used many other sources of information as well. For example, I've conducted many surveys and had many discussions with people about the terms they use to describe terms. I've also thought carefully about what *inner belief structures* are most likely to be present when such statements are made. I have a PhD in cognitive science in addition to my philosophy degree and that has made me very cognizant of the importance of making use of contemporary cognitive science when ascribing beliefs to people. (See Jones 2000a and 1991 for discussions of why using information from cognitive science is very important in modeling people's beliefs.) Besides looking at how ordinary people talk and think about groups, I've also paid a lot of attention to how *social scientists* write and talk about groups. Before going into philosophy, I got a masters degree (and completed all the coursework for a PhD) in anthropology. I did field-work among the Gaenes of Nepal. And I've continued to monitor the work of many different scholars discussing the social realm as a member of the Cultural Studies Committee at the University of Nevada, Las Vegas. Hope-fully, my background puts me in a good position to have some insights about what people from various walks of life mean when they make different sorts of "the X people do Y" statements.

WHY SHOULD WE CARE ABOUT THE MEANING OF SOCIAL STATEMENTS?

I've said that it is hard to know what people believe when they make state-ments about groups. Such statements are often ambiguous. And philosophical and social scientific attempts to clarify such statements often don't make fine grained distinctions between very different social situations, or make distinc-tions that are more fine grained than ordinary language, leaving ordinary statements unexplored. Many people clearly have some awareness of the lack of clarity of such statements. Our awareness of our lack of clarity is readily apparent in the number of philosophical and social scientific works that go out of their way to try to carefully define and clarify social terms. But we also see evidence of this awareness in a commonly expressed *distaste* for general statements about groups in everyday discourse. We often express disapproval of statements that seem to imply *all* group members do something. "Don't generalize" is a commonly heard criticism when someone comments about a group. The psychologist Perry Hinton writes that stereotyping, a common subtype of talking about groups in a general way, "is viewed as indicating a flaw in human nature, as 'evidence of the unfinished mind'" (2000, 68).

Yet, we want to do more than just dismiss group claims. The three fami-lies of meanings for X-do-Y statements represent three kinds of situations that are especially important for people to know about. People want to know what lots of the individuals around them tend to do (and believe). They want to know what the net effect of a lot of individuals acting will be. And they want to know which kinds of activities will be praised or punished by the group. People making X-do-Y statements are trying to tell each other about these situations. But what, exactly, are they trying to tell each other? When speakers say, "Catholics don't believe in using birth control," what do they believe? Do they think that *all* Catholics believe birth control is wrong? Are they saying that this is part of Catholic doctrine? And what is it that *listeners* typically believe upon hearing such statements? While these statements might well be vague and imprecise, we still want to know what people believe about their social surroundings, and these expressions can provide some clues. People make plans for the future based on their beliefs about what group members will do. They also make plans based on their understandings of how groups have caused things in the past. They make moral judgments based on their thinking about group causation as well. If we want to better understand why people behave in certain ways, we need to better understand what they *believe* about groups in various circumstances. Looking at what people *say* about their social worlds, and at how what they say is linked to underlying beliefs can be an important part of understanding some central mental causes of behavior.

But besides using such statements to better understanding other people's beliefs about groups, each of us makes plans and makes moral judgments based on our beliefs about how others' actions cause certain results. We, too, want to know what is actually there in various corners of the social world. One possible source of information about social goings on are other people's statements about the social world. We shouldn't just dismiss or ignore what others say. It's better to have a clear idea about how such statements can and can't give us useful information. We want to know when a statement can tell us certain sorts of information about the social world, and when such statements can't be expected to give us much more than information about the mental states of the speakers—if even that. Understanding what such statements can tell us about the world is most valuable when we combine an ability to decipher what people are claiming, with an understanding of the basic metaphysics of how the social world works. In this book, then, we'll look carefully at the relationship between what people say and what is true about the social world. Then we can use such statements to tell us more about what people believe and also tell us about what social circumstances are actually there. With such knowledge, X-do-Y statements could be quite useful to us, rather than just being a source of confusion. Successfully navigating through the world requires understanding what people in the groups around us are doing, and what others think about what they are doing. Knowing how to use the information that other speakers give us is an important part of this. Being clearer about how these social statements work is more than just a matter of reducing our bewilderment when reading popular magazines.

STRUCTURE OF THE BOOK

We see, then, that it is quite important to understand what it is that people are claiming when they say that the X do Y, but also that we frequently do not understand what people are claiming when they say such things. The purpose of this book is to improve that understanding. To that end, the rest of the book is structured as follows: In chapter 1, we'll look carefully at the methods I've used for understanding the kind of statements about groups that this book is about. I'll talk a bit about the methods used to understand the actual social circumstances existing in the world that speakers refer to when they make X-do-Y statements. But the bulk of the chapter will focus on how we can try to uncover peoples' beliefs about social circumstances, based on what they say. Figuring out what people believe on the basis of what they say is no easy feat, and in chapter 1 we'll look at the complex methods and assumptions I'll be using in trying to uncover the beliefs underlying these statements about groups.

In chapters 2, 3, and 3, I will look in detail at the three different major families of X-do-Y claims that I discussed previously. As I noted there, chapter 2 will focus on X-do-Y claims where what is being said is that a number of individuals within the X group tend to do Y. When a teacher says "UNLV students show up late to their final exams," she is talking about individual students. But she is clearly not talking about *all* individual UNLV students. This chapter discusses what a statement about a collective can mean if it's a claim about individuals without necessarily being about all the individuals in the group. Chapter 3 discusses how X-do-Y claims can sometimes be talking about a group as a whole—often as if the group is an intentional agent, as in sentences like "Germany worried about whether Greece had any intention of paying back its loan." In this chapter, I look at whether it is really possible for a group to have a belief that is different from the beliefs of the *members* of the group. I argue that there are conditions under which it may be possible for groups of people to be arranged such that these groups, as a whole, can have its own goals and representations of the world. I also discuss the difficulties involved in knowing which internal states are present in such groups at a given time. Chapter 4 looks at cases in which X-do-Y statements are best interpreted as meaning that the X group has a custom or norm of doing Y, as in sentences like "The Kaska practice cross-cousin marriage." It also looks at sentences where terms like "custom," "norm," or "tradition" are explicitly mentioned. We talk about norms and customs frequently, but exactly what sorts of things they are remains mysterious. What's the role of imitation vis-a-vis social reinforcement in norms? Why do individuals punish other individuals who depart from what's usually done when punishing is costly? In this chapter we'll look at the meanings of various different kinds of norms claims and at the mechanisms that can enable norms to exist in certain environments.

In chapter 5 we move from looking at the various different meanings of X-do-Y statements to the question of how much such statements can really tell us about the *causes* of various social phenomena. X-do-Y statements, be they claims about individuals acting in a similar manner, a group acting as a unitary whole, or a group maintaining a norm, often aim to tell us that the X group *causes* a certain phenomena. A major question about group activity concerns just how the kinds of things we talk about in typical group statements *can* cause certain behavioral activities. How can the existence of a social norm of shaking hands when meeting someone cause or explain Bill's shaking hands when meeting Bob? Can CBS's desire for a younger audience causally explain what anchorperson got hired for the nightly news? Such questions are much harder to answer than one might think. In chapter 5, I look at questions of whether and how knowledge about norms, whole groups, or sets of individuals enables us to explain social behavior that we want to explain.

Whether or not we can use our beliefs about groups to explain behaviors is a question for social metaphysics about the nature of relationships between features, but it is also an epistemological question about what we can know when. Chapter 6, the final chapter of this book, looks further at epistemic questions regarding groups. If there are difficulties using group statements to explain what happens, what good are such statements? How informative can nonexplanatory statements be if they are as vague and ambiguous as I will be claiming they are? And isn't there something wrong with statements such as "black people are good athletes" just in virtue of their being stereotypical? I'll discuss these and other epistemological questions about group statements in this chapter.

In chapter 6, I'll also look at some ethical questions that often arise regarding statements about groups, especially statements involving stereotypes. Among Americans, there's often a feeling that there is something morally wrong with making sweeping generalizations about collections of people. Most of the worries are based on the idea that, whether negative generalizations about groups are true or not, people's belief in them raises the probability of various harms coming to group members. These harms can run the gamut from the psychological harm done to an individual simply by being looked at with suspicion all the way to genocidal ethnic cleansing. But, while the fact that negative generalizations can harm people is a strong reason not to make them, it is not automatically a definitive reason not to do so. Some people hold that free expression is a more fundamental value and that people should be able to say whatever they wish about groups. These are important ethical issues about statements about groups that need to be resolved, and I will grapple with them in this final chapter.

To get along in this world, few things are more important to know than what we can expect from the people around us. And the people around us regularly try to help us in this understanding, by making statements about what groups of people do and believe. Statements about what groups do or believe, then, are everywhere in our culture. You can't open a newspaper or look at a website without seeing a comment about what Democrats or Republicans really want. But while we are inclined toward making these statements, it's not clear how we should think about them. While we make such statements often, we are also clearly uneasy with them, and we sometimes scold each other for zealous generalizing. Is there really something morally wrong with X-do-Y statements? How much does the vagueness of such statements limit their informativeness? Can these kinds of statements about groups really explain social situations? In this book, I hope to clarify just what we should make of these ubiquitous social claims. I hope to put us in a position to better understand both what speakers really believe about the social world, and what we can really expect to find there. My wish is that this will help us use peoples' comments about the social world as sources of knowledge or entertainment, rather than as sources of frustration and bewilderment.

Chapter One

Groups Acting and Beliefs about Groups Acting

What We Are Looking For and How We'll Find It

The central problem in this book is to try to figure out what people are saying when they make statements like "Bolivians run up debt." We can divide questions about what people are saying with these sorts of statements into two sorts: 1) questions about what people believe when they make such statements, and 2) questions about the social features that are really in the world. I said in the Introduction that when people make these kinds of statements about Bolivians they might be thinking something about individual Bolivians, or about the dispositions of the country as a whole, or about the customs or norms of Bolivians. The first set of questions concerns which kind of these three things speakers have in mind when they make such statements. The second set of questions looks at what actual collections of people in the world are doing—perhaps beyond what speakers think or know that they are doing. (When a speaker talks about a group having a norm, for example, she might know few details about what is enabling there to *be* a norm in that group.) These questions, of course, overlap with each other considerably. Since people often believe what is actually the case, our knowing what is out there generally goes a long way toward telling us what people believe is out there. Conversely, for many kinds of situations, knowing what people believe about the situation is a pretty good guide to what is true in that situation. In this book, we'll look a bit at both questions. Some chapters focus more on what people believe when they say certain things, while others focus more on external social structures. In the present chapter, we are going to be discussing a) exactly what it means to be looking at questions of the first or second sort, b) which of the sections in the book tend to concentrate on which of these questions, c) what methods and techniques will be used to answer questions about what people believe and what is really there when people make X do Y statements. In the section below, we will look at the

1

nature of questions about the external social world and at how this book will try to go about answering such questions. In the third section we will look at questions about people's beliefs about the social world and at how this book will try to answer these sorts of questions.

WHAT'S ACTUALLY THERE:
SOCIAL METAPHYSICS AND IBE

For a number of reasons, we would like to know what we can expect to find in the external social world when someone makes a statement about a group. What are people actually doing in situations that speakers describe with phrases such as "Starbucks wants McDonalds to know they are serious about selling sandwiches"? We not only want to know what people are thinking when they say such things, we want to know about the social structures people are talking about in their statements.

To understand what is happening in various social circumstances, we often have to begin with what scholars or other people *say* about the situation, since we are seldom in a position to make direct observations of most situations for ourselves. What others say helps us uncover what they believe—which gives us some information about what's likely true about a social situation. But the relationship between what is said and what is true about the social situation is a complex one. In the section after this one, we'll extensively discuss the difficulties involved in uncovering what people believe about a social situation from what they've said about it. In the present section, however, we'll assume that there are ways of getting from utterances to beliefs. The question for this section concerns how this book will address the issue of determining what is true about social situations when people make X do Y statements.

In certain kinds of situations, people's beliefs about what is going on generally tend to be fairly accurate. In others, however, it is very common to have mistaken beliefs based on errors or on incorrect assumptions about what tends to be there. To understand what social situation we have, then, it is not only good to know what people believe about it, but whether or not it looks like the general kind of situation where people's beliefs tend or tend not to be accurate. People tend to be good judges of whether others are speaking their own or a different language dialect (see Aronoff 2007; Brennan and Brennan 1981). On the other hand, people tend not to be good estimators of things like crowd size (Sturges 1972) (though the collective averaging of individual estimates tends to be a good predictor of the actual magnitudes (see Surowieki 2004)). With political claims, people tend to discount evidence that runs counter to their own previous political beliefs, while latching onto evidence confirming their prior views, often giving them inaccurate views of situations (Lord, Ross, and Lepper 1979, 2098–2109). Throughout this book we will try to note some situations in which people are prone to have mistaken beliefs—situations where we probably can't regard their statements as giving us accurate social information.

But even where people's beliefs are roughly correct, there will always be many features about the world that their utterances and theories don't say anything about. A person who sees another person sniffling might accurately judge that the person is infected with germs, but have no idea about whether the germs causing the cold are bacteria or viruses. Similarly, an observer might correctly say that it is a custom among truck drivers to honk at attractive pedestrians, but have no idea as to the details of what it means to have such a custom. To know about what is actually there in the social world when someone makes an X do Y statement, then, we also need to have some additional detailed theories about how groups can arrange themselves in certain ways.

Some of what this book hopes to do is supply such theories. Views about what can be there in the social world exist in many different fields: anthropology, sociology, psychology, history, political science, geography, and philosophy. Philosophers tend to label any kind of theory about *what there is* a "metaphysics" theory, to differentiate it from theories about what's valuable (belonging to ethics) and theories about how we know (epistemology). Coming up with theories of what kinds of social structures can be there, then, is to do a kind of social metaphysics. Philosophers may typically look at different aspects of what's there than scientists do, but in my view, there is no sharp dividing line between a philosophical and a scientific theory. Some of the chapters in this book, then, focus to a large extent on "social metaphysics" theories regarding the characteristics of collections. In chapter 2, for example, we will look at the underlying metaphysics behind situations described by statements like "Congress is anxious about how the EPA will react." The basic metaphysical ontology of what is being claimed here is very unclear. This contrasts with claims that are about lots of individuals doing something— claims where the underlying metaphysics is usually fairly clear. Semantically, we may have trouble figuring out if someone is really claiming that all Columbia students love the new gym, or only the athletes do, when she talks about how much the students like the gym. But the underlying metaphysics of claims about individuals tends to be straightforward. We understand what it is for a set of individuals to each be feeling some emotion. Not so with claims about "what France wanted."

Such a locution might indicate that the speaker is saying or believing that the country of France is like an individual desirer. In chapter 3, I will look at what our best underlying metaphysical theory should say about whether and how a collection like this could actually want something. Chapter 4 will also look at some mystifying social metaphysics. While numerous social sciences and others often talk about norms, customs, and conventions, it's not clear what these are and how they work. Can something be a custom if few do it? Can there be a norm prohibiting an action if people merely believe that they will be punished for doing it? The fundamental metaphysics of collective action, and the metaphysics of customs and conventions, are among the most vexing questions in the philosophy of the social sciences. We currently lack a good understanding of the underlying structures and mechanisms in either of these kinds of cases. Without a good understanding of these sorts of things, we might know the meanings of people's statements about groups but not really understand what is happening in the situations being described. In chapters 3 and 4, then, in addition to discussing the meaning of statements about collective wholes and statements about customs, I will also put forth some idea about the underlying metaphysical structures to which these statements refer. In chapter 5, I'll look at the further metaphysics questions about whether and how various kinds of collections are in a position to cause certain things to happen.

The reasons that I advocate the particular metaphysics theories about groups that I do, differ, of course, for different aspects of the social. But I've often generally utilized, among other things, a method termed "inference to the best explanation." Using inference to the best explanation (IBE) here, I collect a variety of data—here, about social behavior; then I look for what structures and arrangements best account for this data. When I find models that best explain all and only the data regarding these situations, I make an inference to the best explanation, that the structures in the model are the ones that actually generate the social happenings we observe. In the inferences to the best explanation I make here, I have benefited greatly from previous social scientific and philosophical theories of certain group activities. I've taken various parts of other social scientific and philosophical theories and tried to find ways to combine them into theories that best account for our observations about what groups can do.

Utilizing various observations, theories, and inferences to the best explanation in this manner, I hope I can say some important things about what we can actually expect to find in the social world when someone makes a claim about it. Helping people know more about what they can and can't expect to actually find in the world when one hears a statement about a group is one of the main things I hope to contribute with this book.

UNCOVERING WHAT PEOPLE MEAN
WHEN THEY MAKE SOCIAL CLAIMS

Finding out what's actually going on when people make comments about the social world is important, but often we can best do so by trying to understanding what people believe when they make a social claim. And, for all the reasons stated in the introduction, it is important to understand what people believe about the social world in its own right as well. So if one major focus of this book is on what people are talking about when they make certain kinds of social claims, the other major focus of this book is figuring out what people believe when they say that the X do Y.

Beliefs, of course, are not directly observable. What, then, are some of the ways we can uncover what people believe about the social world? One family of ways to uncover beliefs is to use our knowledge of the various external social circumstances people have encountered (or been told about) and combine this with knowledge of human belief–forming strategies to make inferences about what people's likely resulting beliefs will be. Holland, Holyoak, Nisbett, and Thagard (1986), for example, have looked at the ways in which people make inductive generalizations from the samples they've been exposed to. In this book, I'll be doing some of this to help uncover what people's beliefs about groups are likely to be. My main approach, however, will be to work from the other direction. If certain behaviors are reliably correlated with certain underlying beliefs, we can use the observation of these behaviors to work backwards to help infer what the beliefs likely are. All things being equal, the more highly correlated the behaviors are with the beliefs, the more useful they are as belief-indicators. If one wished, he or she could even try to use precise numerical probabilities to calculate the Bayesian likelihood of an underlying belief, given the observational evidence. (Whether we use numerical values or not, however, looking backwards requires that we know something about base rate regularities of certain beliefs and behaviors. For we need to know if that behavior, however well correlated with a certain belief, isn't more likely to be the result of some other more common underlying cause.) Among the behaviors best correlated with certain beliefs is the propensity to utter certain sounds. Looking at what people *say*, in other words, is one of our most useful tools for telling what they believe.

Now, the relationship between what is believed and what is said is a complicated one. (Indeed, the bulk of this chapter will be focused on discussing this relationship.) Some of the things helping determine what is said (e.g., pronunciation difficulties) have little to do with belief, and some of the factors that do involve belief do so in a way that is complicated, non-robust, or hard to discover, making these factors difficult to use to help in uncovering the beliefs. What we might call social/linguistic rules, on the other hand, are quite likely to be useful to us. My general view of language is that we can describe people's linguistic behavior in terms of the propensity to follow a rule of roughly this form: Say Y, when you believe B is the case and want other people to believe B is the case. Figuring out what a speaker is trying to get a listener to believe (the B claim) is roughly what we mean when we speak of "understanding the meaning" of a sentence. The existence of certain social/linguistic rules makes for a very strong link between utterances and beliefs, and we can use our knowledge of such rules to understand what particular speakers believe and are trying to get others to believe. The strength of the rule-based link between beliefs and utterances is a reason that looking at social/linguistic rules is important in trying to uncover beliefs. Looking at rules can also be useful in coming to better understand which beliefs are generally associated with certain concepts. Sometimes the best way to understand what we implicitly believe about X is to ask ourselves the questions, "Is it appropriate to call this situation an 'X'? How about this other situation?" Rules are also important to focus on, because, unlike other belief-behavior links, rules linking beliefs and behavior can be investigated fairly straightforwardly. A lot can be learned from just looking at one's own and other's intuitions about what it does and doesn't feel permissible to say to describe various scenarios. In the next subsection, I will describe in more detail what social/linguistic rules are and how we uncover them.[1]

A big part of the project of this book, then, involves looking at some of our social/linguistic rules about how to describe groups. These rules tell us when it is appropriate to say things like "the airline pilots have reservations about the new contract." They tell us that when we believe certain particular things about the world, it is appropriate to say things like, "it's our custom to have a cocktail when we get home from work" (but it is not appropriate to say this when we believe some slightly different things). If we know what the rules regarding when we can say these phrases are, we can use them to help us discover a number of other things. We can combine knowledge of social/linguistic rules with information about the speaker's propensities to follow the rules, or to intentionally break them, or to make mistakes, to work backwards and to help make inference about what the speaker believes about the world. We use the tendency of listeners to use utterances to find out what the speaker believes (and their tendency to assume that what the speaker is saying is true) to make inferences about what the listener will believe after hearing the utterance. And in certain circumstances (we'll explore which) people's beliefs about the world tend to be fairly accurate. Using social/linguistic rules to uncover beliefs in these circumstances, then, can help tell us what we should actually expect to find in the world. In this book, we will be looking at many things beside rules for speaking about social groups. But looking at social/ linguistic rules is centrally important for understanding what people believe when they say that people believe.

What Is a Social/Linguistic Rule?

What sort of thing is the rule 'Say Y when you believe B and want your listener to believe it too'? Social/linguistic "rules" of this sort are cousins of the entities in the "what's done" family described in chapter 4, which includes norms, customs, conventions, and traditions. A rule is an injunction that an action should or must be done (or should/must not be done) unless it is superseded by another rule. The most prototypical sort of rule is probably a divine commandment (e.g., "Thou shalt not commit adultery"). Rules for games (e.g., "You cannot castle out of check") are also very prototypical. Linguistic rules are somewhat different from these more prototypical ones, but are still called "rules" nonetheless—most likely because of the rough idea that it is "wrong" to use certain kinds of words or sentence structures in certain situations. Rules, linguistic or other, while similar to prototypical norms, are also somewhat different from members of this "what's done" family, in that there need not be any special emphasis on social learning or reinforcement. An individual can be thought to have a personal "rule" that he follows regarding what he must always try to do in certain situations (e.g., "If you see an unaccompanied woman your age, you should always go talk to her"). But in most actual cases where we are likely to speak of "rules" being present, there are social reinforcements—just as there are for norms or customs. For the social/linguistic rules we are discussing here, if there are rules that certain things should be (and should not be) said in certain situations, that means there could well be (perhaps mild) disdain expressed toward those thought of as not following them.[2]

Some would undoubtedly consider rules of the form "Say Y when you want a listener to believe B" to be psychological dispositions—they are descriptions of what individuals feel an obligation to do and say. Others would refer to these as "sociological norms," since they are standards of appropriate conduct held by a social group. Others would call them "cultural practices" since we are dealing with habits of language behavior that differ from society to society. Still others would call them "linguistic rules" since they deal with what can and cannot be said. Those calling them linguistic rules would likely disagree about whether they are best classed as syntactic, semantic, pragmatic, or sociolinguistic rules (see Bach 1997 for a good discussion). Certainly numerous different mental and social factors are involved in the sort of rules I am talking about. I call them "social/linguistic" rules to cover all bases. They are psychological compulsions felt by individuals concerning what they

ought (and ought not) to say. At the same time, these same compulsions tend
to be shared by the members of a group. These group members tend to feel
these compulsions, in part, because of how they believe others will treat them
if they don't behave in this way, so these rules are a type of sociological norm.
(If others tend to roll their eyes when a speaker says things like "no one else
supports you on this" when five out of twenty group members do, speakers
will presumably modify their future speaking patterns.) Since these norms are
norms about what one ought to say, we can speak of them as linguistic rules.
There are, of course, numerous theories about what linguistic rules are. In this
book, I'll be assuming the fairly commonsensical picture of how language
works that I've been describing. In this picture, societies have normative rules
specifying that certain sounds are and aren't appropriate to make when you
want people to believe that the world is a certain way. These rules consist of
each person in the group having some sort of mental structure specifying that
when he wants others to believe that the world is a certain way, he can cause
this belief in others by making certain audible sounds. You have a linguistic
rule in a group when enough of the group members have a mental structure
that dictates: Say Y if you want people to believe B.

This view of language rules strongly resembles one developed by the
philosopher Paul Grice. In Grice's view, understanding the meaning of a sentence centers on trying to uncover the propositional attitudes of the speakers.
Within this propositional attitude–centered view of meaning, Grice distin-
guishes between "utterer's meaning," which is what a speaker is trying to get
listeners to believe at the time of utterance, and "sentence meaning," which is
what a group of listeners, over time, generally consider speakers to be trying
to get them to believe when they utter this string of symbols. My description
of a language rule is an informal version of one of Grice's complicated definitions of timeless sentence meaning:

> At least some (many) members of group G have in their repertoires the pro-
> cedure of uttering a token of X if, for some A, they want A to Ψ^+ that p, the
> retention of this procedure being for them conditional on the assumption that
> at least some (other) members of G have, or have had this procedure in their
> repertoires (1989, 127).

Describing the Gricean "sentence meaning" that social/linguistic rules give
to statements about groups, then, will be one important focus of this book.

Multiple Versions and Idealization

A central problem with trying to figure out what people mean by working
backward from our social/linguistic rules about what to say when is that it's

very likely that there are a large number of idiosyncratic variants of a particular social/linguistic rule in any given language. Bill may follow (and believe others follow) a social linguistic rule that says, "You can say that the X group does Y, if over 50 percent of the members of X do." Jill on the other hand, may follow a rule that says, "You can say the X do Y, if over three fourths of the X do, unless the most visible members of the X-group do not." Bill and Jill may also follow different variants even of their own rules at different times. How then, do we describe the rule that Bill and Jill have for speaking about groups? How do we describe *the* rule that speakers of English have? Whenever we have to describe a certain variable characteristic that members of a large group of things have, we commonly resort to talking about an "idealized" description of that characteristic. Here, the group we are interested in is the group of beliefs held by a group of speakers about what is permissible to say when. In this book, too, then, I will be using an idealized model of the social/linguistic rules about what can be said when. My idealization will be to focus on a single exemplar version of a given sociolinguistic rule, one which lots of speakers' idiosyncratic variants are similar to. This will enable me to avoid the unmanageable task of having to describe and utilize each English speaker's personal idiosyncratic version of a rule.

There are many different ways to construct an idealized exemplar, so let me be clear about what I will be doing regarding social/linguistic rules for speaking about groups. One family of idealized variants centers on variants that are simpler to describe. This is not the kind of idealization I am interested in here. I am trying to describe a rule exemplar that is close to the rules that lots of different people are actually using—not one that is necessarily easily described. My interest in focusing on the rules that are actually being used also leads me to avoid using the intuitively strongest rule as the ideal exemplar. Speakers might well recognize a certain phrase as the very best way to describe what they are thinking. But the "best fitting" phrase might well be a very obscure one that speakers would be unlikely to think of or remember when actually expressing their thoughts. Another general family of exemplars consists of various kinds of *central tendencies*—a kind of averaging of the various instances. Means and medians are paradigm cases of a central tendency. These are not the kinds of idealizations I will be making here. I'm not sure what it would even mean to talk about a median linguistic rule. And trying to talk about a mean linguistic rule seems as inappropriate for describing what people actually say and think as "2.2" is for describing the number of children Americans actually tend to have. (Furthermore, if a word or phrase is systematically ambiguous in that it can be used to describe many different kinds of situations (as claims about groups can), it would be more accurate to speak of different rules used in different situations, rather than try to describe one central tendency for all of the situations.) The sort of idealization that I will be employing here is using the exemplar that I think is the most common variant of the rules for describing this or that kind of group. They are the versions more speakers have and the ones that each speaker tends to use on more occasions than other versions.[3]

Figuring Out What the Rules Are

As described in the previous section, trying to understand what someone believes when they make a group belief statement like "PR firms are dishonest," involves making an inference based on hearing utterances and knowing our social/linguistic rules. But how do I have any idea what our social/linguistic rules are? What's my method for knowing what these are?

Philosophers like me are seldom clear about the methods they use in coming to the conclusions they do. This is unsurprising. Philosophers often come to conclusions by sitting in a chair, thinking very hard about a problem, and being satisfied when a solution "seems right." What makes a particular conclusion seem right is often unclear, even to those drawing the conclusion. But I think it's important to be as clear as possible about the methods I've used here to try to uncover our social/linguistic rules.

The method I've used to uncover linguistic rules, like the method I used for uncovering the social metaphysics I described earlier, also involves making an inference to the best explanation. I collect a variety of data about when people make statements about social situations and I look for what best accounts for the data. When I find a model of conceptual structure that best explains all and only the data regarding these statements, I make an inference to the best explanation, that this conceptual structure is probably what underlies our statements about groups. With my roughly Gricean picture of language, what I aim to find is the rule people have about which phrases they should say when they have certain beliefs and groups and want other people to have them. When there is a rule of the sort I am talking about, there is a strong correlation between the beliefs they want others to have about the situation (usually the same ones that they have), and certain utterances.

Knowing that there are certain rules helps enable us to infer what people's beliefs are on the basis of the utterances they make. But to find out what rules are there to begin with, one of the main things we can do is go in the other direction: we start with what we think that people believe, then we look for what people find appropriate to say in these circumstances. Sometimes we can get some evidence for the existence of certain rules, based on people's writing and conversation and our best context-based guesses about what the people believe when they make these statements. I've scoured scores of books in which people use the terms "norm," "custom," and "convention," looking carefully at the surrounding words and ideas accompanying the phrases. I've paid close attention to when people around me talked about "what UNLV students are like." What did they seem to perceive at the time? What information had they received in the past? How did they behave when they uttered these terms? I looked at seemingly similar situations in which they tended not to use these terms. I've looked at how listeners respond when hearing these statements. I've looked at when people tend to try to correct or argue with another's use of phrases like "Russia thinks . . ."

But another source of information about which utterances are the right ones to say about groups is to look at what feels appropriate to say oneself in numerous situations. I have used introspection like this to look, not only at what I believe during actual times when these phrases are used, but in hypothetical cases as well. Would it be permissible, I'd ask myself, for us to say, "Tibetans eat meat," if 80 percent of Tibetans eat meat regularly? What if 80 percent do, but only once a year? What if only 60 percent do? How about if 40 percent do? How about if 60 percent do, but there is a religious prohibition against it in Tibetan culture? Would it seem right to call a graduating class's chanting "what now?" a norm if it had been done by the previous two graduating classes? What about the previous five? Investigating this way is called consulting one's linguistic intuitions (Laurence and Margolis 2003). Looking not just at what one actually says, but at what it feels right to say, serves two purposes. It helps tell us what terms we are disposed to say most of the time when we believe something, not just on this or that occasion. It also tells us which utterances strongly feel right in which circumstances, letting us know what we will likely say in situations where we want to communicate well (even though we will also sometimes sloppily utter these phrases at other times when it doesn't feel so right).[4]

We can often get better information using our own linguistic intuitions than we can get from other sources. With ourselves, there is far less guesswork about what is believed when certain utterances are made. There's also little guesswork about whether the phrases really feel appropriate—information that other speakers may not automatically volunteer in the flow of a conversation. Another nice feature is that intuition collection provides one with a kind of virtual laboratory, where one can examine feelings of linguistic appropriateness for many different situations quickly. Is vegetarianism the norm in a group if 55 percent of the group practices it? What about 45 percent? With little cost, I can quickly examine the appropriateness of phrases in an enormous amount of variable situations very quickly without having to move from house to house with a clipboard.

After asking myself these questions for a while, I end up with a list of intuitive judgments about what does and doesn't seem permissible to say in our language. I then get to work describing what seems to be the general internal rule that underlies these intuitive judgments. Suppose I've found that one can't comfortably say, "The university believes that it should sell all its shares of RJR Nabisco" after just one of the professors said it should. Is the rule one that stipulates we cannot describe things like "the university" as believing something when a single person says it does, or is the rule one that stipulates that a faculty member cannot decide what the university believes? Or is it because we don't think that the university, as a whole, can believe something? I hypothesize a rule version: "its okay for us to say an institution believes Y, if an official spokesperson says it, but it's not okay if an ordinary employee says it." I then try to see if this rule really covers all situations like S. If that rule is right, I should be able to use a statement like that one to describe situations S1, S2, and S3. Does that really seem permissible? If it does, I get more confident that I'm describing the rule accurately. If not, I can modify it. I then look and see if it also covers slightly (then increasingly) different types of examples to figure out the true scope of the rule. To take another example, would it be appropriate to say "Biglervillians hate the new school" if 65 percent did? It seems so. What if only 45 percent did? It still seems so, so long as the rest are relatively indifferent. This seems to indicate that our rules say that we can talk about an X feeling Y, not only if a majority, but if a plurality does. But what if, while 45 percent hate the school, 20 percent love it—and those 20 percent include the town's most prominent citizens? Does it matter who makes up this plurality? What if the teachers and students really like the new school, and the rest of the townsfolk mildly dislike it? I propose various versions of the rule and see if I can find situations in which my proposed rule would say it was OK to say something that really doesn't feel OK to say. If the proposed rule does that, I discard it in favor of a rule that better accords with intuition in a wide variety of cases. After playing around like this for an embarrassing amount of time, I come up with what seem to be the rules for how a certain group situation is permissibly described.

If one's own feelings about a term's appropriateness are the same as those of other members of the group, intuition-collecting quickly tells you a lot about how group members in general feel they should describe situations. This tells you the rule they are using about what can be said when certain things are believed (allowing you to later infer beliefs from utterances). But is the rule that others use really similar to the one you are using? It seems likely that it is at least pretty similar. Group members who grow up in the same language communities will be imitating similarly speaking people, and will get corrected in similar ways. As with grammatical intuitions, each group member's intuitions about descriptive appropriateness are likely to be highly similar to everyone else's. Consulting my own linguistic intuitions, then, gives me a pretty good guess at what the rest of my group member's intuitions will be. Still, it's always possible that one's own usage of a term is idiosyncratic. I therefore try to look at others' intuitions and phrase usage, and to compare them to my own. Being a philosopher, and not a social scientist, I haven't conducted the formal studies that are really needed to see if my intuitions are the same as others. (If others were to do such studies that would benefit this project greatly.) But I certainly have made many informal observations. After coming up with my own judgments of appropriateness (and the rules that seem to underlie them), I start asking the same questions I've been asking myself to the people around me. I start with my wife. Then I ask my parents, my siblings, and my wife's parents and siblings. I next ask colleagues, students, and even strangers on the street. I look at dictionaries and at articles in philosophy or linguistic journals that focus on similar words and phrases. When I can, I ask my students (who come from a wide variety of backgrounds) questions like this:

Imagine that a group of friends has a dinner party every week. Every week it is held at a different friend's house.

Situation 1

In the week after each dinner party, each of the friends usually sends the host or hostess a thank-you note for hosting the party. If they don't send it, the host is usually a bit angry with the non-sender. Non-senders tend to feel very guilty about forgetting to send it. Is there a *norm* of sending a thank-you note to the host after a party among this group of friends? In a sentence or two, say why you think they do or don't have this norm.

Situation 2

In the week after each dinner party, each of the friends usually means to send the host or hostess a thank-you note for hosting the party. But each of them usually gets distracted, and ends up forgetting to do it. The hosts are usually upset with their guests about this. And the non-senders tend to feel very guilty about forgetting to send it. Is there a *norm* of sending a thank-you note to the host after a party among this group of friends? In a sentence or two, say why you think they do or don't have this norm.

Situation 3

In the week after each dinner party, each of the friends always send the host or hostess a thank-you note for hosting the party. But none of them feels any obligation to do so. Each sends the note because he or she feels happy about the party. The hosts are always happy to get all these thank-you notes. But the hosts would not be angry with any of the guests for not sending a note. Is there a *norm* of sending a thank-you note to the host after a party among this group of friends? In a sentence or two, say why you think they do or don't have this norm.

Looking at others' intuitions in this way helps tell me if my own intuitions are really in line with those of other members of my group.

At the end of this process, I arrive at what I think are our social/linguistic rules for speaking about groups. We can then work backwards in the ways I've described to try to figure out what a speaker believes is going on, when he makes one of the hard-to-interpret statements about what group X does or believes.

I think that in using the methods I've described here, I've made a good start toward figuring out what people are thinking when they make various sorts of X-do-Y statements. In the chapters that follow, I describe what I've found using these methods. Obviously, however, my findings will not be the last word on this subject. While the techniques I've described are good ones for uncovering beliefs from statements, they will be more successful when done on a larger scale with bigger sample sizes of speakers. In my research, I've looked in an informal way at my own intuitions about what can be said about groups, and those of my friends and my students. But we would quite likely improve our theories of our social/linguistic rules if we looked at additional data by examining the intuitions of a much larger group of speakers, using more formal surveys. In recent years, a group of scholars doing what's become known as experimental philosophy (or X-phi) has begun doing exactly this kind of systematic large scale work investigating peoples intuitions (see Appiah 2008; and Nadelhoffer and Nahmias 2007 for overviews). Additional work of this sort could surely improve on the preliminary starts I've made here in uncovering our rules for speaking about groups. Further empirical work, like ethnographic observations of people's actual speaking behavior, and additional content analysis of various kinds of texts in which people make X-do-Y statements could also help us learn more about what people likely believe when they make these sorts of statements. Hopefully, the work I've started here can help point the way toward more empirical studies that can help us refine our views on what people believe when they say that people believe.

In this chapter, I've described the way I've been looking for answers to questions about people's statements about what collections of people believe or do. I've described how we can try to extract what speakers tend to really believe about groups from the often confusing statements they make. And I've talked about how such statements and other information can help tell us about what is actually going on with the groups that speakers are trying to talk about with X do Y statements. Let's now begin looking at what people are saying when they say things like, "The American people think it's time for a change."

NOTES

1. I want to be clear that getting from rules and utterances to speaker's beliefs is a very complex matter. (Indeed, see Jones (2000a), and chapter 3, for a discussion of why examining neither behavior [like speaking] nor environmental input is sufficient for enabling us to adequately model inner structure.) To begin with, we need to rely on a set of social/linguistic rules, not just those about sound-making. Some social/linguistic rules are about the speaker making Y sounds when she believes X and wants others to do so too. But there are situations where speakers do not want other to believe what they believe, and one needs to understand these too, if one is to use people's utterances to make inferences about their beliefs. A social/linguistic rule specifying that this situation calls for honesty mandates that you should try to make others believe what you believe. But a social/linguistic rule specifying that this is a situation where deception is called for means that you try to avoid this. Sometimes, for example, it is relatively socially acceptable to deceive people about certain things out of politeness. (A person who masks his true views to avoid seeming to make ethnic slurs comes to mind). If one knows that such politeness is customary then one should not assume that the person's statement could be any guide to either what he himself believes or what is true. At other times, what is expected is not an accurate description of the social situation but an entertaining one. Here, we can expect that someone's statement is not a description of what she believes, but an amusing exaggeration. Linguistic and sociological studies of conversational conventions, then, are highly relevant to our understanding what people believe when they say certain things about groups. I've tried to utilize current knowledge and speculations about these areas in my attempts to understand people's thinking.

2. The question of the precise ontology of things called "rules" is a very unsettled one in both philosophy and the social sciences. I consider rules to be mental representations that one has an obligation to avoid doing (or to do) some action. But how brains actually implement these representations is a mystery. It is also unclear whether rules are actually themselves causal or whether the feelings of obligation that we identify as rules merely indicate that certain types of actual underlying causal mechanisms are present. I suspect that many of the same worries I raise about norms

as causal mechanisms in chapter 5 apply to the notion of rules as causal. At any rate, no commitment is being made here to rules necessarily being causal entities.

3. Even the notion of the most common version of a rule is a very tricky matter. On the one hand, if each person's mental representation of a rule is unique, there will be no versions that are used more often than any others. Each is used only by that speaker, herself, so there is no version that is used more than any other. One can try to get around this by stipulating broad categories of "versions" of a class, then counting the number of people holding one or another instances of these versions (e.g., "A person is counted as having the rule 'Say the X do Y when most of the X do,' if that's what they are disposed to say when somewhere between all and three quarters of the X do.") One can then (in principle) count which broad version is used most often and/or by more speakers. On the other hand, one could easily artificially help make a certain rule emerge as the most commonly used one (with versions used more often than other rules' versions), by making it broader than other rules. But the broader we make it, the more information we lose about what, precisely, people are most likely to say. My solution is to construct the most specific version of the rule possible, consistent with it not being so specific that that version is used by only a very small number of speakers. My suspicion is that we can find versions of particular socio-linguistic rules, very close variants of which are used by large numbers of speakers (with "very close" and "large" being judgment calls.) Such difficulties are endemic to attempts at idealization in nearly any area.

4. The use of intuitions in philosophy has recently come in for a lot of criticism—and for good reason (Swain, Alexander, and Weinberg 2008; Depaul and Ramsey 1998; Bishop and Stich 1998). I largely agree that there's no reason to think that we can use our intuitive uneducated judgments to tell us the true essential nature of justice, oxygen, or reference (if there are such things as essential natures). I don't believe that we can find out what the boundaries of blueness or truth are by seeing what our intuitions tell us.

But in this book I am looking at the boundaries of when it feels appropriate to use utterances like "the French . . ." to describe. For this, intuitions are just what you want. Social/linguistic rules are like the syntactic rules of language. For syntactic rules, people's inner feelings about how phrases should be structured are intimately related to being a rule (see Stich 1983). In my view, a rule is just a representation of obligation to avoid doing (or to do) some action. A rule of language is the representation that one ought to string together kinds of sounds in certain ways in certain situations and that other strings are inappropriate then. A phrase is the appropriate one to say in a certain situation for an individual when she herself feels it to be appropriate. A phrase is an appropriate one for the group when enough individuals in the group take it to be so. A group of people could be wrong in their beliefs or guesses about the general principle underlying their intuitive judgments. But (with a few exceptions) a majority of the group can not be wrong in their intuitive judgments that certain ways of describing situations are or aren't appropriate. Linguistic appropriateness just is largely a matter of group members' feelings of appropriateness. Getting people (including one's self) to describe their inner intuitive judgments of appropriateness, then, really is a good way of uncovering social/linguistic rules. The use of intuitions here, contrary to certain ways of using intuitions in other philosophical projects, is certainly legitimate. We can use intuitions of phrase-appropriateness for uncovering social/linguistic rules, in the same way that linguists can use intuitions of grammaticality to help figure out our grammatical rules.

Intuitive feelings about a phrase's appropriateness could have various sources. But, for the point at hand, the sources of the feelings are unimportant. The point is that in these types of cases, having strong intuitive feelings that something is or isn't permissible is all there is to being permissible. Where the sources of the feelings are important is in speculating about how widespread the intuition is. If these intuitions are genetically pre-wired (like syntactic intuitions are claimed partly to be) then everyone will have them. If they come from social conditioning by a society, they will be less widespread, since not everyone is likely to have been conditioned in exactly the same way. If the feelings come from ideas about what is consistent and rational, they can be even less widespread, since people may well differ in their views of what it will be rational to say.

Chapter Two

Collective Claims about Individuals

How Many Chicagoans Need to Like Thick Pizza before You Can Say "Chicagoans Like Thick Pizza"?

In the introduction and in the previous chapter, we've said that people frequently make statements of the general form "the X (group) does Y" (e.g., "UNLV students do things late") and that these statements can mean quite different things. Let's now start looking at one of the main kinds of things people mean when they make these sorts of statements. In chapter 3 I will be discussing the status of these statements when they are interpreted as talking about the X group acting like a unitary agent. When speakers say things like, "What Microsoft really wanted to do was to put Apple out of business," they seem to be saying something about the actions and desires of the Microsoft Corporation and not just those of individuals who work for the corporation. Other times, when speakers say things like, "In America, people eat three meals a day," they seem to be saying that it is an idealized norm or custom in America to eat three meals a day (whether or not this is actually done by large numbers); in chapter 4, I will be talking about understanding claims that are interpreted this way. In this present chapter, however, I will focus on X-do-Y statements where the speakers are merely trying to convey the more mundane idea that *many individuals* belonging to group X do or believe Y. The "Many Individuals" family of X-do-Y statements, as I'll call it, is certainly not as flashy or exotic a category of statements as claims that attribute intentional states to groups. But it's still an important one. It's relatively easy to come to believe that large sets of a group's members do something, so this is probably what people have in mind most *often* when they make X-do-Y statements. The frequency of statements in this category alone makes it an important one to scrutinize.

But it's also important to examine this family because of what such statements can and can't tell you. Of the various types of statements about group belief and action, this is the only type that can directly say something about how

19

any *individuals* actually behave. And statements about what the individuals in a group *believe* probably tend to give people better information about what these individuals will actually do, than statements about the norms of the group. On the other hand, the statements in this category have a very large range of possible meanings (*how many* of the group's individual members do or don't believe Y is usually left vague with such phrases). So it's worth carefully examining which of the possible interpretations are most apt at which times. But even when X-do-Y statements aren't able to tell listeners much about the behavior of people in groups, they can still tell them something about what speakers *believe* about group member's behavior. This, of course, can tell us something about the stereotypes people hold about group members (e.g., believing that Italian men like to pinch attractive women). The study of stereotyping is an important area of psychology and criminal justice. Knowing what people tend to *believe* in the different circumstances in which they'll *say* that the X people do or believe Y can undoubtedly improve our knowledge in this area.

Despite the importance and commonality of using X-do-Y phrases this way, this family is given short shrift in the literature discussing group activities and intentions. While numerous authors (e.g., Bratman 1999; Gilbert 1989; Miller 2001; Pettit 2002; Searle 1995) have devoted a great deal of time to discussing the details of the requirements for being a norm, or for the creation of "social facts," few devote much time to exploring what we can say about sets of individuals. As mentioned previously, philosopher Raimo Tuomela, in his otherwise comprehensive work, *The Philosophy of Social Practices,* is typical in this regard. Writes Tuomela: "A mere aggregate of facts about people having the same attitude (say fear) is not fully social, because it lacks an appropriate doxastic connection between the participants" (2002, 24). But we shouldn't ignore claims about aggregates as not being sufficiently social.[1] I don't think that what we ordinarily think of as "social" is restricted in this way. But even if the term "social" was restricted in such a way, understanding what "aggregate" groups of individuals do, and how we tend think about them, is certainly an important part of understanding what goes on in the world. This chapter, then, will try to help rectify this deficit and make clearer what people tend to be talking about when they make statements about the thoughts and actions of individuals in groups.

STRATEGY: UNCOVERING RULES, ERROR, EXTENSION, AND TOLERANCE

To understand what social circumstances we should expect to be present when we hear X-do-Y statements, we can start by looking at the social/

linguistic rules governing when such statements are appropriate. (Note that all the X-do-Y statements I will discuss in *this* chapter are ones about sets of individuals, as opposed to ones about collective agents or norms.) As I said in chapter 2, what I will mean by a social/linguistic rule is people's beliefs in various Gricean maxims along the lines of "if you think P is the case, and you want to communicate that to others, say S." When the rule is being followed, we can work backwards to try to infer what speakers *believe* about the world, given the utterances they've made. In circumstances when people's beliefs tend to be accurate, people's utterances also provide good information about the state of the world they are trying to describe.

In trying to best assess what circumstances are present, however, we have to remember that people don't always *follow* the social/linguistic rules and that their beliefs about the world aren't always *accurate*. So understanding what we should expect when we hear such utterances involves more than understanding such rules.

We must also understand when and why people make *errors* forming their general beliefs about the social world. Speakers often say things like "Hawaiians like to surf," because they erroneously believe that most Hawaiians like to surf. At other times, people will say things like "Students hate doing pushups in gym," even though they are aware that *most* students don't really hate it—but the number that do is seen as being *similar enough* to *most*, to allow them to use the same linguistic phrase to describe the somewhat different situation. People doing this may be said to be making *extensions*, rather than errors in their descriptions. People's willingness to make extensions may be influenced by the beliefs they have about other people's *tolerance.* "Tolerance," here, refers to listeners' reluctance to correct a speaker's statements, even when these statements aren't accurately describing the world via current linguistic conventions. Beliefs about people's tolerance levels will not only affect speakers' dispositions to make extensions, but will also affect how cautious a speaker will be in avoiding making errors in their statements or beliefs about groups.

The relation between the social/linguistic rules, errors, and extensions, is a tricky one, since such rules are always evolving. The existence of errors, extensions and tolerance can create new (more enforceable) rules whereby the initial rules concerning when one can make X-do-Y statements come to have a number of "exception clauses" that allow speakers to make these statements in a wider range of circumstances. We may come to realize that the social/linguistic rule that is actually being used is a complex one that allows a description to be used in many more circumstances than it initially was. Such descriptions are permissible for both the initial "basic" circumstances and for additional "extended" ones. And then, error, extension, and tolerance can also occur with respect to *these more lenient rules*—meaning that we should expect that the utterance might be made in circumstances different than what the rules allow, and that the rules may be further evolving. Below I will examine what I think our rules have come to be regarding statements about individuals in groups.

STARTING POINT: A GENERAL RULE ABOUT QUANTIFIERS

Understanding what people believe when they make X-do-Y statements about groups must begin with an understanding of a more general social/ linguistic rule. When a speaker says "A majority of the P . . . ," "some P . . . ," or "2 or 3 P . . . ," a hearer is obviously supposed to think of a majority, some, and 2 or 3 of whatever P one is talking about. But when a speaker says *the P,* without any quantifier, then the convention is that (exceptional cases aside) the speaker should be understood as referring to *all* or almost all of the members of the P class. When a speaker says, "Copper has a boiling point of 2567 degrees, " the conventions of English decree that she is saying that all samples of pure copper have a boiling point of 2567 degrees. When a speaker says "Snakes are deaf," we are supposed to take him as saying that *all* snakes are deaf. When a speaker says, "Oranges are not really orange when they are picked," we are supposed to take her as telling us that hardly any oranges are orange when they are picked. When the group is known to be fairly heterogeneous, it seems to be permissible for a speaker to use this locution when she is referring to *most* as well as almost all. A person can say, "America's chestnut trees were killed in the great blight of the early 1900s," even if some survived.

Since this social/linguistic rule seems to be a rule about how we talk about categories in general, our default assumption should be that when speakers use such phrases to talk about groups of people, they do this with the awareness that listeners will take them to be saying all or most of the category *X people* do Y—unless a particular case counts as one of the many exceptions to this rule. When someone makes an X-do-Y statement that seems to belong to this family, then, our default expectation should be that that person believes that all or most of the individuals in X do or believe Y. When we hear "Hamilton College students like the new library," we assume that the speaker is trying to tell us that, if you ask any given Hamilton student, they will tell you that they like the new library. We can see that this is, indeed, the rule, given the frequency with which people will respond to such phrases with countering statements like, "That's not true, my daughter and her roommates think the new library doesn't have the character of the old." Such responses would be non sequiturs if the person making this response had *not* been interpreting the X-do-Y statement as meaning that "almost all the X do Y."

But people clearly make X-do-Y statements in numerous circumstances in which it's not really the case that all or most of the X people do Y. If people used such statements only when all or most X people really do believe Y, then we would hear such phrases far less frequently than we do, given the diverse membership of so many groups. I've heard it said that San Franciscans hate hearing their city called "Frisco." I'm willing to believe that large numbers don't like it, but I find it implausible that all or most really hate it. Why do people so often make X-do-Y statements when far less than most do Y, in spite of the fact that our conventions say that "no quantifiers = all or most"?

As I said above, I think that the answers are that people frequently make errors in their beliefs about the number of people doing something, and that they feel comfortable extending a description to cover cases that are similar to ones that are conventionally described by that utterance. Speakers tend to believe that these rule violations will be tolerated. These, by themselves, will lead to people making X-do-Y statements when fewer than most do. But I think that error, extension, and tolerance also create *new* rules, whereby specific exemptions are allowed. Later in this chapter, I will discuss what I think are the most important *particular* rules governing when the "no quantifiers" rule can be suspended. Before that, however, I want to discuss, in a more general way, how exceptions to this linguistic rule might develop.

THE GENERAL DEVELOPMENT OF EXCEPTIONS

Error

What sorts of things would cause people to *erroneously* believe that all or most of the X do or believe Y? One way is for them to perform faulty *inductive generalizations* on *samples* of X that they've seen or heard about. They see most (or perhaps even just some) of the Xs doing Y and, on the basis of this, they come to conclude that all or most of *the rest* of the X do Y. Why would people overgeneralize this way?[2] Perhaps the simplest reason it may seem like *all* the X do Y is that the viewer is in contact with a very small number of Xs and all of *those* particular examples of the X group do, in fact, do Y. It's a well known statistical fact that, if the sample size of a class is small, the odds of a random sampling error are high. If your sample size is small, it would not be unusual to have all the Xs that you observe do Y, even though less than half the population of X does. If 50 percent of Miss Tara's preschool students wet their pants regularly, for example, then if you randomly pick samples of four children, then one of every *eight* times you pick a sample, either *all* the children will be pants-wetters, or all will be non-pants-wetters—despite that fact that this trait only appears in half the population as a whole. Many cases in which people believe that all the X do Y are likely to come from seeing all the X do Y in a small sample, and not realizing that seeing this was due to the kind of random sampling error that happens frequently with small samples.[3]

Another obvious thing that can cause an erroneous belief that most of the X do Y, is for a person to be viewing a *biased* sample of X—in which some Xs are much more likely to be sampled for viewing than others. Israelis and Palestinians are far more likely to die of natural causes or traffic accidents than to be killed by each other. But the only samples of Palestinian or Israeli deaths American TV audiences ever see are when one is killed by the other. Based on the biased sample of deaths that they see, it would be easy for Americans to believe that most of deaths are by killings.

In the two types of cases just described, most of the sample Xs that people have seen *really do* do Y. The problem is that people were looking at a faulty sample of the X class. But there are also many cases in which people come to believe most of the X do Y, even when the samples they've seen contain *both* Xs that do Y, and Xs that don't do Y. Various factors can lead people to pay *too much attention* to the Xs that do Y and too little attention to the Xs that don't do Y, or to *think* they see X members doing Y far more frequently than they actually do. Something that psychologists call "one sided events," for example, are activities that in Thomas Gilovitch's words, "stand out and are mentally represented as events only when they turn out one way." The phone ringing while one is in the shower, for example, is classified by the victim as a certain type of mildly unpleasant event. The phone *not* ringing while one is in the shower, however, is not mentally represented as a happy, ring-free shower. Consequently a person's belief that "the phone always rings when I'm in the shower" gets confirmed over and over again, while the myriad of disconfirmations are never noticed (see Gilovitch 1991, 63 for an excellent discussion). A similar error can easily happen in the social realm. Suppose a teacher comes to believe that "the eighth graders at Franklin Middle School are always picking on the seventh graders." Children being who they are, the teacher will probably get numerous confirmation of her belief every day on the playground. Meanwhile, the much more frequent occasions in which an eighth grader walks by a seventh grader without doing anything are *not* going to be mentally recorded as events that disconfirm that view. They will tend not to be noticed at all.

Besides one-sided events, another thing that can make people think that (almost all of) the X do Y, even though they have been exposed to X people who don't do Y, is people's propensity to pay more attention to information

Table 2.1.

	Getting an A on the test	*Not getting an A on the test*
Extra hour of studying	Box 1	Box 2
No extra hour of studying	Box 3	Box 4

that *confirms* some idea than to information that disconfirms it. This well documented psychological phenomenon is called the confirmation bias. To see how confirmation bias works, first consider a simple example of someone trying to figure out whether people who study longer get better grades. If we want to know whether studying for an extra hour does or doesn't make students more likely to get an A on the exam, it helps to have information about how many of a test case class's students we'll get in *each* of the four category boxes in table 2.1.

Researchers have noted that people who want to know if an extra hour of studying is more likely to lead to getting an A will tend to focus on the number of students in box 1—the one that tells you the number of instances that *confirm* the suggestion in question. Now to really know if studying longer leads to getting an A, we need to know, not only if people who study longer did tend to get As, but what happened in the *other* categories as well (e.g., did people who studied a shorter time also get As?) But this is not what people do. They tend to focus on the category with confirming evidence. This is unsurprising, since positive information is easier to process than negative information. But it means that lots of errors will be made when considering whether the X really tend to do Y. If the school principal, for example, is asked to investigate whether eighth graders really do pick on the seventh graders, his automatic inclination will probably be to see if he can find lots of cases in which eighth graders are picking on seventh graders, rather than also looking at cases in which they don't, and rather than looking at the rates in which students pick on other students *in general*. This confirmation bias can easily lead people to erroneously think that the Xs tend to do Y, even if they've actually also seen lots of cases in which the Xs *don't* do Y.

And even if a special effort is made to get people to notice cases in which X *don't* do Y, a phenomenon called *belief perseverance* can lead people to continue believing that they *do* do Y. Belief perseverance refers to the tendency for people to maintain their initial beliefs, even in the face of contrary evidence. A particularly interesting example of belief perseverance was demonstrated in an experiment by Leper, Ross, and Lau (Nisbett and Ross, 1980). In this experiment, one set of subjects was given useful instructions on how to solve a particular type of math problem. The second set was given poor instructions. Predictably, the second set of subjects did worse on sample

problems than the first set. In later surveys, students in this second set rated
their own math abilities as poor. Interestingly, when this second group was
divided into two groups, one that was specifically told about the inferior
instruction and one that was not "debriefed," the two groups were indistinguishable in their poor self-rating. The subject's original belief in their own
poor performance was unaffected by subsequent information that showed the
instruction was faulty.

What's especially interesting about this experiment is how automatic and
effortless the belief perseverance was. Throughout the psychological literature and the literature on the history of science, one finds numerous cases of
beliefs persevering through contrary evidence. Often these beliefs persevere
despite strenuous efforts on the parts of scientists and citizens to discredit the
contrary evidence. Disconfirmation of an initially held belief is blamed on a
failure of a minor auxiliary assumption rather than the main belief in question
(e.g., "the substance really was an acid, dirt on the litmus paper must have
made it fail to turn red"). Confirmation of a rival hypothesis can be blamed
on some alternative other than the truth of that rival. In the Ross experiment,
however, the initial belief was maintained with *no* extra effort on the part
of the subjects. Indeed, one would expect here that the subjects would be
motivated to *disbelieve* that they are poor at math, and they would happily
embrace the idea that their poor performance was not due to their own abilities. Ross's and others' experiment shows that a belief can easily persevere
in someone despite their seeing contrary evidence, without their making any
effort to maintain that belief. Given belief perseverance, it's likely that the
teacher who believes that eighth graders tend to pick on the seventh graders
would likely continue to believe this, *even if specific evidence to the contrary
was pointed out to them*. Indeed, the research indicates she continued believing it (and likely acted as if it were true), even if she makes a sincere asser-
tion that she doesn't believe it. If our psychology is such that seeing many
examples of the X not doing Y will not dislodge an initial belief that the X do
Y, we should expect that many people will erroneously continue to believe
the X do Y, despite evidence to the contrary.

One-sided event representation and confirmation bias are two instances of
a more general tendency of human beings to see causal patterns, even in cases
where the relationship between being an X and doing Y is random. Gilovitch
writes, "Human nature abhors a lack of predictability and the absence of
meaning. As a consequence, we tend to "see" order where there is none, and
we spot meaningful patterns where only the vagaries of chance are operating"
(1991, 9). The various mental mechanisms that incline humans to see patterns
can dispose people who see *some* members of an X group doing Y to think
that just being a member of X is causally connected to doing Y. If being an X
really causes Y behaviors, one should infer that all or most of the Xs will do

Y. The mere sight of some Xs doing Y, then, can dispose people to believe that most of the Xs do Y. Small wonder that overgeneralizing about the X group will occur often.

When people see cases of the X doing Y as well as cases of the X not doing Y, then, it's easy for people to erroneously think they've seen a disposition in the Xs to do Y. It's interesting to note, however, that people can also have a tendency to make the *more egregious* error of coming to believe the X do Y even when *none* of the Xs they see clearly do Y. Frank and Gilovitch did an experiment in which trained referees watched videos of a football play in which the team wore white jerseys and another in which they wore black jerseys. In the version in which the team wore black jerseys, the referees judged the players as more aggressive and deserving of penalty than the white uniformed players doing the same activities. Frank and Gilovitch believe that, because the color black has negative connotations in many cultures, the ambiguous activity was seen one way if the people were black clothed and another if they were white clothed (Gilovitch 1991, 53). An X group might be seen as doing a Y activity, in other words, even when they are not, due to prior expectations. To give another example, suppose someone comes to initially believe, for one reason or another, that Irish people are kind to their neighbors. Suppose, then, that they see an Irish farmer leading an old woman to the house next door. Such behavior is ambiguous. Does he want to help the old woman get back home, or is he annoyed with her trespassing on his land and trying to get her off? The event might be seen either way, but the psychological research suggests that this event would likely be categorized according to prior expectations. It would likely confirm the belief that the Irish are kind to their neighbors. Prior expectations can lead people to erroneously believe that the X do Y, then, even if no one has actually made any observations of an X member doing Y (see, Olson et al. 1996 for a review).

There are numerous psychological factors, then, that predispose people to make errors in estimating the frequency of a trait in a population. Consequently, when we hear a speaker telling us that some X group does Y, we should be somewhat wary of concluding that most of members of the X really do do Y. Such statements are more likely to tell us what the speaker *believes* about the X group. But we should also be wary of coming to firm conclusions even about what speakers believe. For we know that speakers do not always try to follow linguistic conventions. Sometimes speakers try to give new meanings to phrases through a process we can call extension.

Extension

The work of Grice and others has made it well known that utterances are commonly used to convey far more than the conventional semantic meaning of the words used. Speakers often go well beyond literal meaning, and sometimes beyond any prior conventions, by communicating using metaphor, metonym, ellipsis, indexicality, and conversational implicature. To understand why people often describe situations using X-do-Y phrases even when we don't have the default situation in which *most* of the X do Y, we need to look at a type of non-literality I will call extension, in addition to looking at error. I use the word extension to describe when a speaker stretches the bounds of conventional usage without radically departing from it. We extend the word "cat" when we use it to describe lions and leopards as well as house cats. Speakers can also extend whole phrases, such as when people started using "jump the shark" to refer, not just to the episode that marked the downturn of the TV series "Happy Days," but to any of the episodes of any TV series that marks when it seems to have run out of ideas. When speakers use an X-do-Y phrase knowing full well that fewer than the default "most" of the X do or believe Y, they are extending the phrase (unless the extension has already become a new convention).

Why do people extend X-do-Y phrases beyond their default "all or most" usages? It's possible that there is little systematic to be said here. Different people may do it for different reasons in different situations. On the other hand, it is also possible that there are some deep general linguistic rules regarding extension, and that the extension of these phrases is just one class of instances within this general disposition. In what follows, I'll examine whether there are some plausible, fairly general reasons for extending X-do-Y claims. Whether extensions of this sort can be further explained by more general linguistic rules is an interesting question I'll leave to others.

We can begin with the observation that there are numerous situations where although it isn't really the case that *most* of the X do Y it *looks a lot like most* of the X are doing Y. This, as we discussed above, is why it's easy to make errors and to *think* that most of the X are doing Y. Speakers may well realize that it's not really the case that most of the X are doing Y, but they choose to say it anyway, extending this phrase's usage. The most obvious reason for saying it anyway is that many of the groups where less than most of the X do Y have most of the same characteristics of the groups where most of the X do Y. A group where a slim majority or a plurality of the X do or believe Y can produce most of the same net effects as a group where most of the X do Y. If the group produces the same effects, why not describe it in the same way?

But there will usually be some differences between groups where most of the X believe or do Y and groups where only a plurality do. The question, then, is why extend the phrase that has a different default conventional meaning instead of just using a *new* phrase? There are several possible answers.

One set of answers revolves around the fact that coming up with new, more precise descriptions of groups involves more work for speakers (and listeners) and it may not seem like the increased precision is worth the extra work. It is more work to *investigate* the group more closely, and ascertain just how many of the X are doing Y. It is more work to *take the time to explain* to others that "it's not that most of the X do Y, but more of the X do Y than do anything in a comparable class." Also, when speakers take the time to speak more precisely, it signals to listeners that they are being given precise information—which puts more pressure on speakers to be careful about speaking accurately. It takes more time to say "About 10 percent of school age children in New York City play handball with someone at least once a week," and "4 percent of New Yorkers under forty years of age who go to gyms play handball in those gyms," than "New Yorkers like to play handball." If you are a new resident who likes to play handball occasionally, the shorter statement will tell you as much of what you want to know as the longer one, in much less time. The more precise descriptions then, have some disadvantages that offset their advantage in precision.

But if speakers wanted to avoid all the cost of providing more accurate, nuanced information *and* the costs of being misleading, couldn't they do both simply by adopting the convention of making sure to say "*some* X do Y," whenever it's not the case that all or most do? I suspect there are two reasons this convention hasn't been adopted. One is that the word "some" is a notorious "weasel word" that can mean anything from a high percentage to a few individuals. No one is strictly violating any rules of English in saying things like "Some doctors don't believe that AIDS is caused by HIV" even if the number that do is less than a tenth of a percent. Unscrupulous people (and everyone else) sometimes use the vagueness of "some" to say something literally true that nevertheless makes something's numbers seem bigger than they really are. Consequently the word "some" is tainted. I suspect that there's a bit of hesitation to say "some X . . ." when the numbers of X are high—since it's ok to say "some X" when the numbers of X are inordinately low. People don't want to choose words that can make the claim sound less significant and interesting than it may actually be.

The other reason the "some" option isn't used more extensively, I suspect, is that listeners often actually *like* to hear somewhat exaggerated claims. An announcer who says, "And Barry Bonds knocks another one out of the ball park" is thought to have more pizzazz then if he said "Barry Bonds hits one into the left field stands." A person who says, "Nobody in L.A. ever takes public transportation," is making a more interesting, although less accurate statement than one who says "People in L.A. take public transportation fewer times per month per capita than people in other large cities." Why listeners like hearing statements like this is something I'll discuss in the next section. But speakers seem to realize that listeners enjoy them, and this creates another disincentive to try to avoid using the more grandiose X-do-Y phrases and an incentive to press such phrase into service—even when far fewer than most of the X believe or do Y. There are many reasons, then, why speakers are willing to use X-do-Y phrases in situations when they realize that not all or not most of the X do Y. In doing so, they extend the use of the X-do-Y phrase, paving the way for an expanded conventional usage if the extension catches on for large numbers of people.

Tolerance

Something we'll call *tolerance* can also have a large influence on when people will make X-do-Y statements. The amount of listener tolerance refers to how many and to what degree people will not overtly disapprove of (or question) someone's describing a situation in ways that depart from conventional rules. For example, most listeners tend not to ridicule or question speakers who say things like, "Every single member of the UNLV faculty was in Tom and Jerry's bar last night," or, "New Yorkers will sleep over on the first date," even when they know these things are not true of most members of the groups in question. This shows a high degree of tolerance for departing from the usual linguistic convention. Speakers are likely to increase their rates of errors and extensions for X-do-Y statements when they think that listeners will not mind or will not challenge their rule-violating descriptions. Tolerance also plays a key part in creating *new* rules or rule exceptions. When listeners know that speakers continually tend to make errors or extensions, they know not to expect the situation to really be as the phrase's old conventional meaning would have it. A person hearing "Jim had a band-aid on his nose" does not really expect that the bandage Jim is wearing must be a genuine Band-Aid® brand bandage. Listeners realize that people have come to sloppily refer to all bandages that resemble the adhesive bandages made by Johnson and Johnson as "band-aids." Speakers, knowing this, then feel freer to make the error or the extension of calling all of these types of things "band-aids." With this way of talking occurring more often, it becomes increasingly awkward to correct those who are speaking this way. Hearing few corrections, people come to believe that listeners have become *completely* tolerant of speakers using words or phrases to describe situations other than ones that prior convention dictated these phrases refer to. At this point, a new convention has developed and these phrases now have new meanings in addition to (or aside from) their original ones.

Why, and in what situations, do listeners tend to tolerate speakers breaking the "no quantifiers = all or most" rule? We must first admit that different subgroups tolerate different amounts of error and extension in different situations. I've found that many political liberals, for example, seem to believe that it is "politically incorrect" to make *any* general statements about any oppressed minorities. It is often considered racist, sexist, homophobic, etc., to discuss people as anything other than individuals. Racists, on the other hand, may consider it intolerable to talk about any *positive* general characteristics of the disliked race. And members of a given subgroup may tend to begrudgingly tolerate certain linguistic behavior from *strangers*, but demand a higher standard from friends. At times, they may also do the opposite. They may understand which less-than-most situation a *friend* is speaking of with a given X-do-Y statement, and not feel mislead, while a stranger might have his utterance met with an icy "Really? *All* the X?" It is clearly going to be very difficult to say exactly when listeners will and won't be tolerant of linguistic convention breaking. But that doesn't mean we can't try to explain some of the *general* motivations people have for being tolerant of certain phrases and discuss when they tend to be most and least tolerant.

When Is There Tolerance, in General?

We should begin our discussion of when listeners are most tolerant by noting that, while listeners usually don't like it if speakers are talking in a misleading way, correcting or questioning a speaker is costly. First, correcting or questioning simply takes time and effort. Taking the time to correct or probe takes resources away from doing other things. More importantly, however, no speaker likes having her honesty or intelligence questioned. It's hard not to feel insulted when you've been contradicted or questioned by a listener. Speakers whose generalizations have been questioned by listeners often feel a degree of hostility toward the questioners. To avoid the discomfort that can come from a hostile atmosphere, listeners may not bother to try to correct what they feel is a misstatement about some group by a speaker. If a cousin says, "Gee, Chicagoans are so friendly," on a trip to Chicago, this is more likely to be met with a nod, than, "yes, but it's said that people in the south suburbs are really cruel to minorities."

Given that it's costly to correct or question speakers, most listeners will likely be tolerant of a range of less egregious violations of convention. When will they tend to be *most* tolerant? In general, it's likely that listeners will be most tolerant of a rule-violating X-do-Y statement when they think that, a) believing the untrue proposition is *unlikely to harm* anyone, and b) hearing the untrue statement actually produces some *benefit*. There are several situations in which listeners are unlikely to be harmed by hearing a less-than-most situation described by an X-do-Y statement. One is when the net effect that a group produces will not differ much depending on whether it's most or merely *many* of the X that do or believe Y. Listeners will likely tolerate people saying things like "The people of this town support Higgins taking over as mayor," even if less than most do—because the result of an election will be the same whether it's most, a majority, or a plurality who support Higgins. In general, small exaggerations in X-do-Y statements will be tolerated, since even if people are misled by them, they are not misled very much.

At the other end of the spectrum, people will also likely to be tolerant of *large* exaggerations. When someone says something like "It's amazing how people in Baltimore buy all their clothes from thrift stores," they are unlikely to be corrected by people describing Gap and Sears stores where people also shop. Listeners are likely to be tolerant of such statements, as they are unlikely to be mislead when it is clear that such statements are blatant exaggerations made for the listener's entertainment.

A different set of circumstances in which listeners are unlikely to be harmed by X-do-Y statements is when information about *how many* of the X do Y is unlikely to have any effect on any of the listener's short or long term goals. If someone tells me that the people of the Lisu tribe in Northern Thailand build their houses on stilts, I will be very unlikely to probe whether or not most do or many do. Nothing in my long or short-term goals is likely to be affected by knowing whether it's most or many. In general, rule-violating X-do-Y statements will cause fewer problems for listeners, the more the people described are *distant in space or time*. Listeners, then, tend to be much more tolerant of statements about distant matters. This is not to say that listeners will tolerate speakers saying anything that comes into their minds about distant people. Listeners do not like people violating the general moral norm of truth telling. But listeners will be far more tolerant of mild violations of convention concerning descriptions of people they will never interact with than they will be of descriptions of familiar people.

There are also times when people will also be very tolerant of convention-violating X-do-Y statements even for descriptions of familiar groups. If, to satisfy long or short-term goals, all one needs to know is that a relatively large number of the X do Y, an X-do-Y statement will give this information. Knowing whether it's many or most of the X who do Y can be unnecessary. Hearing "New Yorkers like to stay out late at night" leads people to believe, correctly, that large numbers of New Yorkers like to stay out late. It can wrongly lead them to expect this of *most* New Yorkers. But the owner of a small restaurant with five tables deciding what hours to keep her shop open is not going to be harmed by thinking that *most* people stay out late at night when it's really only *many* people that do. All she really needs to know is that there are lots of New Yorkers who stay out late. People like her will tend to be tolerant of slight convention-violating X-do-Y statements.

Sometimes people's goals only require them to know that Y behavior *exists* among the X. If knowing that is enough, a person may not care at all about the *number* of X that do Y. Suppose on a road trip you heard that the people in the town of Kirby, Arkansas, were so hostile to nonlocals that Elks Club members there liked to beat up unsuspecting motorists who are passing through. The appropriate response would not be "Look, perhaps there have been incidents of violence, but it's implausible that *most* of the Elks Club members are involved in beating up non-locals." The appropriate response would be to thank your informant and give that town a wide berth. Why take the costly action of criticizing a speaker when the information she has given you is perfectly adequate for giving you all the understanding you'll need? We tend to be tolerant of all kinds of X-do-Y phrases when we are more interested in knowing *what can be found* in the group, than *the extent* of that trait in the group.

Sometimes renegade X-do-Y phrases are tolerated, not because of their adequacy for various practical goals, but because of the way the information in such phrases can *surprise, fascinate, or amuse* us. Such phrases not only don't harm us, but can benefit us by giving us important information while producing enjoyable emotions. Listeners tolerate speakers making some X-do-Y statements when less than most do, because they find such statements, like other exaggerations, amusing. We like hearing statements like "Your baseball team spends more time in the jailhouse than on the field" because we find such statements funny. Other times exaggerations amuse people simply because they paint big dramatic pictures that give people a certain degree of arousal. "The faucet is broken and now there's a flood rushing though the bathroom" gets the adrenaline running. "Everyone is buying the new Pokemon doll" creates curiosity and excitement. Hearing that "people in Japan idolize The Ventures" is more interesting than hearing that "a large number of Japanese baby boomers idolize The Ventures." Listeners often don't probe or question such statements because they like the small thrill that comes from hearing them. And there isn't a worry about being misled, since people are well aware that such statements are made primarily to entertain, not to give accurate information.

Related to amusement is fascination. There are some subjects we are wired up to be very interested in or have learned to be interested in, whether or not they affect our goals. I remember once being told that in the colonial United States, the Puritans used to practice something called bundling—going on dates where the couple gets into bed with each other fully dressed, and giggles with each other under a blanket. I was very interested to know *that* there were numbers of Puritans who did that. I had little interest in knowing *how many* Puritans did that. Indeed I was probably much more interested in the claim, given that it wasn't qualified (leaving me to picture the default "most Puritans"), than it would be in the claim that "*some* of the Puritans used to do something called bundling." The fascination with the fact that there existed some X people who did Y outweighed any interest in finding out how many truly did Y (which might create a less interesting picture.) And when the situations described in the convention-violating X-do-Y statements have little to do with any of our goals, of course, that only increases our toleration for them.

Pleasant or neutral surprising claims can have an effect on our emotions that is similar to amusing or fascinating ones. When we hear surprising X-do-Y claims, we don't want to lessen the thrill by questioning or probing their accuracy. And we don't want to insult a speaker who has told us something so interesting. If a person tells us that the women in Burma elongate their necks using towers of gold rings, we don't tend to immediately ask "How many Burmese women?" We are probably hard-wired to be interested in surprising claims because such claims tell us that the difference between what we generally expect from the world, and what's true in this case, is very great. The greater the difference is between what we thought was true and what is true—the more we could potentially be harmed by this ignorance. So hearing about surprising things, in general, tends to interest us more than finding out things that would not be unexpected. Now when listeners have heard that the X people do something especially surprising, this information, by its very nature, will contradict previously held beliefs about the world. The stronger sense of urgency in listeners, then, is to a) "absorb" this information and think about which prior beliefs need to be revised and b) get more evidence from the speaker *that* it is, indeed, true that some of the X do Y. In such situations, listeners generally will *not* feel as compelled to try to get *more accurate* information about how many of the X do Y. Listeners will tend to be pretty tolerant of pleasantly surprising rule violating X-do-Y claims. (Unpleasant surprises, however, will be less tolerated, as listeners are more likely to probe speakers, hoping to establish that such claims are untrue.)

THE MAIN EXCEPTIONS TO THE "NO QUANTIFIERS = ALL OR MOST" RULE

Having looked at the general processes of rule-modifying due to error, extension, and tolerance, I now want to look at how these factors may have made it permissible to make X-do-Y statements in a number of particular types of situations other than when all or most of the X do Y.

Caricature

One of the most highly tolerated usages of X-do-Y phrases is when the speaker is blatantly and obviously exaggerating. Speakers can say things like "Philosophy professors never work on Fridays" without much fear of being contradicted because they know that listeners know that such statements are meant to amuse. Humorous X-do-Y exaggerations are the most permissible, because people like being entertained. But other X-do-Y exaggerations are permissible when it is clear that most of the X *don't* do Y, so few listeners feel anyone is trying to mislead them. One can get away with saying, "I can't believe how people in this town spend all of their paychecks at the bars" because people know that most don't really do this, and that the speaker is merely forcefully stating his exasperation. Listeners know that people make strong statements when they are angry, without regard for accuracy. *Blatant* exaggerations that are growled out tend to be tolerated, since few feel any danger of being misled by them. Paradoxically, the less clear it is that an X-do-Y statement like this *is* a blatant exaggeration, the more listeners will be inclined to probe and question its veracity. It is sometimes permissible to break the rules, if they are broken in a big way.

High Surprise/Fascination (and Low Importance)

Another set of circumstances in which it seems permissible to say that the X do or believe Y, even though fewer than most do, is when its very *surprising* or interesting that there are a large number of X who do or believe Y. Suppose Joe hears from a friend that "The players on the Xavier College football team have "Avenging Angel" tattooed on their buttocks." Joe later does some checking up on this. He finds out that fifteen of the thirty-five players do indeed have this tattoo. Would Joe feel that he had been misled? It's not likely he would. He would feel that he had confirmed an interesting piece of gossip. He would probably not be bothered at all that the number of the X that do Y is less than half. We seem not to be disturbed to hear that the X do Y when it's quite surprising that some of the X do Y, even when it's a relatively small percentage that do. And the more surprising it is, the smaller the percentage of Y-doers there can to be without listeners feeling mislead. You can't clearly get away with saying "workers at the Musselman Applesauce plant bring their lunches from home" unless most do. But you could get away with saying "workers at the Musselman Applesauce plant like to play chess during their lunch breaks," even if only ten out of seventy workers did. The effort it takes to absorb the surprising idea *that* this is done by a fairly large number of people makes listeners less interested in finding out precisely *how many* do it.

Why might it have become acceptable to say that the X do Y when merely a surprising (possibly low) number of the X do Y? First, it is likely quite common for people to *erroneously believe* that most of the X do Y, when a surprising number do. Numerous cognitive scientists have commented that people most easily remember surprising facts (Hamilton, et al. 1985; Wyer and Srull 1986). In remembering a group, it's more likely that the surprising, rather than the mundane, features come to mind. When what comes most readily to mind is the group members that are doing the *surprising* activity, then it can be difficult to remember that fewer than most group members engage in this activity. Many speakers will, thus, often erroneously believe and use phrases that mean most of the X do Y, when merely a surprising number do.

Secondly, even when speakers know that fewer than *most* of the X do Y, they may be quite willing to extend this phrase to cover cases where merely a *large* number of them do. Speakers know that such phrases evoke large numbers. But they may not want to do the extra work it takes to find out *how* large the number is. And they may also think (usually correctly) that listeners don't mind the use of this more comprehensive phrase. Indeed, speakers who amuse their listeners get some type of social reward for doing so.

But why would *listeners* tend to be tolerant of speakers using X-do-Y phrases to describe cases where there's merely a surprising number of X who do or believe Y? Well, for the reasons stated above, the numbers of times people describe surprising situations this way, both in error and as extensions, is likely to be very high. Since listeners don't want to be in the position of *constantly* questioning and correcting, they are probably willing to let surprising X-do-Y claims go unchallenged quite often. This makes it look to others as if surprising X-do-Y statements can legitimately be made, regardless of the actual numbers of the X doing Y. Surprising information about group activities also tends to be especially valuable in and of itself—even without much information about its extent. Listeners, then, have less incentive to probe to get more accurate numbers, given that the information they have is already valuable. Listeners may also be reluctant to risk lessening the emotional thrill of surprising information by finding out how few of the X really do Y. Listeners also know that speakers would be less willing to provide them with interesting surprising information, if such information would likely provoke skeptical questioning whenever it was potentially misleading. Because listeners like to hear surprising information, they are willing to encourage speakers to *just make* X-do-Y claims, rather than slow down and describe the group's activities in a careful accurate manner. Surprising information—with no annoying qualifications—is interesting to hear.

It is not true, of course, that speakers can make X-do-Y claims *completely* irrespective of the number of X that do or believe Y. One would probably not get away with saying that Clevelanders like to eat insects, if it's a *very* small number—no matter how surprising this may be. And some claims about what the X do are so surprising that they invite questions about the number who do. If I were told that the patients at the Michael Manor Home for the Elderly liked to do cocaine in the bathroom at dinnertime, I would immediately ask skeptically, "*How many* patients do that?" Also, if people's goals depend on having accurate information about a group, they may well also probe, no matter how surprising the information is. A city councilman hearing the surprising news that the residents of his district actually hate the new jogging track in the park will want to know how many residents really hate it. The concern with accuracy regarding goal-related subjects means that surprising X-do-Y claims, like other rule-violating X-do-Y claims, will be far more tolerated if they are about groups that are *distant* from the listeners in time and space. There are limitations, then, on when you can describe a surprising situation with an X-do-Y claim. But when the claim is surprising, we should expect that speakers are describing situations in which the actual numbers of X doing or believing Y can fall within a very large range.

Plurality

Another set of circumstances that can permissibly be described with X-do-Y claims are when the X people do or believe Y—more than they do or believe any other comparable thing in the domain of interest. While in the *distinctiveness* class, discussed in the next section, X-do-Y statements can be made to emphasize that *the X* (and few other) frequently do Y, the plurality class is one where such phrases are used to emphasize that the X do *Y*, and not something else. It seems acceptable to say, "The people in Humbolt County mostly drive pickup trucks," even though, put together, more Humbolt County residents drive either motorcycles, SUVs, or regular cars. But if more people drive pickup trucks *than any other vehicle*, it is acceptable for speakers to say that this is what those people tend to do, even if less than a majority drive pickup trucks. In other words, speakers can say that the X do Y even if a majority of X doesn't do Y doesn't but a *plurality* does.

We should note that the idea of "plurality" is actually a more complicated notion than it may first appear. The paradigmatic use of the term plurality is to describe the results of an election contested by more than two candidates, where none of the candidates gets a majority of votes. When candidates A and B each get 30 percent of the vote, while C gets 40 percent, candidate C has won a plurality of the vote. In general, a subgroup of a group can claim to have a plurality of the group's members if more members are in this subgroup, than any other subgroup, within a particular division scheme. The phrase "within a particular division scheme" is important here, since nearly every subgroup of a group always has *some* type of subgroup of that group that is bigger than it. People might farm in Adams County more than any other single line of work. But there will certainly be more people who are "farmers or accountants" than there are farmers. There will be more blue-collar workers than there are farmers, and there may well be more Lutherans than there are blue-collar workers. So a plurality is not just the biggest subgroup of a group—it's the biggest subgroup within a particular division scheme. Now speakers talking about pluralities know *which* division they are picking the largest subgroup from because they themselves are the people who have the division in mind. When a speaker says, "Adams Countians tend to be Lutherans," he has in mind that Lutherans are the biggest subdivision of the various types of *religious denominations* in the county. He is not mentally dividing the county's population as to membership in fraternal organizations. Listeners who know that subgroups are being compared in such discussions also often have some awareness of the division scheme being used, as soon as one of the subgroups is named. Only subgroups of the same "grain size" within the same general superordinate type make sense to compare, as opposed to comparing apples and oranges. And only some sorts of comparisons tend to be interesting ones. When a listener hears that "Adams Countians are farmers," he knows that what is being said is that the number of farmers is large compared to the number of people belonging to other occupations. And he knows that "farmers" and "farmers or accountants," aren't classes that people tend to be interested in comparing. The same goes for "farmers" and "blue-collar workers." "Farmers" can still be the largest group in an occupational division scheme, even though there are more blue-collar workers. When speakers talk of the size of "farmer" class, listeners know that few are interesting in comparing its size with the size of a "blue-collar worker" class. So listeners know that the division scheme that the speaker has in mind must be one comparing farmers to other *particular* occupations, rather than a division scheme in which "blue-collar workers" can be the largest subgroup. On the other hand, when listeners hear things like "blue-collar workers have bad manners," they know that the speaker is trying to convey that the number of blue-collar workers with bad manners is the largest one in an occupational division scheme that divides people into just blue-collar and white-collar workers. A plurality, then, is the biggest subgroup according to a particular stated or implied division scheme of a group. When someone makes an X-do-

Y statement with the idea that a plurality of the X do Y, they are thinking that the Y-doers form the biggest subdivision within a certain division scheme for the X group that they are thinking of.

How could we get a rule by which situations with plurality as well as majority Y-doers could be described with X-do-Y phrases? First, it's likely that many speakers describe pluralities using "X do Y" because they erroneously believe that *most* of the X do or believe Y. It's not hard to see how people could be prone to this error. When searching one's minds for information about what members of a certain group tend to do—in general, or within some category of activities—one is likely to come up with the activity that group members do more frequently than they do other things. (Surprising things are likely to come to mind even more often, of course, creating our second 'exception' category.) If one thinks of the occupations of Oceanview, Maine residents, and fishing comes to mind first (as more people fish than do any other job), then it's easy to mistakenly believe that *most* members of the group are fishermen. Most residents *are* fishermen *in the mental sample* that one is scanning. And if there are no other activities that are done as frequently in that domain (the very definition of a plurality), it is all the more difficult to envision people in X doing anything but Y. It is easy, therefore to erroneously believe that most of the X do Y, when only a plurality do, and then to consequently describe this situation with the phrase that has the default meaning "most of the X do Y." As usual, when a situation is mistakenly described in a certain way with great frequency, there are pressures on listeners to simply tolerate that phrase as an alternative way of describing that situation (as when one "xeroxes" a page on an IBM copier).

It is also straightforward to see why people would want to *extend* the usage of X-do-Y phrases to cover pluralities. For one thing, many of the same things are true of a group where a plurality of members do Y that are true of a group where a majority of the members do Y. Eddie Shara will become the student council president when the majority of students prefer Eddie Shara *or* when a plurality of students prefer Eddie Shara. Why not use the same label ("The students prefer Eddie Shara") to describe states of affairs that are so similar?

And why would listeners tolerate the use of such phrases to describe pluralities, given that phrases of this sort are so often used to describe the belief that *most* of the X do Y? The answer, again, is that questioning and probing gives "diminishing marginal returns." Probing needlessly insults the speaker and takes time. And on any plausible interpretation, hearing that "The people of Humbolt County drive pickup trucks" tells listeners that Humbolt county dwellers do drive pickup trucks, and drive them in large numbers. Furthermore, if conversational context tells them that the speaker is comparing Y-doers to other activity–doers, they now know Y-doers are more numerous (even though they may not know *how numerous* the Y-doers are). A listener who believes that such a phrase has correctly informed her that *large numbers* of the X do Y, but who thinks that it may not actually be *most* of the X who do Y, will probably be unlikely to pay the cost of probing for the small benefit of getting slightly better information than she already has.

Distinctiveness

A different set of circumstances in which it seems acceptable to say that the X do Y when less than most of the members of X do, is when "the X" are a group in which a high percentage or a high number of the members do Y, while few other *comparable groups* do Y to that extent. When speakers talk this way about *pluralities* they are emphasizing that the X do *Y*, and not other comparable activities. The distinctiveness class emphasizes *the X*, and not comparable groups, do Y. Speakers often say things like, "In Cajun country, the people are always eating a spicy soup called Jambalaya," even if it's the case that *most* people in this region eat Jambalaya rarely. People are rarely censured for making such statements. I suspect this is because we have developed the rule that it is permissible to make X-do-Y statements when merely high percentages or high numbers of the X (as opposed to most) do Y—but far more of them do Y than people in *other* groups do.

How could such a descriptive convention have developed? Again, it's likely that many speakers describe distinctive groups using X-do-Y phrases because they erroneously believe that *most* of the X do or believe Y. It's not hard to see how people could be prone to this error. When someone wracks their brains for information about which group does Y (say, who eats deep dish pizza), it would be unsurprising if what comes to mind first is the group that has the highest percentage or numbers of X members that do Y. If, when thinking of deep dish pizza eaters, they think of Chicagoans, one is *not* picturing the many Chicagoans who don't like pizza at all. And if one is picturing Chicagoans when one is picturing deep dish pizza lovers, then it is easy to slip into thinking that you are picturing what *most Chicagoans* like. (Psychologists call this the "representativeness heuristic.") And when a situation is mistakenly described in a certain way with great frequency, again, there are pressures on listeners to simply tolerate that phrase as an alternative way of describing that situation.

Speakers also have motivation to *extend* the usage of X-do-Y phrases to cover cases where doing Y is distinctive to a group. A speaker may want to tell a listener where he or she will find *the most* Y-doing. Upon eating her first bagel, a delighted Midwesterner may wonder what group has a practice of eating these regularly. An easy thing to say in response to a question along these lines is "New Yorkers really like to eat bagels." Using this phrase tells people *that* it is the case that large numbers of New York City dwellers eat bagels regularly. The context of the conversation often lets a listener know that the speaker is telling her in *which* group, compared to others, we'll find large numbers of Y-doers. Now this context doesn't explain what the percentage of Y-doers in this X group is. So such a phrase does run some risk of misleading listeners, if it is interpreted as meaning that most New Yorkers eat lots of bagels. To avoid the potential to mislead a speaker could say, "New Yorkers eat a higher percentage of bagels than people in other cities—though it's not clear that people who eat a lot of bagels are really a majority in New York." But it is difficult and time consuming to sift through one's knowledge and come up with this idea. And it's awkward and time consuming to *speak* this way. "New Yorkers really like to eat bagels," is quicker and easier. Speakers also likely know that listeners are tolerant of hearing things described this way.

And why would listeners be likely to tolerate an X-do-Y phrase used to describe a distinctive group, when the default meaning of such phrases is *most* of the X do Y? After hearing such phrases, listeners know that there *are* Xs who do Y—something that they may not have known before. They also know the fact that there are *large numbers* of Xs that do Y. It is seldom acceptable to use X-do-Y phrases when the numbers of the X doing Y are quite small. The context in which the phrase is uttered can enable listeners to infer that the speaker is contrasting the large number of X members who do Y to the small number of members of comparable groups that do Y. All of this is good information to have.

What listeners will not know, when they hear such phrases, is *how many* of the X do Y. But they will know it has to be a large number or large percent. They will also know that such phrases are frequently made (and tolerated) when less than most of the X do Y. So the number must be *somewhere between a large number of the X and most* of the X doing Y. To know which it is, speakers will have to probe further. But since the information they have is good enough for most of their goals, and since probing is costly, listeners will seldom probe or question the speakers. The result is that speakers seldom get negative feedback for saying that the X do Y, when talking about a distinctive group in which high numbers (but less than most) of the X do Y. As speakers feel free to say it, it becomes part of our convention to say that the X do or believe Y when the X have more Y doers than comparable groups.

A Particular Subgroup of the X Group

Another set of circumstances that has become acceptable to describe using an X-do-Y phrase is when the Y activity is being done by a *specific salient subgroup within X.* A dance teacher at a local gym recently told me that, "people in Las Vegas are really into belly dancing these days." Surely she didn't have in mind that a *majority* of Las Vegans like to belly dance. What she had in mind most likely was that *Las Vegans who take dance classes in gyms*—the class of Las Vegans that are of interest to her (and to me in the context of this conversation)—like to belly dance. Making an X-do-Y statement to describe a situation in which a particular subgroup of X does Y is, I believe, at the outer edge of permissibility in conversational English. A speaker may well say, "People in Barcelona love to go dancing," while believing merely that *young people of dating age*—rather than a larger group of Barcelonans that includes toddlers and the elderly—love to go dancing. She may well know that Barcelona residents of other ages don't dance much. But she has no interest, at least at the present moment, in these other Barcelonans, and believes her listeners don't either. She is not worried about a listener misunderstanding her and saying, "The grandmothers there really like to go dancing?" Indeed, a listener who said that would be making a somewhat unacceptably cranky probe. Our rule seems to be that a speaker can make an X-do-Y statement while speaking about only a subgroup of X. A listener should not, then, uncharitably interpret her as making a statement about most members of the group.

The permissibility of using an X-do-Y statement to talk about a salient subgroup of a group lowers the threshold of when someone can make an X-do-Y statement considerably. Most of the X group need not do Y, only the members of that subgroup do—and that number can end up being far less than most of the whole X group. And the requirements are even more permissive than this, I believe. How many members of the particular *subgroup* have to do Y before we can make an X-do-Y statement? I think the requirements are similar to those of the larger groups. That is, we can make an X-do-Y statement about the group, not only when most of the subgroup does Y, but when a plurality of the subgroup does, when a surprising number of the subgroup does, when we want to make a caricature of what the subgroup does, and when this subgroup is distinct in doing Y. It has become permissible in some circumstances, in other words, to say that the X do Y, when possibly only a small percentage of a small subgroup of X does Y.

How could such a convention have arisen? It could have started in part, by people making errors concerning subgroups quite frequently. An example of such an error would be where a speaker sees that a large number of fellow dating-age Barcelonans go out dancing often. Whatever else one might call this group of young revelers, they are all *Barcelonans*. This might be the first label that comes to mind for various reasons. Other Barcelona residents may be completely "off the radar screen" for this person, so she doesn't think about the fact that the vast majority of Barcelonans don't go out dancing frequently. She doesn't think about them at all when she's thinking about dancing. Without thinking about other residents, she erroneously believes and says, "Barcelonans like to go out dancing often." Seeing Y-behaviors frequently in a subgroup, not paying attention to the activities of the rest of the group, and referring to the subgroup by using the name of the superordinate group that they belong to, leads to frequent erroneous X-do-Y statements. With an unwillingness to correct or question such frequent statements, this erroneous way of speaking gets on the road to becoming an acceptable convention.

Another way this convention could begin is by extension. A speaker might want to say something about the activities of a particular subgroup of X. He knows what subgroup he has in mind, and he believes that his listeners know exactly what subgroup he has in mind. He does not, however, know exactly how to *describe* the makeup of this subgroup and doesn't want to take the time to figure it out. He knows, however, that people in this subgroup are members of a well known X-group. He knows that most of the X-group do not engage in Y behaviors, but he isn't worried about his listeners being misled, because he has good reason to believe that they, too, are thinking of the same subgroup that he is. He decides that it's reasonable to just quickly label this subgroup with the more general X group name. Here an X-do-Y phrase is being extended to mean that a subgroup of X does Y. If this extension gains widespread acceptance, it becomes a new rule.

And why would listeners be tolerant of such errors and extensions, instead of correcting speakers when they make X-do-Y statements in such circumstances? The main reason, I suspect, is that the context often makes clear which subgroup the speaker is really wanting to talk about. Even though the speaker gives the name of the larger group, listeners, in these circumstances, usually realize that they aren't really being given information about the larger group. They realize the speaker is talking about a particular subgroup, so they don't feel misled. A listener may well assume that a speaker saying "Barcelonans" is talking about young potentially dateable Barcelonans between eighteen and thirty. Since the listener knows that, she likely would not even want speakers to take the time to say all the quantifying adjectives. A feedback cycle begins where X-do-Y statements in these circumstances become less corrected, and therefore more frequent and acceptable. Tolerance of such errors and extensions regarding subgroups can lead to a new kind of "exception" category for X-do-Y statements. I find it highly plausible that such an exception category has developed in this way.

Saying that the X do or believe Y when only part of a subgroup might is a very lenient requirement. One might wonder if such a requirement is one that is so lenient that it allows a person to say that the X do Y in just about any circumstance. After all, there will often likely be some or other small subgroup of X whose members do Y. This needn't be a worry, for this exceptional category is more structured and restrictive than one might think. To make it permissible to say that the X do Y when only a subgroup of the X does, the context of the conversation must make it fairly clear to the listener *which subgroup* of X is being discussed. It seems permissible for a speaker to say, "Actresses are now rushing to their dentists to get botox injections every month or so," if it is clear to the listener from the context of the conversation that he is talking about Los Angeles movie actresses between forty and eighty years old. If the context does not make this clear, and there is no clear subgroup he is talking about, then the listener may likely assume that the speaker is talking about actresses in general. The default "no quantifier = most" rule suggests that the speaker is claiming that most actresses do this. This seems very implausible (actresses in their twenties don't have wrinkles, and botox limits the number of expressions your face will make). And a person making such a statement can expect corrections, questions, and probes. Just because saying that the X do Y can sometimes be permissible when a subgroup of X does, that doesn't mean that *any* subgroup of X doing Y makes this description permissible. This is why people will fairly often be challenged when they claim things like "People are really into reading the Kabala these days," when all that they've seen is stories about a handful of celebrities.[4] The category of *celebrity* is not the kind of clear distinct subgroup that a speaker could count on her listener as assuming she was talking about—so such a statement could easily mislead listeners. In the right circumstances, however, even a small percentage of a subgroup of X doing or believing Y can make it permissible to make an X-do-Y statement about them.

We learn much of what we know about the world through listening to other people's descriptions of it. Some of the most important information we can have about the world concerns what collections of people tend to do or believe. This is a topic of discussion in numerous everyday conversations and among journalists and scholars. The topic is often discussed using X-do-Y phrases. But despite the importance and commonality of these phrases, the amount of good information they can give you about the social world is limited. When we hear someone say, "Some fire-fighters put out the fire on Seventh Avenue," it is usually pretty safe to conclude that the state of the world is such that there was a fire on Seventh Avenue, which some fire-fighters put out. But when we hear a speaker say, "fire-fighters like to play poker while they are waiting for an alarm signal," it's not clear what we should believe about the world. Estimating the frequency of a trait in a population is something people tend to be bad at, for a variety of reasons we have discussed. The probability of a speaker's having erroneous beliefs about how many of the X do Y is quite high, so their statements about such matters should be taken with a grain of salt. And even if a speaker's belief is not erroneous, speakers frequently extend the meaning of words and phrases and use them to describe situations they aren't conventionally used to describe. A listener expecting that the "no quantifiers = all or most" convention is being followed will be misled. And even when speakers are following sociolinguistic conventions, our conventions have come to be loosened, so that hearing X-do-Y phrase might signal any of a number of different things a speaker has in mind. It is permissible to say that the X do Y when most of the X do, when a plurality do, when it's surprising that some of the X do, when the X and no other group does to that extent, when a particular subgroup of the X do, and when one wants to caricature the activities of the X group. When we hear such a phrase, it can be unclear which situation the speaker really has in mind (or which situation in the world he or she is trying to describe). When a journalist writes, "Albany residents are increasingly annoyed at high property taxes," is he thinking of most Albany residents, a plurality of them, a surprising number of them or of just the homeowners? According to our evolved social/linguistic conventions, he might be thinking any of these when he says this. (Indeed, he might also be thinking of *still other* meanings of such phrases, such as *collective* belief, which we will discuss in the following chapter.) Academics are sometimes more choosy about their wording when describing groups. Political scientists sometimes take care to write things like, "A plurality of voting age Americans did not vote at all in the 2000 election." But such scholars are writing in English, and they just as often write according to the conventions of colloquial English. (Notice how easy it is for *me* to be unchoosy in my descriptions of "academics" as I write this.) Thus we quite often see highly regarded anthropologists using phrases like "the Balinese are aversive to animals and treat their large number of dogs not merely callously but with a phobic cruelty" (Geertz 1973, 420). A student reading such a phrase cannot be sure if the anthropologist is referring to the beliefs of most of the Balinese or if he is saying that the Balinese are far more averse to animals than comparable populations (or if the anthropologist has just made one of the errors that people often do in such matters).

What are we to do, then, given the importance of such information in our lives, and the frequency with which such phrases are uttered? Well I would hope that once the unreliability and ambiguity of such phrases have been pointed out, academics, at least, will be motivated to write more carefully. Political scientists should be more careful to say things like "Upper class voters tend to write letters to newspaper editors more than they practice any other single form of political dissent" rather than "Upper class voters tend to write letters to newspaper editors when they get angry." I would like to see journalists, too, become more careful in their language. They should work harder at saying things like "a higher percentage of Southern adult males own guns than adult males in other regions of the country" instead of "Southerners tend to own guns." Perhaps if academics and journalists began writing about groups in a less vague way, people's speaking patterns would slowly follow suit.

But academic and ordinary patterns of speech about groups, of course, will likely be very slow to change. What should listeners do, in the meantime? Readers of X-do-Y phrases should remember to be cautious in making inferences about the populations described in this manner. Given errors and extensions, there are a large number of different situations that could lie behind people's X-do-Y statements about groups, besides most of the group doing or believing Y. Hearers of such statements should remember that such statements can't be counted on to be accurately describing a single type of situation.

But listeners should also remember that my claims in this chapter have not been entirely negative. There do seem to be some rules regarding when X-do-Y phrases are most permissible. Now, given that the rules may not be followed, we can't tell which *actual* situations we have when speakers make such statements. But, since people at least try to follow rules more than they try to extend phrases to mean new things, knowing what our conventions are will usually be able to tell listeners what speakers at least *believe* about the world. Knowing what speakers believe about groups is an important thing to know. My examination of our social/linguistic rules tells us that when we hear a speaker making an X-do-Y statement, they can't have just anything in mind. Speakers are likely thinking that most of the X do Y—or they are thinking that the situation is one of the other five we have described here. Conversational context often helps make clear which one. And knowing about these six beforehand can make it easier for listeners to know how to question a speaker to figure out which of these she really has in mind.

Our situation is such that we want to know what the people in the groups around us are thinking and doing. It is important enough that speakers are constantly giving us descriptions of things the X people do and believe. But understanding what people around us are up to is also important enough that we should try to get a better understanding of what we can and can't conclude when people give such descriptions. I hope this chapter can help increase that understanding.

NOTES

1. While this way of talking about the social has been neglected by philosophers looking at "social facts," it has not been completely neglected by linguists. Saying

that the X do Y belongs to a class that linguists call "generic characterizing sentences." There have been many interesting studies of the semantics of generics by linguists (see Carlson and Pelletier 2003).

2. Before faulty inductive generalization can be fully understood, it would help if two prior things were first understood: A) It would help to know why something is categorized as an X at all, and B) It would help to know when we generalize at all, beyond the particular event seen. Suppose a Russian writer comes to New York and sees three young Puerto Rican men stealing hubcaps. He may inadvertently come to believe a generalization. But which of the following generalizations is he most likely to make?

- Americans steal hubcaps
- young Americans steal hubcaps
- New Yorkers steal hubcaps
- Hispanics steal hubcaps
- black haired people steal hubcaps
- men steal hubcaps
- young men steal hubcaps
- young men in white shirts steal hubcaps

Or perhaps he will infer

- young men steal
- young men steal from cars
- young men steal from red cars
- young men steal from off the street

I will not attempt to discuss such issues here. Psychologists currently tend to be very unclear about why things are labeled as they are, and which generalizations people make (McCauley, Jussim, personal communication). Perhaps many different factors are responsible, and it's idiosyncratic to environments and personalities as to which dominate. Some clear things can be said, however, about what sorts of things tend to cause error, once labeling has occurred and once generalizations are happening.

3. In this chapter we are discussing potential epistemic problems with such general claims. In the final chapter we will discuss possible *moral* problems with such claims.

4. This is not to say that people (and gossip columns) won't often make claims like this. What I am saying is that statements like this do not rise to the status of being justified by a new social/linguistic rule the specifies something like "when a lot of the country's *celebrities* do Y, it's okay to say that the country's *people* do Y." Unlike instances of the "exception clauses" discussed in this chapter, such claims do tend to be fairly frequently criticized.

Chapter Three

What Starbucks Really Wants

CONFUSION ABOUT COLLECTIVE ASCRIPTION

In the previous chapter we looked at X-do-Y claims where speakers intend to say something about individuals in the X group doing something. But, as we said in the introduction, similar linguistic constructions can mean something quite different as well. "UNLV students drink gallons of water every day," can mean that each individual student drinks gallons of water every day or (more plausibly) that the group as a whole consumes gallons of water every day.

Sometimes we are interested in talking about what a group as a whole can do, rather than what each of the individuals in the group can do—since there are things that groups, as a whole, can do that the individuals in them cannot. All the individuals in the group, each doing a certain activity, can produce a different effect than a single individual can. AIDS patients (collectively) could use 10 percent of the world's antiviral drugs, though AIDS patients (taken individually) cannot. It's also true that each of the individuals doing different actions can, together, do something an individual can't—like when the employees of Maloy and Jones Construction build a shopping center or win a sandlot baseball game.

When people make X-do-Y statements, they are sometimes talking about what the X, together as a group, do, as a net effect. In this chapter, I will be talking about such collectivist X-do-Y claims. Sometimes, such statements about groups don't say anything particularly unusual or controversial. No one doubts that a knitting club, as a whole, can make a giant quilt. Other times, however, statements about groups seem to be saying something quite noteworthy.

Sometimes, when people say that the X do Y, they seem to be saying the group is acting like an intentional agent with beliefs, desires, hopes, or fears

49

of its own. "The government was happy to take my money, but then forgot about fixing the fence," a taxpayer may say. It is these sorts of claims I mostly want to focus on in this chapter. We see claims of this sort everywhere. They are frequently found, in newspapers, for example. "As part of a strategy devised almost a year before, CBS had decided it would make separate bids on National Conference games, American Conference games and Monday Night Football," writes *New York Times* writer Richard Sandomir (1998). Such attributions of beliefs to groups aren't restricted to locker rooms or newspaper headlines. Social science texts also contain many attributions like "But what the U.S. government and the foundations most wanted to do was make sure that American history and literature would be taught on a permanent basis in Europe" (Pells 1997, 104). What should we make of such statements? On the one hand, we quite commonly hear groups being discussed where it seems like the speaker clearly thinks of the group as acting and maybe thinking like a unitary agent. And some scholars have specifically endorsed the idea that groups can be agents (see, for example, Nelson 1990; Rovane 1998). On the other hand, common sense seems to suggest that collections of people as a whole don't seem like the sorts of things that can have thoughts and feelings (though the individuals in them can). And one of the founders of social psychology, Floyd Allport, once famously declared, "There is no such thing as a group mind; it is a misleading and harmful conception in every way, whether it is applied to crowd behavior, social conflict, revolutions, or the theory of the superorganic" (1924b). When people make group intentionality statements, then, what are they really thinking? And can groups be the sort of thing that can really have states like beliefs and desires? Is it helpful to think of group states in this way? If groups can have such states, can we know what they are? These are the sorts of questions this chapter will focus on.

DO SPEAKERS THINK OF GROUPS AS AGENTS?

It is clear that speakers talk as if they think that groups can have belief and desire-like states. It's not uncommon to hear statements like "Walmart is worried about what Target is planning" in everyday conversation. States like beliefs, desires, hopes, and fears and the like are called "intentional" states by philosophers. Sentences attributing such states are also said to be describing actors in terms of a "folk psychology" where internal states are described in more or less the everyday terminology we regularly use to describe the mental states of people. But we regularly use folk psychology to describe more than the inner states of individual humans. "Pick up any newspaper or listen carefully to broadcast news," writes Austen Clark, "and you are bound to hear governments described as intentional systems. The usage is remarkably frequent. Most of our international news is reported as a high-stakes soap opera. Its players are impulsive, moody, and heavily armed nations" (1994, 406). It's not difficult to find examples of what Clark is talking about. As I am writing these words on my computer, I stop and type in "China wants" on my search engine, the first headline that comes up is, "China Wants US to Set Timetable on Removal of Curbs on Trade in High-Tech Products." And the first sentence of this article reads, "China hopes that the US will set a timetable and road map on the removal of curbs on trade in high-technology products" (Low Seng Guan 2010). Surfing the web a bit, I find that "Germany Thinks Greece Should Sell Islands to Reduce Debt" (Chattahbox.com. 2010), and "India wants spotlight on per capita emissions" (Sinha 2010). On the official website of the French Government, I learn that "France believes that 'promoting and protecting all Human Rights are a legitimate concern for the international community' and it gives equal consideration to civil and political rights, as well as economic, social and cultural rights." These sorts of statements are not limited to claims about countries; "Toyota Hopes to Price Hydrogen Cars at $50,000" states a recent headline in *USA Today* (Woodyard 2010). "The stakes are high, not only for the sufferers of Type 1 diabetes who stand to benefit from the leaps in research *Harvard hopes* the program will generate," says an article in *Wired* (Van Buskirk 2010, emphasis mine).

Note that language of this sort strongly suggests the idea of an individual actor thinking or doing something. The claim is that "China hopes"—with the verb form of hope being the one used for *singular* agents, unlike the plural form used in "the Chinese hope." Similarly, Germany thinks (not Germans think), India wants (not Indians want), and France believes (not the French believe). The language used in these kinds of sentences, then, commonly and consistently invokes individual agency.

But what do speakers actually believe when they say or hear such sentences? One possibility is that people are speaking completely metaphorically and never really attribute belief-like states to groups. We do seem to be using intentional terms only metaphorically when we say things like "the earth feels the same force against it as the rocket feels lifting off." Perhaps we are doing something similar when we make intentional ascriptions to groups. Many scholars, however, believe that articulating or hearing metaphorical expressions leads people to conceptualize things in terms of the metaphor. The linguist George Lakoff, for example, argues that "metaphor is fundamentally conceptual, not linguistic, in nature" (1993, 244). Daniel Casasanto (2009), on the other hand, gives careful evidence showing that the relation between metaphorical language and metaphorical thought is a tangled and complex one, with language sometimes strongly effecting how people think about something and sometimes not doing so. There is, here, some relevant intriguing evidence that when the stock market is talked about using the metaphor of an agent acting (e.g., "in the glamour group, Telex *climbed*") listeners were more likely to believe that the stocks would rise (and act like they were trying to achieve the goal of increased profits) (Morris et al. 2007). If thinking about groups of people works in a similar way, then, when someone says, "Walmart wants to fire Bob," the speaker is thinking a similar thought to the one he has when he says things like, "Mr. Bechtel wants to fire Bob," only he thinks of the collective (Walmart) as the agent wanting to do the firing. Such a speaker might *say*, if pressed, that he doesn't really take such talk literally. But perhaps such denials would just be to avoid admitting to a seemingly unusual ontological commitment that one actually holds (like a person who says he doesn't believe in vampires but can't refrain from sleeping with a crucifix).

Confusions about what people are thinking when they ascribe folks psychological states (like desires) to groups this way is increased by the fact that philosophers and psychologists are not at all clear about what folk psychology is committed to even when intentional states are ascribed to individuals. What people believe about others beliefs then is unclear even in seemingly straightforward cases involving other human beings (see Stich and Ravenscroft 1994; Morton 2002). What does Jill end up thinking about what Bill believes when she believes that Bill hates all women but loves blondes? What speakers are thinking when talking about groups in intentional terms, then, is not that clear.

My suspicion is that both the kind of folk psychological theory a speaker is committed to and how literally one takes it regarding groups is highly variable across individuals and even within the same individual at different times. At this point, I have little evidence telling me what people who talk about group intentions actually believe about them. My focus in this chapter, then, as I'll describe below, will be elsewhere. In this chapter, I'll mainly look at questions of whether or not and how it could actually be possible for groups to possess something like goal or representational intentional states, and on how productive it is to try to ascribe such states. I'll be assuming that when people make statements like "Walmart wants to teach Target a lesson" they are thinking that Walmart has something like an intentional state. But I'll leave open the question of how much like an intentional state (exactly like? a bit like?) people tend to really think it is.

Let's assume, then, that, with some X-do-Y statements, speakers are saying that the group as a whole is thinking or doing Y in an agent-like manner. We'll assume that some speakers and listeners think that the group quite literally has intentional states very like those of individual agents, while other speakers think what groups have is something only vaguely analogous to intentionality, while other's views lie on continuum in between. But what kinds of states are speakers ascribing to the group they are giving an intentional X-do-Y ascription? This raises the questions of what it is to literally have an intentional state (or something close to one), and whether and how groups could have such states. In the sections that follow, then, I'll mostly be leaving behind questions about what speakers are believing about groups and focusing on questions about whether the groups in the world that speakers are talking about should really be thought of as having intentional states. I'll first discuss what it is to have an intentional state. This will set the stage for a discussion of whether and how groups can have such states. I will argue that they can. I believe then, that sometimes when people make X-do-Y statements, they are saying that the group is acting like an intentional agent (or something very close)—and that speakers can be saying something true with such assertions. I'll then talk about the difficulties of knowing what these group intentional states are, and the advantages and disadvantages of thinking of groups in these terms.

Investigating whether and how groups can actually have intentional states is important. Whatever the precise details of what people are thinking when they say or hear a group has a hope, it seems likely that the use of the folk psychological vocabulary will do some skewing of people's ideas toward thinking the groups are agents governed by the regularities described by folk psychology. If thinking this way about group activity is quite wrong, it's important to know that. If it's wrong we should begin doing our best to encourage the use of different, more accurate terminology (as my college instructors seemed to be doing when they would circle my "but Germany thought" statements with a red pencil).

Now one might think that we could save ourselves some time and just begin talking about why we should stop using intentional terms to describe groups, and how we could describe group activity better. We already know, it might be thought, that groups can't really have intentional states. Groups, after all, are often composed of people spread out in space and time, with each pursuing his or her own agenda, sometimes with very little knowledge about other group members. How could such an entity really think or behave as a unitary agent? But having such pessimism before our investigation starts is unjustified. We already know that there are some groups of far flung independent units that act together as a unitary agent—namely the cells that make up each of us. All of us are presumably made up of nerve and tissue cells, with each cell doing its own activities with little information about any but locally adjacent cells. Still all of these cells miraculously manage to coordinate their individual activities in such a way as to produce unitary eating, sleeping, arguing, and ticket-buying activities, unitary desires to win the lottery and unitary beliefs about separation of church and state. If groups of cells can somehow pull off this trick by being organized in the right way, perhaps groups of people can, too. We can't just dismiss the possibility without investigating. If groups really can have intentional states, many fields of study would surely benefit by having clear understanding of how this is possible. Social sciences focusing on higher-level collective activity would benefit by knowing the types of organization required for a group to begin thinking on its own, perhaps thinking differently from the members composing it. Psychology (and philosophy) would also gain a clearer understanding of what intentionality requires and entails.

While it would be interesting to discover that groups actually can have intentional states, we should remember that this, by itself, need not mean that we ought to focus on describing groups with intentional terms, or in the intentional terms we do now. We should think about whether describing groups with intentional vocabularies is useful compared to other kinds of descriptions. And if ascribing intentions to groups does help us understand group activities, we should ask how we could do it well, and how we avoid doing it badly. Ascribing intentional activities to groups is something we do all the time, but we should neither casually assume that this is an appropriate practice, nor casually dismiss it as an unworthy one. This chapter should help clarify how we should think about it.

OUR INITIAL TASK—
SAYING WHAT INTENTIONAL STATES ARE

In order to examine whether a group can have beliefs and desires and the like, a natural way to begin is to lay out the criteria for what it is to have an intentional state, then examine whether or not a certain arrangement of people can meet this criteria. The problem, however, is that there are a number of different accounts of what it is to have an intentional state (see Haugeland 1990; Lyons 1995; Stich and Ravenscroft 1994; Ramsey 2007 for good surveys). If anyone successfully shows that by this or that account of belief, groups can have them (or can't have them), they will invariably face opposition from proponents of other accounts of intentionality. These critics will say that groups only counted or failed to count as having beliefs because the criteria used to decide were too loose or too stringent. (Claims about animal belief face the same problem.) Dan Dennett's instrumentalist theory of intentionality, for example, holds (roughly) that an entity should count as having beliefs and desires merely if ascribing such states to entities enables us to predict behavior with a certain degree of accuracy. So in Dennett's theory, if "taking the intentional stance" and ascribing beliefs to groups enables us to predict the group's behavior, then a group counts as having those beliefs. On John Searle's theory of intentionality, on the other hand, even an android that behaves exactly as I do wouldn't count as having intentionality unless the activity of its artificial "brain" very closely mimics the activity of my organic one. On this view of intentionality, there is almost no way a group could ever really have anything like a belief state, since no group has any parts closely mimicking anything like an actual organic brain.

With such diverse opinion about what intentionality truly is, one must proceed cautiously in investigating group intentionality. One must begin by doing a bit of quasi-stipulation. A theorist investigating whether some or other entity has intentional states should start by saying, "by intentional states what *I* will mean here is this." Without a clear specification of what an author means by intentional state, it's never clear whether something's apparent failure (or success) at counting as intentional comes from something the entity lacks or from some unjustified (and maybe unarticulated) requirement in the author's criteria. Now to be useful, of course, the definition of intentionality one proposes must be very carefully chosen. First, given that there's a lot of suspicion (despite the way we talk) that groups can't literally have beliefs, it's important that we adopt fairly demanding criteria for counting as having intentional states. The burden of proof should be on the person who wants to make the initially implausible claim that groups can literally have representations. So he or she needs to show that demanding criteria for having intentional states can be met. This means we should look to see whether a realist and not just an instrumentalist definition of criteria can be met.

Next, in investigating whether groups can have intentional states, we should make sure that the definition of intentionality proposed cleaves fairly close to our folk theory of intentionality (sometimes called "folk psychology"). If a scholar is using terms like "goal," "belief," or "hope," in ways quite different than we ordinarily use these terms, listeners will have no idea what they can or can't infer, since ordinary expectations don't apply. What is and isn't in our folk theory, of course, is something still being studied by scholars. But if the states we are talking about are clearly substantially different from other states we label with these terms, we are better off not using these labels. The intentional theory one should work with to examine whether groups can have intentional states should resemble our ordinary folk theory.

But while the theory we work with should resemble our folk theory, it need not be exactly like it. Scientific astronomy has uncovered facts about stars that are different from our folk astronomy suppositions. Yet we don't say, "X is not really a star, but a burning ball of gas millions of miles away." Similarly, we could find out there are characteristics of actual goals, fears, or representations that are not in folk theory at all. Nevertheless, we can still refer to these entities as goals or fears, even though they have some differences from our folk theoretical beliefs about these entities (just as we still are referring to stars, even though are beliefs about them change). It is only when our scientific beliefs about these entities become so drastically different from our folk beliefs that we begin thinking that it is too confusing to continue to use the old names, with the old connotations these names have. (See Stich 1983, chapter 6, for a good discussion of these issues.) We want our theory of intentionality for groups to accurately describe features of intentionality that are really there in the intentional states we typically refer to (even if some of these features are not in our folk theory).

If we start with an intentional theory defined in this careful way, we can go quite far in understanding what we should say about group activity we so often casually describe in intentional terms. We will clearly understand how a group can (or can't) have intentional states, according to the conception of intentionality described in this theory. If we conclude that they can, people who dispute that groups can have intentional states should be able to look at the theory proposed and say precisely what additional features need to be added to have real intentionality, and why it is that groups must always fall short of this standard. (Conversely, if we conclude that they can't, proponents of group intentionality should be able to say why the intentional theory employed was too stringent.)

I will proceed, then, by outlining a theory of intentionality (meeting the criteria I describe above), and then examining whether groups could qualify as having intentional states on that view. Even though I will be quasi-stipulating, I will have to describe the view at some length, since the question of whether groups have beliefs will largely depend on what a theory of intentionality says intentional states are. Hopefully, others will find the view of intentionality I describe to be a plausible one. If not, then this article should still help advance our understanding of the social by explaining how groups could have belief-like states, whether or not these states should be considered instances of full-blown intentionality.

Note that in what follows, I am less interested in the question of whether groups specifically have "belief" states than in whether they have intentional states of some sort. It might turn out that "belief" is a complex hybrid intentional state, perhaps even conceptually linked with the human mind (see Stich 1983). Below, then, I'll more often focus on whether groups can have the broader "representation" and "goal" states than the narrower "belief" and "desire" states. Looking at whether more fine-grained distinctions can be made concerning, say, whether a particular "goal" state counts as a "desire" state is a project I'll leave to others.

AN ACCOUNT OF INTENTIONALITY

What does it mean for a creature to have intentionality? Let's begin with the bare bones of our common sense folk theory of the subject. Jonathan Bennett describes the core idea of our commonsense view this way: An intentional system is one that "*does* what it *thinks* will bring about what it *wants*" (1991, 176). What does this mean? How does any system do this? Let's begin with a general overview of intentionality. I find it most useful to begin understanding intentionality by getting clear about what it is for a creature to want something, or to have a goal. The basic idea of goal-seeking is that there are some entities in the world that have a robust disposition to do some activities that result in some (fairly narrow) state, G, and are disposed to change their activities if the original activities aren't getting them closer to G. There are various ways to describe these tendencies, but one convenient way is to describe them in terms of the state they are disposed to produce. We do this by saying that these entities have the goal of G. However else one would describe a person who picks up a variety of litter from an area and puts it in a trash can, we say that that person has the goal of putting litter in the trash can. A frog that flicks its tongue and moves various small dark objects to its stomach is said to have the goal of eating them (or to "want" to eat them, or to be "trying" to eat them.) The early MIT robot that roamed the rooms and halls scanning them for electric sockets and plugging itself in, recharging its batteries, is often described as having the goal of charging its batteries. In the process of doing the things it takes to achieve G, a goal-seeker has to a) "know" what obstacles are in the way of achieving the goals, and b) "know" how it is doing in terms of achieving the goals. There are various ways we can describe the system's abilities to use information about the world in achieving its goals. One way is to use our descriptions of the external world that the goal-seeker has become "tuned" to be able to successfully interact with to describe the mental states used governing these interactions. We call these mental dispositions "representations" (and other cognate terms) of the world.[1] Let's look at goals and representations in a bit more detail.

Goals

The intuitively central characteristic of a system said to have a goal is not merely that it has a robust disposition to produce a similar range of end states ("a goal")—after all, raindrops make things wet without their having that as a goal. A true goal-seeking system has the ability to change its activities if what it is doing is not getting it closer to the G-result. The term "goal" seems to be most prototypically used to describe systems that use a number of different tricks to get to similar end states. We would be hesitant to say that a mousetrap that guillotined rats (and everything else) that poked their heads in had a mouse-killing goal. John Haugeland points out, however, that we'd feel little hesitation in using goal language to describe a "supertrap" that used numerous different mechanisms for killing mice in different circumstances (1990). If a battery-charging robot that did not locate an outlet began moving furniture and scanning behind it, or finally drilling holes and tapping electric lines, we'd be even more inclined to talk about its behavior in teleological terms. In general, the more different ways a system has of producing a certain end state from a variety of initial states, the more comfortable we are of speaking of the system's "goals" and "wants" (see Bennett 1991 for a similar account of goals).

Another requirement for counting as goal-seeking is worth mentioning here. Suppose we have a system that is a candidate for being a goal-seeker and we also have another system connected to it in some way that does count as a goal-seeker by the criteria we have discussed so far. If, in every environment, this other goal-seeker is required to produce the energy or signals necessary for the candidate goal-seeking system to produce the target end state, then this candidate system is not itself a goal-seeker. A remote controlled robot that works like this might be called a *tool* or *slave* or *organ* of a human goal-seeker. But its abilities are too parasitic on those of another goal-seeker to call it a goal-seeker in its own right.

How could a goal-seeking system, readily describable in teleological terms but difficult to describe in mechanical terms, come to develop in nature? The basic story of how nature builds these sorts of entities is the familiar one from evolutionary biology: During the course of its history, some entity or entity cluster randomly undergoes a change which makes it behave in a manner that helps prevent it from being destroyed—or helps it create a replica of itself. The persistence of the entity or its replicas helps ensure that the source of the helpful behavioral disposition also survives. Eventually, various entities continue to exist because they have come to acquire a number of such mechanisms, which help them in various ways. If the number of mechanisms an entity has is large enough, and different enough in different circumstances, we begin to speak of an "organism" with a "goal" of survival.

Now the set of mechanisms helping an organism survive are likely to be ones that enable it to engage in, as the old joke goes, the four F activities: feeding, fleeing, fighting, and reproducing. Each of these activities achieve certain end states via mechanisms that lead to some or other portion of that end state, or mechanisms creating an intermediate state launching pad for reaching that end state. Each portion or intermediate stage is subjected to the same evolutionary pressures as the organism itself. Over time, through trial and error, the organism can come to be structured such that the attainment of these portions or intermediate stages can themselves come about via a number of different mechanisms. When this happens we begin speaking of each of these "sub-system" mechanism sets as having its own goals, or alternatively about the organism having a "subgoal." An organism that eludes predators in a number of ways is said to have not merely the goal of survival, but a sub-goal of eluding predators. An organism that develops a number of means of hiding comes to have what we'd call a subgoal of hiding. An organism that develops a number of ways of locating and identifying rocks to hide behind has a subgoal of finding rocks. This process can continue indefinitely. Over millennia, there emerge complicated machines, best described as organisms with the overall goal of survival and with numerous subgoals, and sub-sub-goals, the pursuit of which normally help (or helped) insure the organisms' successful interaction with and survival in its environment.

Things can also develop new goals in a relatively short period of time if they can do what we colloquially call "learn." Some learning takes place via processes not dissimilar to the way species of organisms develop over millennia. Some organism, via various causes, can begin emitting certain non-genetically specified movements following the presence of certain sensory input combinations. The practice of making *these* movements in the face of *that* sensory information can become "fixed" in the organism for a long period of time—if the organism has some sort of feedback mechanism which enables such input-output dispositions to remain operating in the system when (and only when) they help satisfy higher-level goal-dispositions. (A familiar part of such mechanisms in ourselves are pleasure and pain.) Over time, an organism can come to be disposed to make different movements that also result in that end state. Or it can come to be disposed to make those same movements in response to a number of different sensory inputs. With a variety of different mechanisms involved, it becomes useful to describe the organism as having acquired the goal of producing that end state in those circumstances.

In organismic evolution, the ability to achieve certain goals is enhanced when a number of alternative routes come to exist for ensuring a portion of the end state (or a certain intermediate state) results. Similarly, in learning, various subgoals come to exist when an organism "fixes" a number of movement mechanisms in place that all result in the creation of that intermediate/portion state. An organism, for example, can come to have the goal of identifying and consuming nuts as part of its diet. Over time, as part of this process, it can come to develop a number of different mechanisms for achieving an intermediate stage of this end—it can develop a number of mechanisms for cracking the shells of nuts. It has thus acquired the subgoal of cracking nuts. As with species evolution, an individual organism over time can develop more and more sophisticated subgoals enabling it to successfully interact with the world.

For organisms that are advanced learners, sets of movements and states of readiness need not be randomly generated and then "pruned." An organism can evolve or develop a subsystem which tends to produce only certain sorts of movements in the first place—ones which have a fairly high probability of being successful in certain environments. (Mechanisms which produced inferior movements could themselves have been pruned earlier on.) An organism can thus learn to be a better learner. Alternatively, advanced learners can develop complicated mechanisms by which certain possible movements are rewarded and punished before the movements are actually made, and before rewards and (potentially lethal) punishments are rendered by the world. This potential for "internal simulation" also tremendously enhances what an organism can learn. (For a discussion of these different kinds of mechanisms, see Dennett 1995, 378–80.)

Our world, then, is structured such that through trial-and-error processes an entity can come to acquire complicated clusters of dispositions to make movements that usually enable it to achieve certain ends, or, as we say, "to try to achieve certain goals." This, then, is how it is that certain entities in the world have the capacity to want certain things.

Representation

Our intuitive notion is that a creature possesses intentionality when "it does what it *thinks* will bring about what it *wants*." I have claimed that talk of wants or goals is a way of describing a state of having numerous dispositions that usually bring about a certain end state. Now in order to successfully achieve its goals, an entity must interact with the obstacles in the world that are in its way, by achieving a set of fine-grained sub and sub-subgoals. We can describe this fine-grained system for interacting with a particular world state as being "tuned to" W or as "having information about" W, or having "knowledge of" W, or "representing" W, or "being a representation" of W. These fine-grained steering signals in pursuit of sub-goals are the essence of representation.

Presumably, the evolutionary and learning processes described above can get more and more sophisticated, enabling the organism to overcome an inordinate amount of different types of obstacles that stand between it and the end-state goals (or subgoals) that it's disposed to try to achieve. It can do so by developing a large number of nested "if-then" dispositional mechanisms. These can emerge in this way: Through trial and error (in evolution or learning), mechanisms for registering different kinds of energy signals from the external environment develop. (For example, an organism can come to have carbon-atom arrangements called rhodopsin molecules, which react to the presence of certain colors by absorbing light at longer wavelengths.) Through trial and error, the organism can also develop different kinds of behavioral responses, moving various appendages to produce movements. Through feedback mechanisms, which may involve pleasure and pain, it develops pathways that coordinate certain input signals with certain responses that are appropriate for achieving goals. Over time, organisms develop regular sensory-motor repertoires such as this one: If a light occlusion occurs above (a likely predator), move your tail muscles in a way that gets you away from the occlusion, unless it is a very small occlusion (likely prey), in which case, you should move your tail muscles to move in the direction of the occlusion, and move your jaw muscles in a way that enables you to ingest its source (see Churchland 1980). Creatures may also learn that the best thing to do at a given time is nothing, save be in a state of "readiness" to make particular movements when in the near or distant future certain conditions arise.

Now how can we describe the set of conditional dispositional mechanisms an organism has developed? The most elaborate description would be to actually name the sets of physical mechanisms involved in these activities. We could, for example, describe the entire physiological process that enables say, a fish, to detect, track, and ingest its prey. A very minimalistic way of describing these conditionals, on the other hand is simply to refer to them as "those mechanisms disposed to achieve XYZ end states." Giving a minimalistic description saves us time but gives us little information about the exact ways in which the organism will be interacting with the world or cogitating about how it will interact. The middle way is to give people a fair amount of information about the internal mechanisms indirectly by describing the sort of world with which the creatures are set up to make appropriate interactions. One of the phrases we use for describing a state of being set up to interact effectively with that kind of world is "having a representation" of that world. When a thirsty creature has mechanisms that enable it to push a rock, gage how far it has moved, dig under it, stick its tongue there, and move its throat muscles in a certain way, we describe this by saying that the creature believes or has the representation "water is under the rock."

Why would we describe a set of internal steering signals using words we typically use to describe states of the external world (e.g., a representation of *a tall tree*)? The answer is that this terminology provides a very efficient way of communicating to people what an agent's inner state is like. What's inside the agent is an organized set of steering signals enabling it to maneuver through the nooks and crannies of the world to fulfill its goals and subgoals. It's very difficult to describe these inner states directly. We don't directly see the millions of (usually neural) inner connections and couldn't easily describe them if we did. We also seldom have any interest in communicating much detail about these mechanisms. But it is relatively easy to convey rough information about what these mechanisms do. Giving the name of the things interacted with when we talk about a representation (or some cognate term) of X, directs us to think about the many familiar features of Xs. From a knowledge of this external structure and a knowledge of the agent's goals, we can infer much about what kinds of subgoals an agent would have to have to be able to successfully interact with this part of the world. We also have information about this based on knowledge of our own inner reactions to these external structures. We have reason to think that people we talk to also have this information based on their experiences with these structures. The fact that one knows lots about one's own (and other's) dispositions regarding X, allows a speaker to communicate a lot about what's inside an agent with just the name of X and terms like "representation."[2]

Note that in talking about representations, it needn't be the case that in the world a creature has come to be "tuned to" matches the world it's currently in. It can be prone to dig for water under a rock because that's where water has been in the past, even if there is no water there now. In these cases we are still often inclined to say it "believes" there is water under a rock. Indeed, the term "belief" seems to be used more prototypically to describe situations in which the real world doesn't match a creature's tunings. The "internal" aspect of beliefs is more highlighted in these cases.

Over time, then, along with developing goals, creatures come to have fine-grained internal dispositions, which guide them through particular worlds in order to get their goals. When we want to describe these internal systems, we call them "representations" and portray them quickly and indirectly by describing the sort of world that that the creature has come to be wired up to navigate through. Such representations and goals constitute a creature's intentional system.

COULD GROUPS HAVE INTENTIONAL STATES?

We now have a theory of how something could be an intentional system and how some such systems could have developed in the natural world. Could groups of people come to be intentional systems, according to this theory? I don't see any obstacles, in principle.

The criteria of having a goal I've described here, holds that a system with a robust disposition to produce a certain end state by switching movement-producing mechanisms when it is not getting closer to that end state is a goal seeking system. Any materials that can act this way can be said to be a goal-seeking system. If a group of people can be arranged so it robustly acts in this manner, then that group of people is acting as a goal seeking entity. Whether or not a given group actually meets this criterion, in practice, is a question that needs to be looked at on a case by case basis. But I see nothing preventing a group of people being arranged thusly, in principle.

Various processes could lead a group of individuals to be arranged so that it has a robust disposition to produce a particular end state. Various processes could arrange that group such that, if one set of activities weren't producing this end state, another set of activities would ensue. If a group was disposed to act in this manner, it would be implementing the same sort of system that we'd have no qualms about calling "an entity with a goal" when such a system is constructed out of smaller, less cognizant units (as when we find it in individual organisms).

Consider an army doing various sorts of activities that tend to have the effect of destroying an enemy army. An army like this is a prime candidate for the kind of group that can be organized as a goal seeking system. There are usually clear end states that this group's activities have the effect of producing. Armies usually have many redundant means for achieving the same end, and if one type of means is not achieving the end, another means will be switched to. If an army that is thwarted in engaging the enemy in a ground based invasion would switch to a sea landing, and then, an air barrage, continuing until the enemy is destroyed, that army has the goal of destroying the enemy army. The people making up an army can easily be arranged to do various activities and to stop doing them, in favor of others doing different kinds of activities—since every individual can easily be steered toward doing a specific activity that will help the goal be achieved. Furthermore, in a group like an army, the people comprising a system can also be arranged so that numerous different ways of bringing about a portion of the end state can be activated. Or there are numerous ways of bringing about an intermediate state that's required for bringing about the end state. When a system made of smaller parts is disposed to produce an intermediate state in a large number of ways, we recognize this to be a system with *subgoals*. Different army units can readily be said to have subgoals. An army unit which first tries to remove an enemy's heavy artillery, first by bombing the grounds where the big guns are stored, then by blasting annoying music, then by trying to get the guns to fire until the ammunition runs out, is a unit that has the subgoal of removing the threat from the enemy artillery.

If the intentional theory described above is adequate, then one can see how groups of individuals can come to have representations as well. A representation, on this account, consists of numbers of fine-grained subgoals that are set up to appropriately interact with the world in order to succeed at the goals and subgoals. We describe this set of subgoals by describing the world they are "tuned" to. In the case of the army then, we can imagine units that have sets of fine grained sub-subgoals for achieving their end goal—subgoals that constitute a representation of the terrain of obstacles that will need to be overcome in order for the subgoal and overall goal to be met. Imagine a unit charged with kidnapping the enemy king. Suppose this unit has a number of plans about how to enter the palace, go down the secret passageways, seal off the exits, engage the guards in certain types of combat, and capture the king. This unit could be said to represent the king's whereabouts and the ways in which he might try to avoid capture.

I see nothing that shows we can't use terms like "goal" and "representation" to describe the dispositions of an army group I've described. The system is composed of a cluster of entities that employ different mechanisms to produce a particular end state. It is able to do so by being able to engage in fine-grained "subgoal" activity that enables it to overcome the obstacles in its environment—with these stored subgoals being a kind of representation of the environment. Now one thing that might make us hesitate to say a group like this one has goals and representations of its own is that we already use terms like "goal" and "representation" to describe the thinking and behavior of the component parts of that system. Each of the people involved in the group's goals has goals and representations of their own—representations at a grain size that is quite familiar to us. It's tempting when we hear talk about group goals or representations, then, to think in terms of the goals and representations of the people within the groups. (In a robot with goals, we usually couldn't ascribe goals to the robot's parts. So we seldom are inclined to say the goals of the robot were only the goals of its parts. But since the parts of a group of people (the individuals) do have goals, there is a temptation to say that all we have here are the goals of the parts.) But note that there's nothing stopping there from being two sets of goals here—those defined by what the group as a whole does, and those based on what the individuals within the group do. Furthermore, it's quite possible that the goals of some of the people in the group happen to be the same as the goals that our theory of intentionality would lead us to identify as the group's goals.[3] In this case, the army commanders will probably have the same goals as the army. It's even possible that all the individuals in the army have this same goal as well. But an interesting aspect of the intentionality given above, is that the goals (and representations) of the group and those of the people in the group need not be the same. In the theory of intentionality I've given, the goal of the entity is what it has a robust disposition to achieve through multiple means. It doesn't matter what each of the parts is doing (or, in the case of groups of people, what each of the people is thinking). As long as it has a robust disposition to produce this end state, through these various means, that's the goal it has, irrespective of what the parts within are doing to help enable this end-achieving. This means that it's perfectly possible for a group to have a goal or representation that none of the people in that group has. In the next section, we'll look at a more complex example of a furniture manufacturing group with goals and representations that none of its members have. But the point can be made in a straightforward way with the military case just considered. We can see that the group's goals, here, need not be identified with those of any of the people in it when we realize that we would still be inclined toward giving descriptions like "that unit is trying to knock out the enemy artillery," even if every soldier and commander were gradually replaced by ones with different beliefs and desires as long as overall activities remained highly similar. Indeed, imagine we replaced each soldiers with three soldiers, each with a third of the previous soldier's knowledge of what he or she was supposed to do (along with better information about how to coordinate with one's fellow soldiers). Each commander could also be replaced by three commanders, each having a third of the knowledge and plans. Imagine, further, that each of these replacements is eventually himself replaced by three replacements—with the end result that each of the soldiers could have goals and representations that were unrecognizable by the original soldiers. But as long as the overall end states and intermediate states they accomplish are the same as before, we would not say that the goals of the unit have changed even though the particular representations and goals of each of the people involved has changed. Most of the replacements might even be conscripts with little interest in destroying the enemy. Yet destroying the enemy could, in principle, remain the robust disposition goal of the army nonetheless. (See Lahroodi 2007 and Mathiesen 2009 for other arguments a group can have for goals or beliefs that are different from its members.)

Groups, then, could have goal and belief-like states different from those of the individuals in them. What's more—if the above argument is correct, there is no reason that groups of groups cannot have goals and representations as well. If the army example shows how clusters of people can meet the criteria for instantiating goals and representations, then it's easy to see how clusters of armies could do the same thing. A cluster of different armies could join forces to defeat a common powerful enemy. A subgroup of this super group—a unit made up of four different armies, could be responsible (via various means) for the subgoal of knocking out the enemy's artillery. A coalition of five armies could coordinate their activities to capture the enemy king, and structure their conditional activities in a way that constitutes a representation of the king's possible escape routes. In theory, whatever a group can do, a group of groups can do. With the above definition of an intentional system, as in functional role theories generally, it doesn't matter how the requisite activities are performed—with metal parts, organic parts, individuals, or groups of individuals—it just matters that they get performed. Again, I see no in-principle obstacle to a group or a group of groups fulfilling all the criteria for being an intentional system.[4]

THE POSSIBILITY OF FORMING
SUSTAINED INTENTIONAL GROUPS

Origin and Continuance

How could a group that could be thought of as an intentional system (henceforth an *i-group*) come to exist? Organisms with intentionality can come to exist and continue to exist when systems appear that have a robust disposition (through various means) to produce end states that happen to help that system continue to exist or reproduce itself. I-groups, similarly, could come to exist and continue to exist when there are groups of individuals that collectively have a robust disposition (through various means) to produce end states that happen to help that arrangement of people continue to exist or reproduce itself. As with organismic evolution, exactly how the various parts (in this case people) first come together in a certain arrangement, and what makes them stay there is unimportant. What matters is that something moves a person who does a certain activity into the right place, where he or she happens to contribute something to the activities of a set of actors who collectively help produce a certain end state. Something keeps that actor doing that activity. Eventually, what helps keep these activities continuing is the fact that such activities contribute to the survival of the group in that form, so those are the activities that the group has come to be disposed to do. This process of groups continuing to exist because of the way that clustering enhances the survival of that cluster happens in nonhuman, as well as human, groups (see Wilson and Sober (1994) for a review article in which they mention over two hundred articles which discuss group selection). Writes biologist Tom Seely:

> By virtue of its greater size and mobility and other traits, a multicellular organism is sometimes a better gene-survival machine than a single eukaryotic cell. ... Likewise the genes inside organisms sometimes fare better when they reside in an integrated society of organisms, rather than in a single organism because of superior defensive, feeding and hemostatic abilities of functionally organized groups" (1989, 546).

Biologist Richard Dawkins (1976) calls any stable interacting assembly of traits a vehicle which natural selection can operate on. The example he uses to explain this concept is instructive for our purposes. A vehicle, he writes, is like a rowing team in which the success of any individual member is dependent on coordinating activities in such a way that the team as a whole wins the race. An i-group could continue to exist because of the way that the clustering of individuals, as a vehicle, enhances the continued survival of that cluster.

What kinds of things typically move people to the "right" places where they contribute to the goal-seeking activities of a group? At one extreme, we have the activities of independent self-interested individuals, rewarded for doing the activities they do by impartial forces of nature. At the other extreme, we have hierarchical groups behaving as they do because other people direct them to do certain activities and punish them for not doing them. (In general, entity A has power over entity B, when A can make it costly (in terms of goal-achievement) for B not to do what A wants it to. An A-entity can make activities costly to a B-entity by its ability to inflict punishment, or its ability to deny rewards that it is in a position to give (see also Emerson 1962). In between these two extremes we have groups of socially-minded individuals, without bosses, who do what they do specifically because they want the group to achieve certain goals.

It's easy to imagine examples of different i-groups coming and continuing to exist in these different ways. We are very familiar with hierarchical groups like corporations that are usually founded by a small number of powerful individuals and have their day-to-day activities managed by "bosses" at the top. But it is possible for such a corporation to evolve into something with a type of "mind of its own" that systematically tries to come to a particular end state through various means. We could imagine a lumber company, for example, with a subgoal of sending wood from Brazil to England via the Gulf Stream shipping route. It could be, for example, that getting wood from any other place, or shipping through any other route, turns out not to be profitable. Over time, a complicated set of implicit policy rules could evolve, along with a system of checks and balances between different departments within the company that makes it the case that, whatever the wishes of the executives or the workers, the company always reverts back to shipping wood from this source through this route. The group's initial set-up and day-to-day activities are hierarchically managed by bosses, but it is still the case that such groups can come to be organized so that the group as a whole has various goals and subgoals. Each worker or manager at any level can be replaced, and while the goals of the workers and the company as a whole can coincide, they need not. Like a beehive colony, the company can continue working to produce its overall goals, whatever the intentions of its (temporary) workers.

At the other extreme from i-groups organized or managed hierarchically by bosses, are i-groups composed of independent self-interested individuals that could randomly come to be organized and reinforced by nature to act in ways that serve a group goal. Imagine a pacific atoll populated by random clusters of hut-dwelling hermits. Storms routinely flood the island and inhabitants often drown, despite their best efforts to save themselves. A common strategy for holding off water when storms are approaching is to build a small sand wall, below one's own hut that's on higher ground, hoping to divert water to each side of the wall. Imagine, however, that each of the hermits in a cluster of huts in the southwest corner of the island wisely decides to extend his wall to the point where the walls of his neighbor's end—ultimately creating a circular wall which spares this cluster of houses more than any other cluster on the island. While none of these hermits has much interest in the well-being of his neighbors, this southwest group continues to build circular walls in various ways, and survives for decades, while the individuals in other groups perish. This group's disposition to build protective walls around their "compound" could keep this settlement surviving long term. Over time, the dam building could improve, with the dam design coming to implicitly represent the typical patterns of flood danger. This could happen, despite each individual's acting in his own self-interest without any plan for the group.

In between the groups whose members' day-to-day activities are organized by powerful bosses, and ones composed of individuals with little concern for what others are doing, are groups of equals that together work toward some social goal. A good example of this is a group with a goal of rescuing a fellow motorist from a ditch spontaneously forming. In such a group, different people direct themselves, or direct their fellows, to do the various tasks needed to get the job done. Some people stop and redirect traffic; others find dirt or gravel to shove under a wheel. Some push, while others pull. There is no leader of such a group, and each person decides for herself what activity will be most helpful (and/or perhaps makes a suggestion to an immediate neighbor). But the assembled group members are all trying to get the car out of the ditch together. The philosophy of social science literature is full of all for one and one for all "joint-action" activities like this. In groups like this, it usually does tend to be the case that the goal of each of the individuals in the group is also the goal of the group as a whole. Here, a set of institutions creating a stable net effect didn't need to slowly evolve in order to make sure the group continually strives to achieve the same goal. Here, each group member has the goal of the group achieving a certain end, and does what it takes to help achieve it. In these kinds of groups, the explicit social goals of the individuals involved provide one of the main means of making sure a group works to achieve a certain end.

Even in this kind of group, however, it need not be the case that the goals of the individuals in the group and the goals of the group coincide. Suppose a group of homeless people who met in a Salvation Army meeting decide to form a company to sell cheap bookshelves and put the nasty local furniture store owner (who was always kicking them out of his shop) out of business. In the back of a donated storefront warehouse/factory, these homeless men build bookshelves out of materials they salvage from their wanderings. In a display room in the front, they sell the bookshelves. The store turns out to be a surprise success. The rustic-looking very sturdy bookshelves built of old beams and doors turn out to be immensely popular with a group of wealthy hippieish "bourgeoisie bohemians" that David Brooks parodies in his book *Bobos in Paradise*. It is this market, however, and no other market in which such bookshelves are a success. Imagine that the company members (who have never heard of bourgeoisie bohemians) occasionally try to make various types of bookshelves out of more conventional materials. But such book-shelves don't sell at all. Group members slowly become conditioned by their successes and failures to build shelves made only of those salvaged materials that really appeal to the bobo market—even if the homeless workers have no conception at all of who bourgeoisie bohemians are. While the explicit goal of the co-op members is still to compete with the despised furniture store owner (whose business is unaffected), what this company actually has a robust goal or subgoal of doing is producing furniture for the bobo market. Indeed, the group comes to develop a good fine-grained representation of bobo tastes (buyers prefer slit railroad ties to roofing materials), even if none of the individual group members have much information about who their customers are. The goals of joint action groups are usually the same as the goals of the members. But they need not be, as long as the group comes to be a system that seeks a particular goal (perhaps unknown to them) through some means or other.

The idea of an i-group, where the intentions of actors need not determine the goals of the group, is importantly broader than the groups focused on by Margaret Gilbert, whose works dealing with group intentionality have been among the most sophisticated to date. In *On Social Facts* and *Living To-gether*, Gilbert argues that the main focus for the study of the social should be on a type of group she calls "plural subject" groups. Plural subject groups are ones whose members could describe themselves by talking about what "we believe" or "we intend." Her paradigmatic social groups are those like poetry circles, baseball teams, or even two people "taking a walk together."

Groups that are plural subjects seem to be organized to do something or other according to a hybrid combination of peer pressure (others could sanc-tion them if they don't act a certain way) and rational self-interest (acting in ways that help achieve one's goals—the goals here being the goals of the group which one has made one's own for the time being). Having a group of people whose members hold a "we intention" is indeed sufficient for having an i-group. And there are interesting generalizations about plural subject groups. But having members with such attitudes is not necessary for being a collective intention group with interesting generalizations true of it. Habit, peer pressure, extreme weather, rational reflection, or military force could all compel individuals to act in ways that collectively realize a robust disposition to achieve an end goal. Groups might have members whose activities are organized hierarchically by bosses to achieve certain goals in a way that permits all sorts of rich intentional descriptions and understandings of the group's activities (while still, as I argue above, having the activity result from the group's and not just the boss's intentions). The group can act in this way, even if none of its members ever explicitly identifies her activities with that of the group and thinks, "we intend." Similarly, a cluster of individuals who each engages in activities that are rewarded by Mother Nature through benefiting the group as a whole can be an i-group even if none of them knows or cares how the whole benefits in a way that "we intend" requires. Groups of cells work this way, but so could a group of dam-building hermits. Now sometimes individual actors can see how various activities coordinate, and want them to coordinate successfully, and this can be an important part of creating and maintaining the sort of social group about which useful collective intentionality generalizations can be made. But this isn't necessary for creating and maintaining such groups. People interested in plural subject groups should see such groups as one special type of i-group about which certain generalizations can be made.[5]

Various forces, then, can direct individuals to do certain activities, and reinforce their dispositions to do so. Some types of the resulting organization of activity-doing are such that in the short or long term they do what goal-seeking and representing entities do: have a robust disposition to produce a certain end (changing what's done if that end isn't being achieved), and keeping track of what's needed to overcome the obstacles in the way of achieving that end. Clusters of cellular materials (which compose cells) and clusters of cells (which compose individual organisms) all do this. It looks as though clusters of organisms, including clusters of people, could work along the same principles.

Types of I-Groups

There are several types of situations in which i-groups could emerge. Whether or not a given group formed in one of these ways actually does constitute an i-group is a question that must be answered on a case-by-case basis. But let's look at the kinds of i-groups that one could expect to commonly emerge. Among the kinds of groups where people could easily begin to have self-sustaining goal seeking activities are ones in which people cooperate to extract consumable resources from the earth. Hunting, gathering, farming, mining, and herding groups could do this. A different type of group, one that can thrive only in the environment of the right sorts of other groups, is a *trade* group. Trade groups are groups composed of individuals who benefit by co-operating in taking materials and transforming them into various consumer goods and services, not for themselves, but to trade and sell to other groups and individuals in exchange for other goods and services. There are a myriad of organized groups that have this type of organization, from toolmakers to software companies. Trade groups that come together could continue to exist for a long time because their activities give benefits to group members, which, in turn, encourages members to continue to engage in those activities.

In environments where people's basic metabolic needs are already taken care of by certain activities, other types of groups could form whose activities are sustained because of their ability to assuage the pain and stress of the members that compose them, or enhance the pleasure of these members. I call such groups noneconomic support (NES) groups. In NES groups, members benefit by joining together not to produce goods and services for themselves and others, but to give each other emotional support or enjoyment. A person can benefit by knowing that there are other people around who can help him through a range of potential problems or who can enhance his enjoyment of various things by using their knowledge to help focus his attention in useful directions. Groups with the emotional support function include Alcoholics Anonymous, Gay Men's Health Crisis, and the National League of Families of Prisoners. Groups with the "share enjoyment" function include the Girl Scouts, softball teams, Masons, Knights of Columbus, and book discussion groups. The American Association of Retired People, like many other groups, seems to be set up to serve both functions. Such groups seem to have the potential to become goal-seeking i-groups.

Note that the general forces sustaining these groups could be the same ones that put the dispositional mechanism together in the first place. Rewards for staying together could be bestowed on lucky individuals whose coming together happens to be beneficial for each of them. Individuals could also steer themselves toward continuing to engage in certain coordinated activities because they see that acting that way will give them certain benefits. Or powerful individuals can punish people for not continuing to engage in certain activities (or reward them for doing so). All three forces can certainly occur at the same time.

If resource extracting groups, trade groups, and NES groups could bear similarities to individual organisms in that they are self-sustaining units which survive because they benefit that arrangement of component parts, other types of groups can be more analogous to the organs of organisms. In goal-seeking creatures, recall that over time, you get the development of specialty organs (and specialty organ-parts) with subgoals of their own. These parts produce portions of the end state, produce states intermediate to the end state, or just enhance some of the activities that help produce either of these. These parts continue to exist (and to evolve) because of the benefits they provide to the overarching group that contains them. Over time, groups of people could develop specialized subgroups that do analogous things. In organisms, some of the most important organs with subgoals are ones that function to protect the organism. Similarly, among the most important specialized subgroups are those devoted to the activity of protecting the larger group from forces that would jeopardize its existence. Groups like armies protect a given group from outside forces like invading parties. Shelter-building subgroups keep group members protected from the hostile forces of heat and cold. Other groups like the police protect members from threats that result from the activities of other group members. (Note that these subgroups could be made up of the same individuals who engage in other activities. In small groups they would be made up of the same individuals.)

Related to protection groups are groups dedicated to insuring the harmonious coordination of other group members. In organisms, the subpart called the brain is an organ that helps make sure the body's other activities are successfully coordinating with each other. In human groups, even small organizations usually develop governing subparts whose task it is to coordinate and regulate the activities of the larger group. Trade groups, for example, develop management teams to make sure the people involved are efficiently doing their part to achieve the group's goals. The larger the group, the more likely it is to further divide governing subgroups into specialized sub-subgroups. Large communities, for example, often have councils or parliaments that specialize in making pronouncements about which actions should be forbidden and which are obligatory. These communities also often have various subgroups such as regulatory agencies that punish people and groups who engage in forbidden activities.

Protection groups and governing groups often directly benefit a larger group containing many different subgroups. Other subgroups most directly benefit the subgroup that contains them. Some soldiers are part of a ground repair team subgroup of an air strike unit subgroup of the Marines (itself a subgroup of the armed forces). Some auto factory workers specialize in producing parts for subgroups that produce motors. Some girl scouts are on subcommittees of recruitment committees dedicated to minority outreach. As in organismic evolution, where goal-seeking entities can develop numerous subgoal-seeking entities, the existence of certain i-groups could lead to the development of increasingly specialized subgroups, which themselves might meet the definition of an i-group. Over time, within a community, then, it would not be surprising to find not only numerous i-groups forming, but numerous sustainable i-groups continuing to exist. As the biological world is populated with various sorts of goal-seeking creatures (and organs), the social world could also come to be populated with various sorts of intentional system groups.

In biological systems, meanwhile, we also find that certain organisms can eventually evolve which have goals and subgoals beyond survival, maintenance and reproduction. A farmer can trade his vegetables for a shepherd's mutton, planning to consume it. But he can also plan to only purchase mutton that has been killed and cleaned in a certain way, he can plan on forming a long-term trade pact with the shepherd, and he can plan on refraining from trading with the shepherd's enemy. Similarly, we can expect that certain i-groups like corporations might also develop elaborate goals, plans, and representations directed at achieving far more complex ends than their own survival and profitability.[6]

ADVANTAGES OF USING I-GROUPS IN SOCIAL THEORY

It appears then, that it is metaphysically possible for collections of people to have goals and representations if they are organized similarly to intentional creatures. It is possible, then, that when people make X-do-Y statements that seem to entail that a group is wanting something, they might be saying something true. Whether and which groups have such goals or representations, as I've said, is a question to be answered on a case by case basis that I will leave to other scholars. Another question we can ask is whether, if we can, we should describe group activity in intentional terms. Bill Ramsey has recently described how the work of Dennett and others shows how it is always possible to assume "the intentional stance" and describe the activities of all manner of things in intentional terms. At the same time, it's never the case that we need to.

> It is always *possible* to adopt the intentional stance and ascribe representational states to just about anything, including rocks and vegetables. And, at least in principle, it is never necessary to characterize actual representational systems in representational terms because all physical systems can be described in purely

causal-physical terms. Instead, the question we are interested in is something more like this: Are there mindless systems in which an internal element is performing a role that is most naturally (or intuitively, or justifiably, or beneficially) viewed as representational in nature? (Ramsey 2007, 196).

Do we actually benefit by giving groups that meet qualifications for having representational state intentional descriptions? I believe that there are a number of advantages to describing group activity in intentional terms, if groups meet the criteria for intentionality (less permissive than Dennett's) that I have described here. There are also some disadvantages to such intentional descriptions that these advantages must be weighed against—disadvantages that will be described here and in other chapters. But let's first look at some of these benefits of giving groups intentional descriptions.

Saying What Would Happen

Individualistic folk psychology contains many true generalizations. Typically, if we know that a person has certain beliefs and desires, and we know that certain surrounding circumstances are present, we can predict what will probably happen. Now if group intentionality works similarly to individual intentionality (and we've described reasons to think they are the same kind of thing), then, if we know that a group has certain belief and desire-like states, and we know certain surrounding circumstances are true, we should be able to predict what the group will do. Whether or not we usually tend to have the surrounding information we need when discussing groups is another question—one we'll talk about in chapters 5 and 6. The point here is that if and when we have the surrounding information, ascribing intentional states to groups should help us make many predictions.

In addition to helping us predict actual future situations, intentional descriptions also tell us, what, counterfactually, would have happened. In *The Intentional Stance,* Daniel Dennett gives an interesting account of the advantage of individual intentional descriptions for counterfactual situations. He tells this tale of Martian super-scientists who can perceive things at a molecular level and predict what will happen, using the laws of physics, as Laplace's Demon would:

Our imagined Martians might be able to predict the future of the human race by Laplacean methods, but if they did not also see us as intentional systems, they would be missing something perfectly objective: the patterns in human behavior that are describable from the intentional stance, and only from that stance, and that support generalizations and predictions. Take a particular instance in which the Martians observe a stockbroker deciding to place an order for 500 shares of

General Motors. They predict the exact motions of his fingers as he dials the phone and the exact vibrations of his vocal chords as he intones his order . . . But if the Martians do not see that indefinitely many different patterns of finger motions and vocal chord vibrations—even the motions of indefinitely many different individuals—could have substituted for the actual particulars without perturbing the subsequent operations of the market, then they have failed to see a real pattern in the world they are observing. Just as there are indefinitely many ways of *being a spark plug*—and one has not understood what an internal com-bustion engine is unless one realizes that a variety of different devices can be screwed into these sockets without affecting the performance of the engine—so there are indefinitely many ways of *ordering 500 shares of General Motors,* and there are societal sockets in which one of these ways will produce just about the same effect as any other. There are also societal pivot points, as it were, where which way people go depends on whether they *believe that p,* or *desire A,* and does not depend on any of the other indefinitely many ways they may be alike or different (1987, 14).

We can easily extrapolate a similar moral when thinking about whether to describe social phenomena purely in terms of the individuals involved, or whether to describe what the group is doing in intentional terms. Giving an intentional account of how an army won a war tells one about lots of other ways victory could have been achieved. Lots of non-intentional accounts of the particular events leading up to the victory, on the other hand, wouldn't tell you anything about other counterfactual situations in which the war would be won. Knowing that the enemy would consider their cause lost if they lost the high ground, tells you that the victory could have been secured if either the 14th Rifleman's Regiment or the 4th Cavalry Corps took Piper's Hill, in a way that just describing the 14th Regiment's activities would not. Describing army A's representation of army B's position and capabilities also gives you lots of information about what army A would do in various situations and why, in a much shorter time than describing a long list of the various disposi-tions of various parts of army A.

Making Predictions Without Using Lots of Resources

We want to know what will and what would happen in the world. But we don't just want to have this knowledge. We want to be able to obtain and use this knowledge in an efficient resource-saving way. We just saw that learning that something has certain goals and representation can help us tell what would happen in a number of different situations. Now various ways of describing the group might be able to tell us how it would behave in each of these situations, but an intentional characterization tends to automatically tell us about a very large number of situations, using a very small amount of descriptive space (e.g., it wants Y, it believes X). Knowing that Boone's Bookshelves has a good picture of the market it is trying to sell shelves to, gives you a huge amount of information about the product they want to sell, and what they are and aren't likely to do. Intentional characterizations not only provide us with ways of getting lots of information, but they do it with striking resource-saving efficiency.

We Are Skillful at Using Intentional States to Predict

Another reason that it's advantageous to describe a group in intentional terms is that we tend to be good at reasoning about what an entity with certain intentional states will do. No one needs any special kind of social scientific training to know how to give intentional accounts. We've all been giving intentional accounts of behavior every day, since we were children. There is even much evidence to suggest that there are parts of the brain that are wired up for the purpose of interpreting things as intentional agents and understanding and predicting their behavior accordingly (see Baron-Cohen 1995; Leslie 1994; Bogdan 1997). If we have "specialized hardware" for giving intentional accounts, it is unsurprising that we should be good at reasoning about the entities we describe in intentional terms. We should also expect to be much faster in our reasoning about entities described this way.

Intentional Descriptions Help Us Understand Lower-Level Arrangement and Activity

Giving a group a high-level intentional characterization may not only be a good way of making predictions about what the group will do. It could also help us by constraining and focusing how we think about what is happening internally to the group at *lower* levels. If we know that a group has a certain goal, this gives us a quick averaging description of a myriad of constraints that reduce degrees of freedom and structurally put pressure on various lower-level parts to behave as they do. When we want to understand the details of how a higher-level task is implemented by the lower-levels in a biological organism, we often do so without just observing them directly. Instead we imagine various ways lower-level mechanisms could implement it, given the constraints of what higher-level task must be accomplished, of having to accomplish it in a certain environment, and having to accomplish it while working with other higher and lower level goals and subgoals. The mechanisms that eventually become fixed as part of an organism's repertoire are ones that can still enhance performance at these tasks, given all of these constraints. Looking at these top-down constraints, then, can provide us with an alternative route to understanding the general outline of the work-ings of the lower-level organs—which, in turn, gives us a more detailed understanding of the higher-level systems they are a part of. What kind of neural mechanisms code for a particular bird's mating song? We know that the mechanisms that do this must move a bird's vocal chords in a way that produces sound frequencies in the range that other birds can hear from a cer-tain distance. They must be mechanisms that are different from the mating calls of other bird species, etc. This sort of higher-level information gives us clues about what the lower-level mechanism must look like. (And, in turn, improves our knowledge of the details by which this high-level mating task is accomplished.) Similar attention to higher-level goals and the environment they operate in could improve our understanding of the lower-level activities of i-groups. How will a company that hopes to sell television-based Internet browsers operate? Conceptualizing the company as a certain sort of i-group tells us to begin with the idea that the company probably wants to sell as many devices as it can, for as much money as they get for them, while keep-ing the costs of production down. But we also know that they will have to make these products in an environment in which most consumers will have already purchased televisions (and don't have space for another one) and that these televisions are capable of having certain sorts of devices attached to them and are incapable of having certain other ones. We can expect, then, that part of the organization of the company will include a division that does research and development work devoted to making their technology work in certain ways with existing TVs. Direct observations, or theories concerning the lower-level individuals who implement this system, provide one route to this information. Having knowledge of the group's environments and the various higher-level tasks and subtasks it is engaged in is an additional route to understanding the detailed functioning of the lower (and ultimately the higher) levels.

Not only is it possible then, for groups to have intentional states, but there are several advantages to giving a group an intentional as opposed to other types of description. I have described ways in which giving groups intentional descriptions can have lots of the same advantages as giving individuals intentional descriptions.[7] My claims in this section have been that once we have assigned an intentional description to a group, if we have certain other information about surrounding internal and external states of affairs, these descriptions could allow us to make pretty good predictions easily and efficiently.

Now in chapters 5 and 6, I will discuss worries about whether we can usu-ally actually obtain the additional information about the other circumstances surrounding these intentional states that we need for successful explanations or predictions. My suggestion will be that, while we typically know what surrounding additional beliefs, desires, and goals our compatriots have, and we typically know what tools they possess and what environmental obstacles they face, this information will often be lacking regarding groups. This means that, while it is possible to predict and explain what groups will do with intentional characterizations, actually doing so will be very difficult. Even if we can clearly and correctly characterize a group as having a goal of P, and a representation of the environment Q, we typically don't know enough about the tools such a group has at its disposal to know how the group with that goal will be able to effect its environment. In the following section, I will describe another problem—the difficulty of being able to give groups a correct intentional characterization in the first place.

EPISTEMOLOGICAL PROBLEMS
FOR UNDERSTANDING I-GROUPS

Difficulties with Regular Representations

While groups can have intentionality as a metaphysical possibility, I believe there are numerous epistemological problems in uncovering particular intentional states and making inferences on the basis of them. In other works (Jones 1997, 1998, 1999, 2000a, 2000b) I have described numerous features that make it difficult to successfully ascribe intentional states to other individuals. All of these same difficulties, plus some new ones, are present for ascribing intentional states to groups. I will first describe some of the problems of ascribing intentional states for individuals, and then say something about how these problems and others arise for groups.

The difficulties begin with the fact that intentional states are unobservable. We can't just look and see which ones are there. How can we uncover the presence of intentional states we can't see? The task of describing unobservable states of minds in others is just one instance of the very common and general problem of trying to uncover information about entities we can't directly observe. There have long been several methods for justifying claims about the unobservable. One method might be termed "the environmental strategy." Here one starts by observing external conditions that are thought to cause certain unseen states of affairs to result. In the case of belief ascription, the environmental strategy begins with the idea that certain beliefs result from exposure to certain perceptual/environmental situations. Showing that a person was exposed to a certain natural or social environment is taken as evidence of her having certain resulting beliefs. The other method, which might be termed "the behavioral strategy," starts with the assumption that only certain sorts of things can cause certain resulting actions, according to our theories. So when those resulting behaviors are observed, that's taken to be good evidence that those purported hidden causes are in fact there. In the cases we are discussing, observing certain behaviors (including verbal utterances) is taken to be evidence that certain internal beliefs must be there, causing such behaviors to occur. Now, of course, the environmental strategy and the behavioral strategy cannot, as a point of logic, get off the ground looking only at environments and behaviors. To come to any sorts of conclusions with these strategies, one must employ some kind of theory of the nature of the entity being affected by the environments, and some kind of theory about the kind of entity that is able to cause certain types of behaviors. (You can't say how a computer will be affected by a certain input, for example, without some idea of how that computer is structured.) Now an enormous percentage of social scientists say very little about what theory of mind they use when they ascribe beliefs to individuals. This is likely due to many social scientists' romantic resistance to utilizing any well-researched scientific theories of the mind or brain. The celebrated anthropologist Clifford Geertz, for example, once wrote of his method of justifying belief ascriptions: "You either grasp an interpretation or you do not, see the point of it or you do not, accept it or you do not." And "This raises some serious problems of verification, all right—or if 'verification' is too strong a word for so soft a science . . . of how you can tell a better account from a worse one. But that is precisely the virtue of it" (1973, 16). But since, as a point of logic, one can't make any inferences about how the mind is producing behaviors, or is effected by the environment without having at least some tacit theories of mind, we can assume that whatever belief ascribers say or don't say about the theories they use, they must be using some theory (or perhaps a simulation as I'll discuss below).

One very minimal theory of mind, sometimes explicitly and sometimes implicitly adopted by social scientists is that the entity affected by the environment and producing the behavior is some kind of rational agent, coordinating beliefs and desires with each other to enable the agent to reach her goals. This is the sort of theory and method Dennettians advocate for ascribing beliefs to people. Using "inference to the best explanation," observers using this minimal theory of mind and the behavioral strategy might collect a large sample of behaviors, and then postulate that belief-desire set S is the one that a rational mind is most likely to have utilized in generating the observed behaviors. We can see an example of someone attempting to make this sort of abductive inference in social critic Warren Farrell's book *The Myth of Male Power*. In this work, Farrell (1993) takes a look at a large range of observations such as these:

1. The military's not giving combat assignments to women.
2. Twenty-four of the twenty-five professions rated as most hazardous are virtually all male.

3. The more hazardous the job, the higher percentage of men it has.
4. Men are twice as likely to be the victims of violent crimes and three times more likely to be murder victims.
5. The suicide rate among men in their early twenties is six times higher than that of women the same age, and the suicide rate of men over eighty-five is 1350 times higher.
6. Breast cancer receives 600 percent more funding than prostate cancer even though death rates from each are equal.

In the course of examining hundreds of observations like these, Farrell, rightly or wrongly, concludes that the beliefs underlying such a pattern must be that women are actually perceived as the valuable gender (especially in evolutionary terms) that needs to be protected and preserved at all cost, while men (a dime a dozen in evolutionary terms) are thought of as essentially disposable. Farrell clearly comes to this conclusion by trying to infer what sort of rational thinking could have generated these observable situations.

Now as many philosophers of science have documented, this sort of abductive inference is one of the central strategies used throughout successful sciences. While social scientists may not have direct evidence for the belief states they postulate, they often seem to be trying to use abductive inference to inform us about the hidden structure of the mind in the same way Perrin used abductive arguments to inform us about the hidden structure of the atom. In belief ascription, as in other areas of inquiry, one proceeds by collecting lots of evidence, proposing that a certain unobserved causal structure best fits the observations, and inferring that such a structure must be present. Observing further behavior that would be predicted by such an inner structure is thought to help confirm that one has hit upon the correct view of the inner structure.

But this common strategy tends to be especially problematic when used to try to uncover beliefs—even garden variety ones. It is a point of elementary logic that merely showing that one can confirm a prediction entailed by a hypothesis isn't enough to show that that hypothesis is true. If there are plenty of viable alternative hypotheses that could generate the observed prediction, then observing that prediction doesn't give you any evidence that the hypothesis in question, rather than its equally well-predicting rivals, is true (see Laudan 1996 for a good articulation of this point). If different beliefs and desires could have led to the same behavior, then observing that behavior provides no evidence for the existence of any particular beliefs or desires. One of the root difficulties of belief ascription is that, unlike the sparse fundamental building blocks of some other sciences, there exist not merely a few dozen or even a few thousand different possible beliefs and desires—but an infinite number of them. We must begin, then, by selecting from an unlimited number of potential belief posits. The beliefs we can reasonably ascribe using a behavioral strategy are, of course, only those that could possibly cause the behavior we observe. This, however, is a fairly weak restriction. We can think of beliefs as something like maps used for getting around the world. A central problem is that many different sorts of maps could usefully lead you to the same destination. Any given behavior is, thus, consistent with positing numerous different core beliefs and desires. To use a social science version of an example Quine made famous: when Malinowski's (1922) Trobrianders initially pointed to an outrigger canoe, for example, and said "Kewo'u," he initially had no firm way of telling whether they were thinking "there's a boat," "there's a group of undetached boat parts," or "there's a stage in a boat's existence."

And there are still further difficulties. Beliefs do not cause behavior by themselves, but do so in conjunction with desires and, often, with other beliefs. A selection of vanilla over chocolate may be based on the belief that vanilla is tastier and a desire for the tastiest ice cream. It may also, however, stem from the belief that chocolate is tastier but also more fattening, and a desire to lose weight. Selecting vanilla could also stem from a superstitious belief that chocolate should never be eaten on Wednesdays and a desire not to offend the gods. The vanilla-choosing behavior alone won't tell you which of these beliefs and desires are behind it. (This realization marked the downfall of the philosophical behaviorist view that a belief statement was merely a statement about a disposition to behave (see Stich, 1983; Churchland, 1988).) If one's task is to find a belief that, along with a string of auxiliary beliefs and desires, would lead to the production of a given behavior—with no prior restrictions on the number and type of such strings—then the task is analogous to one of guessing a number which, added to some string of positive or negative numbers, yields the sum of five. If one makes the appropriate adjustment in the strings of added numbers, literally every number can qualify. Similarly, with the right adjustments in auxiliary beliefs and desires, it is logically possible for any belief to cause any behavior. Increasing the numbers of behaviors one observes can help rule out some possible belief-desire sets by showing that some of the predictions of that set are incompatible with the further observed behaviors. But even large sets of behaviors can be shown to be compatible with any given belief-desire set, so long as one is willing to postulate the existence of enough additional (perhaps very odd) beliefs and desires that make all those behaviors rational. Behavioral observations and assumptions of rationality alone, then, could not justifiably enable one to say what sort of hidden beliefs lay behind them. What one needs are some further constraining theories that say which of the belief-desires sets that could generate the behavior we observe are likely to be the ones that do.

Difficulties with Hidden Representations

While unobservability and the difficulty of inferring intentions from behaviors makes intentional ascription hard for both individuals and groups, individual ascription does have an advantage. When we are ascribing beliefs to other human beings, we also have an additional source of information. If other people are like ourselves, then we can use observations of our own mental states and arguments by analogy to make inferences about others' intentions. Some philosophers and psychologists believe we literally perform simulations to ascribe intentions to others. Ascribing beliefs in this way would require very little prior knowledge about how people's minds work, or about the various other beliefs and desires they hold. What one does to see what they believe is to physically put oneself in their position—or imagine oneself in the other's position—and then check to see what beliefs and desires pop into one's own mind. If others' minds indeed work like ours do, and the simulation is a realistic one, this should provide a good indication about what thoughts appear in others' minds in such situations (see Gordon 1986, Goldman 1993, Davies and Stone 1995).

Other philosophers and psychologists have proposed that in ascribing beliefs to others we do make use of vague folk theories about how minds work ("folk psychology"), and about the types of beliefs and desires people tend to have. When calculating what others believe using these general theories, we look at the particular things they see and do, but we also assume that the beliefs they form are influenced by their surrounding beliefs. We generally make the default assumption that their surrounding beliefs are the same ones we would have—unless there are specific reasons to believe otherwise (see Stich and Nichols 1997).

Whatever the details of how we actually go about ascribing beliefs to others, it's clear that for some beliefs, if others really are like us, we can indeed use ourselves as models, both of what prior beliefs exist and which beliefs get formed in certain circumstances. It's much less clear that we can use this strategy with individuals who aren't like ourselves. And, as we will discuss, we certainly can't use ourselves as good models of what *groups*, as a whole, will be thinking.

Other difficulties stem from the fact that, however well we can use minimal rationality or simulation to infer what ordinary beliefs are likely to be, we can't infer unconscious, symbolic, or "hidden" beliefs and desires this way. Consider this claim about the thinking of one of the officers involved in the 1992 Rodney King beating in a contemporary issue of *American Ethnologist*:

Sergeant Stacey Koon, the presiding officer at the scene of King's beating, also testified to the meaning of this posture and added that at this point King's bodily response and directed speech to the officers beating him signaled the final level of compliance. The successful confinement of King—the symmetry of a body lying at attention with the face in the dirt—and the acquisition of linguistic reciprocity marked the neutering of the animalized body and its internalization of the will of the state. A "gorilla in the mist" a black "bear" that was insistent on rising on its haunches was turned by violence into a speaking subject (Feldman 1994, 410).

Unconscious symbolic beliefs, roughly, are ones in which, without being aware of it, one categorizes things as having far different attributes than the ones that appear on the surface. Unconscious desires are interests different from any the subject is aware of. In the above passage, Koon is ascribed the belief that King was (like) some sort of animal that needed to be turned into a human by being forced to speak. Two motivations have always made unconscious beliefs especially interesting to social scientists. First, ever since Freud, unconscious beliefs and desires have been considered among the most important central causes of people doing what they do. Second, as in the case of exotic peoples, we are generally more interested in uncovering information about things that we don't know much about. Beliefs that are inaccessible to consciousness are especially mysterious.

But the task of ascribing unconscious beliefs has all of the problems that beset ascribing ordinary beliefs—plus several new ones. Our theories of the unconscious leave us with far too many different reasonably posited belief ascriptions. The problems I'll discuss below are: 1) the theories of the unconscious that ethnographers typically rely on are not well supported, 2) even if any of these theories were accurate, their central posited mechanisms don't constrain possible belief ascriptions enough; and, 3) even if these posited mechanisms did constrain them, we often don't know enough about people's personal histories to constrain ascriptions in the needed way.

Consider these more elaborate claims about what the Japanese believe when they are watching monkey performances, described by a well-known anthropologist:

> In an effort to present themselves to the audience during the monkey performance, the monkey and trainer distance themselves from themselves. And this reflexive process enables them to transform their identity with nature into an identity with culture. The performance then, represents the culturalization process in two ways: transformation of nature (monkey) into culture (performing art) and transformation of self into sign. The latter is a basic feature of the human ability to symbolize.
>
> While the monkey and trainer present the self as an agent to transform nature into culture, the audience of non-burakumin Japanese is amused at the animal attempting to be human and at the trainer, whom they see as being human and

yet not quite fully human. The performing art of humans is reduced to an unsuccessful imitation by an animal.

However, when we examine the context of the performance, we see that the presentation of the collective self of the burakumin is to the non-outcaste audience. Therefore, by presenting themselves as the agent of the culturalization process, the outcastes force the non-outcaste audience to be reflexive about their own world, which should represent culture. . . . At the end of the performance, [the audience] realizes that it was they who were the untamed nature to be culturalized by the monkey. Put another way, the monkey and the outcaste are the small eyes in yin and yang. For this reason, I think, even amidst the laughter at the monkey performance the audience is reminded, albeit vaguely, of their darker side, as represented by the monkey and the outcast trainer (Ohnuki-Tierney 1984, 301–4).

In the course of her article we find Ohnuki-Tierney using the behavioral and environmental strategies to try to show that such claims are accurate belief ascriptions. The environmental strategy, for example, is used when she discusses the various ways in which monkeys are depicted in Japanese history and folk tales. What she is doing is showing us part of the cultural environment that the Japanese are exposed to, growing up. We are supposed to infer that people exposed to such environmental influence will come to form the beliefs that she ascribes to them.

Using this strategy, however, we have many of the problems that the environmental strategy often encounters in ascribing beliefs. Knowing what environments readers of Japanese folk tales were exposed to, will tell you little about what they believe unless you also know about the internal environment of other auxiliary beliefs that affect this incoming information. We might try to bypass an infinite regress of belief positing and justifying by projecting that certain beliefs are there based on an examination of our own beliefs—or on the basis of their self-reports. But here, the main beliefs we are interested in and perhaps the auxiliary beliefs affecting them are unconscious. And the most salient feature of unconscious beliefs is that they are . . . unconscious. One cannot find what unconscious beliefs and desires people hold by asking them what their beliefs and desires are. Similarly, we can't figure out what other's unconscious beliefs must be by seeing what our own unconscious beliefs are when we imagine ourselves in their shoes. We can't, for example, see that the Japanese monkeys are seen as nature vainly striving to become culture by merely imagining ourselves to have been brought up in the same culture as the Japanese audiences. The makeshift strategies we commonly rely on to ascribe beliefs in everyday life are not available for ascribing unconscious beliefs.

And there are still worse problems. When we ascribe unconscious beliefs to people, we must also clearly go beyond our usual behavioral and environmental strategies. Up until this point, in discussing the behavioral strategy, I've talked about the beliefs and desires that cause behavior. In discussing the environmental strategy, I've talked about the environment that causes particular beliefs. What I haven't said much about are the intervening mental rules by which behavior gets transformed into action, and by which particular environmental features get turned into beliefs about the environment. This is because we usually rely on mundane rules such as:

When a person desires X and believes that action sequence L, M, N will get her X, she will usually begin moving her muscles in a way that tries to implement action sequence L, M, N.

And:

When a person sees features A, B, and C in front of him, he usually comes to believe that features A, B, and C are in front of him.

Or:

When a person sees A and B continually co-occurring in the past, she will believe they will continue to co-occur in the future.

But these are not mental rules that will tell us much about the unconscious beliefs that are present. Relying on such rules might be able to tell you that Stacey Koon believed Rodney King was trying to get back up. Such rules would not tell you that King was seen as a gorilla/bear that needed to be neutered and made to signal a return to the "internalization of the will of the state" by speaking. For unconscious beliefs like these, the environmental strategy must be supplemented with an explicit theory of the rules by which the mind comes to produce particular unconscious beliefs in various circumstances. The behavioral strategy must be supplemented by rules about the sorts of unconscious beliefs and desires which typically produce certain behaviors.

But the supplementary theories that ethnographers tend to rely on to help them make unconscious belief ascriptions are far more tendentious and speculative than the implicit theories used to make ordinary belief ascriptions. To begin with, the theories of the unconscious that ethnographers typically rely on are simply not well-established theories that we can have much confidence in. There are literally dozens of competing theories about what sorts of unconscious beliefs and desires lie behind behavior, and how they come to be there. Within the psychoanalytic tradition alone there are Freudian, Jungian, Adlerian, Horneyite, Sullivanian, Frommian, Reichian, and Eriksonian theories. There are also the Structuralist and Structural Marxist theories of Lacan, Levi-Strauss, Douglass, and Friedman. This lack of consensus about the nature of the unconscious ought to make one pause before using one of these aging theories as the basis for ascribing particular unconscious beliefs to people. In the face of such divisions, we should at least try to insure that the particular theory we do end up using is one for which we have a great deal of evidence. Unfortunately, most proponents of these theories eschew making systematic attempts to provide evidence for them (see Harris 1979; Grunbaum 1984). Worse, when attempts by independent researchers have been made to test the two most prominent theories, Freudian and Levi-Straussian, the results have consistently been stunning failures for both (see Harris 1979; Erwin 1993).

A far worse problem is that, even if these theories of the unconscious were well established, they are not theories that provide enough constraints to keep dozens and dozens of different thoughts and associations as counting as "the meaning of the symbol," even within the constraints of the theory. When confronted with a candidate for something that has a deeper symbolic meaning, ethnographers of all persuasions, much like psycho-analysts and literary critics, suggest that what's going in is that the observed surface features are mentally associated with some other features, in native minds, because of a vague resemblance or contiguity. Thus Wilson interprets the meaning of eating a banana in a ritual performed by the bride in Nyakyusa culture as a symbol of the sex she will have with her husband. Shells and coral have been said to be symbolically associated with the ocean by Levi-Strauss because of spatiotemporal contiguity. The hearth is frequently symbolically associated with women, according to many interpretive anthropologists, because women in many cultures commonly do the cooking there. It's also possible for things to be symbolically associated with other things based on a resemblance between their more abstract features. Thus, a spinning wheel was used to symbolize India in order to suggest that characteristics associated with spinning, such as simplicity, devotion, ancient traditions, and self-sufficiency, were also characteristics of the Indian people in general. To make things still more complicated, ethnographers also posit that something can symbolize something else, not merely by being mentally associated with it in some way, but just by being associated with something else that is. Hence, something can be symbolically associated with something else through elaborate chains of association. Such a convoluted chain can be seen in Sapir's discussion of the symbolic association of lepers and hyenas among the Kujamaat Diola. Lepers, on Sapir's account, are thought to be burned by a magic fire associated with iron working forges. Leprosy is associated with the forge because the way that leprosy acts on the body is seen to be isomorphic to the way that forge fire works on iron. The forge is thought to send leprosy when someone attacks something that the forge (a source of spiritual power) is thought to protect (primarily cattle or children). If a cow is killed through witchcraft, it is thought likely to have been done by the person in the form of a were-hyena. "Hence," writes Sapir "if you had leprosy, you were caught stealing something protected by the forge; and if you were stealing, you might have been stealing in the guise of a hyena" (1981 533). Thus, the symbolic connection between lepers and hyenas.

The basic problem with using association to find symbolic meaning is that, as Anderson and Bower (1973) demonstrated long ago, virtually anything can be associated with anything else in the right circumstances. Bananas can serve as phallic symbols, but they could also possibly serve as symbols of the tropics, of monkeys, of banana bicycle seats, of the Velvet Underground, or of Bob Dole. Showing an interesting possible set of associated remindings by itself does nothing to establish that such a set of remindings is actually present among the people studied. Above, Feldman suggests that Officer Koon saw Rodney King as a wild bear that needed to be culturalized by submitting to state authority. That's possible. So is the idea that King was seen as a symbol of a black revolutionary movement—one that threatened the American government and way of life. But perhaps Koon saw King as a symbolic snake, and believed that it is proper for snakes to be lying on the ground. Maybe, in trying to put King down, Koon remembered a tree that he chopped and chopped at but couldn't fell as a child, and King became the symbol of Koon's continually straining and failing.

To make plausible the idea that it is one set rather than another of the potentially infinite symbolic associations that is actually invoked in certain circumstances, one needs to make use of constraining theories about what symbols tend to be invoked when. The theories mentioned above do sometimes put some mild constraints on associations, but not many. Freudian theories, for example, posit that associations with sexual matters will be more common than others. But through an elaborate chain, anything can be associated with a sexual matter. What's important here is that none of these theories of our symbolic mental life is incompatible with a huge range of unconscious beliefs we might plausibly attribute to Officer Koon in these circumstances. The additional constraints from theories of the unconscious that ethnographers usually use are just not that helpful for narrowing down the number of possible interpretations that can be given to a symbol.

Finally, even if we knew far more than we do about which syntactic mental mechanisms produce which sorts of symbolic associations at a given time, we would still be left with a problem that is always present in environmental (or behavioral) strategies. To know what symbolic thoughts are being produced at a given time, we must know not merely the form of symbolic association mechanisms involved, we must know the contents of the surrounding thoughts that have become connected with other thoughts. Knowing this, however, requires knowing a huge amount about a person's individual life history. To really know what Rodney King is a symbol of to Koon, it's not enough to look at the situation Koon is confronted with and combine this with a simple or sophisticated theory of symbolic belief formation and use. Ultimately, to be certain of Koon's unconscious symbolic beliefs, one needs to know all of Koon's personal history. The less one knows about this, the further one gets from being able to accurately gage his unconscious symbolic thinking. (This, of course, makes cross-cultural symbolic belief attributions very tricky.) Conversely, knowing everything there is to know about a person's history won't tell you what symbolic thoughts are evoked at a given time, without a far more complete theory of symbols and associations than those we currently use.

With so many different kinds of symbolic association mechanisms potentially at work at any given time, there are correspondingly numerous possible symbolic thoughts that might be ascribed at a given time. Numerous different symbolic beliefs are consistent with the evidence usually cited to establish that particular symbolic beliefs are activated by people. Ethnographers like Feldman or Ohnuki-Tierney who try to assess the unconscious symbolic beliefs of Koon or Japanese audiences have even less evidence for their particular assertions than ascribers of ordinary beliefs do.

There are enormous difficulties, then, with accurately ascribing symbolic unconscious beliefs to individuals. Nearly all of these problems (and many new ones) will carry over to ascribing analogously "neo-subconscious" or hidden beliefs and desires to groups. It is important to be aware that just such internal states are ascribed to groups all the time. In the past, I have called such attributions FIC (Folk-psychological Interpretive Collectivist) descriptions partly to point out their family resemblance to an approach to social science that Geertz labeled "thick description" that has been immensely influential in anthropology, history, and other social science disciplines. Here's an example that once caught my eye in the *New York Times:*

> Among the elements that compose China's complicated psyche today, two stand out: its insular self-satisfied attitude, rooted in the ancient Chinese belief that the nation lay at the center of the world; and the deep sense of inferiority that came with the modern realization that China was actually far behind most of the developed world (Faison 1997, 5).

Ben Colby and his colleagues described the intellectual parentage of this style of social science as lying in

> psychoanalysis, on the one hand, and in the sociology of knowledge, on the other. The primal documents are Freud's (1965 [1899]) *The Interpretation of*

Dreams, with its emphasis on personally generated symbolism, and Durkheim's 1961 [1923]) *The Elementary Forms of Religious Life*, with its emphasis on collective representations and systems of classification and correspondence (Colby et. al., 1981, 424).

These sorts of accounts, which bring together a psychoanalytic-like approach emphasizing the deeper, darker, symbolic roots of social behavior, and a Durkheimian or even Hegelian emphasis on a collective zeitgeist, are found throughout the social sciences and popular media. Thus you have historian Simon Schama saying things like "it is not too much to say that *classical civilization* has always defined *itself* against the primeval woods" (1995, 82, emphasis mine). Or you have social critic Barbara Ehrenreich writing in the nineties that "All that is happening is that our collective values are shifting away from the liberal, unisex ideals of the seventies toward something more belligerent. The national wimp hunt, I have concluded, is an attempt to press men into line for the postdetente militarism of the eighties" (1991, 139). Such ascriptions clearly go well beyond the usual "ordinary" beliefs we tend to ascribe to individuals or groups if we think they have a decent map of the environment that they are navigating through (e.g., "Dan believes the car is close to the curb." "CNN is worried that people will watch the show later on the internet.").

We just described a large number of problems in ascribing hidden beliefs and desires to individuals. Most of these problems will re-arise in trying to ascribe hidden states to groups. If a group's representation of the world contains, not just features of items out there in the world, but features that are symbolically associated with these items, we need a theory to help us narrow down what kinds of associations will be present when. Without such constraints, we are in trouble since just about anything can be associated with anything. One problem is that, even when ascribing beliefs to individual minds, people in the business of ascribing unconscious mental states often don't make clear what theory of mental states they are relying on. (Anthropologist Brad Shore once wrote of his participation in a cognitive science conference, "My assignment at the conference was to try to characterize the implicit theory of mind that anthropologists employed in their cultural analyses. In such heady company, it soon became clear to me that most of our work in symbolic anthropology proceeded innocent of any well-formed theory of mind whatsoever" (1996, vii).) They are even less clear about their theoretical commitments when they are talking about the unconscious minds of groups. And the theories that they do seem to use most often are the outdated and much unsupported, but still popular Freudian, Jungian, Lacanian, etc., theories of the individual unconscious. Now it's not clear that these are very useful at constraining even individual cases. But even if they were, it's unlikely that group minds should work according to principles like those. If groups can have beliefs, there's little reason to doubt they can have controlling internal states that are "hidden" in the sense that they are beyond what our usual folk psychological ascription strategies can uncover. What's less plausible is that groups are likely to really have hidden beliefs with anything remotely like the sorts of content that ascribers of hidden beliefs to groups currently tend to ascribe. Groups are composed of internal parts (people) quite radically different from those that form the brains of individual humans (neurons). These parts are arranged according to quite different principles. The evolutionary pressures and learning histories of groups are likely to be quite different from those of individual humans. And we certainly don't know which sorts of things are going to be associated with what (e.g., through resemblance) for such an entity likely "cognizes" very differently from the way we do. A group might well come to be organized in such a way that certain rough principles of folk psychology are true of it (e.g., it "*does* what it *thinks* will bring about what it *wants*"). But the burden of proof is surely on anyone who thinks that a given group can be organized such that it does anything like feel "a suspicion of counterfeit nurturance" (Lifton 1975, 326). Groups that "think" this way would have to have internal information processing structures that mimic a human unconscious structured along Freudian or Levi-Straussian lines. The idea that any group could come to have that degree of complex organization, realizing just these sorts of structures, is so implausible that one should regard any such ascription to a group with even more skepticism than one should for individual interpretive ascriptions. Such ascriptions should, then, be regarded as muddled implausible speculations.

And even if the beliefs we are ascribing are not deep "hidden ones" we don't have the strategy available to us of figuring out what a group mind is thinking by using ourselves as a simulation model or using ourselves to supplement a folk theory. However successful we are at ascribing ordinary beliefs to others by using ourselves as models, we can't be confident about ascribing certain beliefs to groups this way. We may know many of the long and short-term histories of our compatriots that would lead to their becoming "tuned" to these environments via forming certain subgoals and representations. Our compatriots' histories' are often similar to our own histories. But one can't tell at a glance which environments a group has passed through, which subgoal mechanisms arose, nor which were successful. (This ignorance is multiplied downwards through the sub and sub-sub goals.) Since numerous different subgoals could have developed in tuning an intentional system to parts of the world, it takes a great deal of actual empirical investigation (along with better theories of hidden states) to uncover which are the ones that actually have developed.

A final problem for trying to understand group behavior by ascribing intentional states to them is that, unlike for individuals, we have no guarantee that a given group really even is one that has intentional states. We won't know from casual observation whether a group is really an intentional system that does what it takes to reach its goals through a large variety of dispositional mechanisms. What looks like an intentional system might, in fact, be a mere mechanical "doer" system—one in which if the "goal" end state was not achieved, no systematic further activities would be initiated. Even worse, we can't tell from casual observation even if its mechanical dispositions are robust ones. Perhaps the group acts the way it does only in restricted circumstances. For groups, unlike for human beings, a great deal of observation will be needed to tell if the entity in question is an intentional system at all.

The task of figuring out whether a given group even is an i-group will also likely be a difficult one because of our own inherent dispositions to ascribe intentionality, whether it's there or not. Above, I mentioned that there is some evidence that we are "hard-wired" to ascribe and reason about intentional states. This hard-wiring likely serves us well when trying to understand our fellow humans. But it may also predispose us to ascribe intentional states to an array of entities—even when they aren't intentional systems. We've all heard stories that highlight pre-literate peoples' tendencies to anthropomorphize an array of natural forces: Thunder is seen as the anger of Thor or Jupiter. Stumbling is caused by the witchcraft of neighbors. But such over-ascribing of intentionality is not limited to tribal peoples. In 1944, Heider and Simmel found that people who were shown films of simple geometrical figures moving were inclined to describe the actions as being those of purposive agents. More recently, and more interesting for our purposes, is Bloom and Veres's study showing that people who were shown certain films were inclined to ascribe intentionality even to clusters of objects, with phrases such as "The blue dots would not let the green rectangles pass. However the green rectangles did not seem to mind and didn't try that hard" (1999, B8). With a deeply rooted disposition to see intentionality everywhere, it is likely that we would be easily disposed to say things like "the Upper West Side wants . . ." whether the Upper West Side is a genuine i-group or not. Knowing of this tendency to see intentionality everywhere, we should be wary of too casually ascribing beliefs to groups. We need to do lots of careful study before we can conclude that we are dealing with a genuine i-group with particular goals and representations.

None of these considerations show that we couldn't ever understand a group's activities better by characterizing them intentionally. But they do show that it will take a great deal of effort to accurately uncover and use information about such states. The central difficulty with ascribing beliefs to groups is not that they can't be there, but that it's easy to get them wrong.

BETTER HIGH-LEVEL ASCRIPTIONS

Given that our understanding of group activity can be improved in some ways by characterizing it in intentional terms, are there things we can do to reduce the ascription problems just described? When ascribing beliefs to individuals, I think that one of our most effective (but sadly underused) strategies is to begin with well-supported theories of mental functioning and knowledge of particular circumstances, and make inferences from these. This is a strategy cognitive scientists often use for ascribing intentional states. (And I, of course, try to use such strategies to help uncover what individuals likely believe when they make X-do-Y statements.) Cognitive scientists often start with a theory of the component parts out of which a mental state is constructed, and use theories of how such parts link together to create more complex constructions.[8] The "composite-construction" strategy is pursued at a very low level by neurologists and connectionist modelers looking at how neurons and neuron clusters are linked together to create specific machines that tend to bring certain sorts of ideas to mind in certain situations (see, for example Squire 1987; Morris 1994; McClelland and Rumelhart 1986; Clark 1994). At a higher level, numerous cognitive modelers have investigated how various items of knowledge fit together to form mental models and theories (for example, Bower and Glass 1976; Palmer 1977; Johnson-Laird 1993).

It is easy to see how an analogous strategy could be used for ascribing intentions to groups. Here too, one could start with general theories of the component parts (here, individual people) that would create the "mental" structures of groups, and theories of how such parts link together in space to create more complex constructions in certain circumstances. There are currently few group-level analogues of high-level mental state theories that I have much confidence in using to derive conclusions about particular intentional states. But it's clear what the group analogues of low-level theories of individual human internal states might be. Just as models of individual mental states are sometimes derived from theories of how clusters of neurons combine to create maps of the world and behaviors, models of group intentions might be similarly derivable from psychological (and other) theories of how individuals interact with each other to produce net group behavior (see for example, Burt 1982; Hutchins 1995; Satz and Ferejohn 1994; and Denzau and North 1995).

The idea that we could improve our knowledge of high-level social phenomena by gathering information about the lower-level implementational details should not be a particularly striking suggestion. We regularly try to better understand how goal-seeking and functioning works in biological creatures by examining the details of their lower-level anatomy and neurology. In places throughout the social sciences, too, we try to understand what is happening at a social level by looking at what is happening at the individual level. This is done most often in history, where an understanding of larger social forces is often explained by a detailed look at the particulars of who was doing what to whom, and when. I suggest that we could improve our group intentionality descriptions, if we would make them in light of a better understanding of the particulars of what is happening at lower levels. It is easy enough to say "White Pine County wants to turn itself into a tourist mecca." But that will tell you little about what we can expect there unless we know more about the activities of particular individuals and subgroups. Are there just a number of businesses separately running ads in the papers of the nearest metropolitan area? Is it a matter of the county commissioners giving a developer tax breaks to build a ski resort (and do the citizens support the commissioners' decision)? Is it a matter of citizens or the town council lobbying the state to build a railway stop in their town? We will understand much better what will happen in that county, if, instead of just looking at the group's goals, we look at the lower-level sub-goals and sub-sub goals by which it tries to achieve them via the actions of individuals.

Knowing the facts about the situations of the implementing individuals in a group, of course, will not tell you about what any of them will do or why they are doing it, unless one has some (at least implicit) understanding of the psychological regularities governing how people respond to various situations. If we want more detailed understandings of the way individual activity produces goals and subgoals we'll want to incorporate information about psychological regularities. This, too, is done in some areas of the social sciences (though seldom with an eye to discussing group intentionality). Historians, who explain things on the basis of low-level details, must do so by relying on the reader's knowledge of the regularities of folk psychology (Hempel 1965, Jones 1998) as well as the situations actors find themselves in. Economists often model economic situations by describing the net effect of a certain number of individuals who make choices according to a set of internal decision-making rules (e.g., Day and Chen 1993). The psychology used in these accounts, of course, is of an awfully "thin" variety. I have argued in detail elsewhere (Jones 1997, 1998, 1999, 2000a, 2000b) that our knowledge of the social world could be vastly improved by utilizing more sophisticated, better empirically researched principles of psychology in social explanations in general. Understanding the detailed functioning of particular i-groups is an area where we should expect that paying attention to the psychology of the implementing individuals involved should improve our understanding considerably.

The idea that we should understand social phenomena better if the social sciences more fully utilized information about lower-level individual psychological dispositions should not be a controversial one.[9] In nearly every area of inquiry, from astrophysics to improving choral conducting, careful scrutiny of something's parts tends to yield enhanced knowledge of the whole. For numerous reasons, however, many areas of social sciences have been remarkably resistant to seeking or using information from psychology. Let me briefly mention what I think is the most compelling reason for the resistance, and say why it doesn't really tell against using more information about the lower levels. The most compelling reason for ignoring psychology in many social sciences is the idea that we can explain certain social phenomena in terms of high-level factors alone. We sometimes find a similar inattention to lower levels in other sciences, such as when biologists used (and continue to use) the concepts of Mendelian genetics to predict phenotypic features, without using (and sometimes without even having) information about the DNA structuring that makes such inheritance possible.

There is no disputing that we can sometimes go very far in predicting and explaining with a great deal of ignorance about lower-level details. But the reason that scrutinizing low-level details has always been a central part of science is that we can usually make more predictions with more accuracy when we do know the low-level details. It is standard introductory philosophy of science fare that most high-level laws have exceptions and *ceteris parabis* clauses. We frequently use our understanding of lower-level phenomena to make clear when higher-level laws won't (and will) work. Thus, our knowledge of physics tells us how the chemists' normally unreactive noble gases can be made to react at extremely high energy levels. A knowledge of molecular biology tells us why we don't get certain expected Mendelian ratios because of additional mechanisms of inheritance from the DNA in the mitochondria and chloroplasts. A knowledge of neuroanatomy tells us that certain kinds of language skills will be lost with certain types of head injuries. There's no reason that we should not expect that a similar understanding of lower-level principles of social psychology and contingent facts about individuals involved wouldn't improve our understanding of i-group functioning, even if we already had good high-level models. Using additional information from psychology might help us understand, for example, how the hiring of new mid-level managers with a certain managerial style would dramatically lower productivity at a company (perhaps while dramatically raising productivity at a seemingly similar company).

Understanding how the lower-levels work also often enables us to make predictions about higher-level phenomena for which we don't or don't yet have knowledge of higher-level regularities. Thus the higher-level properties of the element hafnium were predicted on the basis of a knowledge of atomic structure before hafnium was even discovered. One can easily imagine how a knowledge of lower-level individual thought and behavior could similarly tell us some general principles of i-group functioning that we weren't aware existed. We can imagine a look at lower-level details helping us discover, for example, a systematic connection between the ways in which coworkers are encouraged to compete or cooperate and the speed at which companies would alter products in response to changing market demand.

Finally, even when we have relatively stable and reliable high-level laws, one of the best ways to know that we do is to understand how it is that the lower levels guarantee such stability. It is a remarkable fact about our world that natural selection, design, and various combinations of low-level laws and contingent facts have created systems of highly uniform high-level regularities. These high-level regularities are there despite a great variety in initial conditions and manner of composition. A seed will grow into a pine tree in a wide variety of soil conditions. A general-purpose computing machine can be made to print out the square of fourteen through a huge variety of low-level processes. A certain company can continue to successfully sell their services with a large degree of personnel changes. But while the same high-level activities take place despite their being realized by a variety of low-level activities, it's not true that they would take place that way no matter what the low-level activities. This is why we find that high-level laws so often have exceptions. Certain lower-level arrangements or initial conditions sometimes can radically change what will happen at the higher level. As stated above, when we want to understand why a high level activity is not happening as expected, we often look to what special lower-level circumstances account for this. This means that in order to be really confident that a high-level regularity can be counted on, we need to know that the lower-level circumstances are such that they are making this possible, rather than being in an arrangement that produces an exceptional case.

Knowledge of lower-level regularities and circumstances, then, can improve our knowledge of higher-level phenomena, by enabling us to understand exactly when we can and can't count on these higher-level regularities to tell us what will happen. Even when we know about high-level regularities, then, knowledge of the lower levels will usually be of great benefit. There's no reason to expect that more fully integrating observations and theories about lower-level individual interaction shouldn't be expected to improve our understanding of the behavior of i-groups and remove some of the epistemological difficulties of group belief ascription.

Homuncular Functionalism

The usefulness of having knowledge of both high- and low-level functioning suggests that a good way to understand the intentional states of groups is to think about the high-level internal states of groups and the lower-level individual implementers of these simultaneously. One way this is done to better understand intentional states at the individual level is called *homuncular functionalism*. In an early work Daniel Dennett described how artificial intelligence workers typically try to design artificial systems with some kind of intentionality this way:

> The AI programmer begins with an intentionally characterized problem, and thus frankly views the computer anthropomorphically: if he *solves* the problem he will say he has designed a computer that can understand questions in English. His first and highest level of design breaks the computer down into subsystems, each of which is given intentionally characterized tasks; he composes a flow chart of evaluators, rememberers, discriminators, overseers and the like. These are *homunculi* with a vengeance; the highest-level design breaks the computer down into a committee or army of intelligent homunculi with purposes, information and strategies. Each homunculus in turn is analyzed into *smaller* homunculi, but, more importantly into *less clever* homunculi. When the level is reached where the homunculi are no more than adders and subtracters, they need only the intelligence to pick the larger of two numbers when directed to, they have been reduced to functionaries "who can be replaced by a machine." The aid to comprehension of anthropomorphizing the elements just about lapses at this point, and a mechanistic view of the proceedings becomes workable and comprehensible (1978, 80–81).

The idea that the way to understand human or machine intentionality is to conceptualize it in terms of a complex being whose functioning is made possible by nested hierarchies of beings has been developed by Fodor (1968), Cummins (1975), Dennett (1978), Haugeland (1978), and most extensively by Lycan (1981, 1987, 1988). However well homuncular functionalism works for describing intentionality at the level of the individuals, it seems almost tailor-made for understanding group level intentionality. One should not be surprised that I think that the best way to understand the intentionality of a group of people is in terms of a model that explicates intentionality by showing how it can be conceptualized in terms of the machinations of a group of little people. Ultimately, however, it is not really that it employs the metaphor of "little people" that makes homuncular functionalism a good way of understanding group intentionality. Homuncular functionalism gets its power due to the manner in which it brings together the higher and lower levels. In a homuncular functionalist model, one does not merely describe an intentional agent as "trying to decide who to invite to a Halloween séance." One also says what subtasks this divides into: "generating a list of close friends," "checking to see if each one is an obnoxious unbeliever in ghosts," "trying to make sure there's a balance of men and women," etc. Each of these tasks, in turn, is broken down into further tasks. "Checking to see if each one is an obnoxious unbeliever" consists of "recalling conversations about the supernatural with each proposed guest," "looking for derisive words," etc. Ultimately each higher-level activity is systematically linked to a cluster of lower-level mechanisms in which it is implemented. At the very bottom level is a set of well-understood simple devices.

This is just the sort of spelling out of the lower-level implementational details that are usually lacking from many ascriptions of intentionality to groups, but could really help us gain a fuller understanding of what is going on. A good homuncular functionalist account of an i-group would not just seek a top-level description of a group's goals, but would try to build a picture of the types of sub and sub-sub goals it had into the account. A full homuncular functionalist description would not merely say, "The XYZ Company is trying to come up with and market a new Web TV browsing device." The homuncular functionalist account would also contain information about the different divisions devoted to the various parts of this goal, and then about how each of these subdivisions is divided into various tasks. Making sure we focus on getting the low-level implementational details right, means we will get a more accurate picture of the *higher*-level state—one that really reflects what's actually happening with the individuals who make it happen. With these details, one should make much more accurate predictions than if one merely asked, "What would I do if I were the XYZ Company?"

Using a homuncular functionalist approach also gives us ways to understand what is happening at the individual level better. As we said while discussing the advantages of giving a group an intentional characterization, having knowledge of the group's various higher-level tasks and subtasks is an additional route to understanding the details of the constraints that reduce degrees of freedom and structurally, collectively pressure various lower-level parts (including individuals) to behave as they do.

Finally, connecting the high and the low levels, as one does in a homuncular functionalist approach, means one need not have to try to derive our understandings of the social world purely from an understanding of the activities of the low-level individuals involved. If we know something about how low-level individual activities roughly correlate with higher-level group intentional states, we could move from some observations of the low-level to a correlated state in a high-level subsumptive intentional theory. (See Jones 2003 and chapter 6 for a discussion of the advantages of subsumptive accounts.) As Dan Dennett never tires of pointing out, there are many advantages to trying to figure out what someone will come to think on the basis of an intentional characterization, as opposed to trying to derive it from neuronal activity. We've discussed similar advantages that can be expected when we think of groups characterized as intentional agents, as opposed to trying to calculate what will happen based on an understanding of the individuals involved. Reasoning using folk psychology is something we are very efficient at. This should be true for folk psychological reasoning about group intentions as well as individual ones. Whether such high-level intentional descriptions are good for doing things like *explaining* why what happens, happens is a task we will look at in later chapters. And the reader will have to decide how disadvantages there, along with the *difficulties* in ascription (that a homuncular functionalist approach could help avoid), stack up next to the *advantages* of intentional characterization described earlier in this chapter.

Throughout everyday conversation, journalistic reports, and the social sciences, people talk about groups having beliefs and desires. In this chapter, I have shown that this need not be just loose, idle talk. It is quite possible for collections of people to have goals and representations by being organized according to principles that are similar to those organizing organisms with intentionality. Intentional biological organisms are cooperating clusters of cells that, over time, develop capacities to survive and flourish by becoming increasingly well tuned to getting their goals in their particular environments. There is no reason to believe that cooperating clusters of people can't come to be organized in a similar manner.

Furthermore, we have seen that there are certainly some advantages to describing group activity in this intentional manner. Giving a high-level functional description to a group could actually help us understand what various lower-level sub and sub-subparts are doing vis-à-vis each other. (Knowing that a company is trying to boost clothing sales in its youth division, could help us understand why, at various lower levels, investments are being made in machinery that can make smaller buttons and snaps.) High-level intentional ascriptions also have some special advantages regarding making predictions about what will happen. In our everyday lives, we continually make use of folk psychological ideas to quickly infer what an agent will do, without having to use a huge amount of cognitive resources trying to calculate how an agent will behave using low-level information from neurology. Indeed, we might even be hard-wired to quickly and efficiently come to conclusions this way. If groups really have intentional states, we should also, in the right circumstances, be able to use our folk psychological views to quickly and efficiently infer what the group is likely to do, without having to first have a lot of knowledge about the individuals involved in the group activity.

But these advantages should not cause us to lose sight of the fact that it is often difficult to correctly ascribe certain kinds of beliefs, even to individuals.

It is often difficult to use these ascriptions to predict what else a person will think or do. All of the obstacles that make it difficult for us to ascribe intentional states to individuals are present, and numerous more difficulties are there, besides these, when we try to ascribe such states to groups. We can't go from a knowledge of environmental exposure to a knowledge of the internal arrangement of parts unless we know a lot more about how learning and conditioning effects inner representation. We do know a fair amount about this regarding the inner representations of individuals, but we have an enormous amount of theoretical work to do before we can say what kind of inner representation that exposure to a certain environment will create in a group. Similarly, we can only use our knowledge of intentional states to predict how an agent will behave if we know a lot about the other beliefs and desires that surround the state we are ascribing, and if we know how the limbs and tools of the agent are able to interact with the environments the agent typically finds itself in. When we are ascribing beliefs to individuals, we often possess this additional information without explicitly studying the systems involved. We fill-in-the-blanks with plausible ideas about surrounding beliefs and surrounding tools because we have reason to expect that ones the agent in question likely has are probably similar to the background beliefs and tools that we know that we ourselves have. We shouldn't expect that we could get away with using these same default assumptions when we are talking about the surrounding states of groups. The auxiliary assumptions we need for making behavioral predictions regarding groups on the basis of belief ascriptions, are ones we shouldn't expect that we have based on a knowledge of the surrounding beliefs and tools we ourselves tend to have as individuals. We need to actually study the groups involved and the situations they are in to begin to get the information needed. Without collecting a lot more information about the workings of the lower levels that implement group representations, and about surrounding representations and tools, any success at uncovering the existence of interesting metaphysical higher-level intentional states will be matched by epistemic failures regarding which intentional state a group has and how it will act.

We can make things better by adopting a homuncular functionalist approach to i-group description. A homuncular functionalist approach means that when we say that a group wants something to happen, we try to also say what is happening in the parts and subparts that implement this desire several levels down. We try to develop theories of what high-level intentions typically can and can't tell you about low-level implementations, in what conditions. With a homuncular functionalist approach, we also look at how individual low-level activity can create high-level group intentional states. And we have a much more accurate picture of exactly what is involved in having this high-level intentional state. Knowing these details also puts us in a better position to know how, exactly, these states are likely to interact with surrounding states and with the group's tools for interacting with the environment.

If we take this homuncular functionalist approach to understanding group intentionality, we will also have a rare situation in which our ordinary and social scientific ways of describing things can work together. Our humanistic and scientific knowledge could complement each other considerably. This way of understanding group intentionality could allow for a widely shared but still sophisticated understanding of the ways in which important parts of the social world operate. When we ascribe beliefs to groups in ordinary conversation or in the social sciences, we don't usually do it with the idea of cashing these ascriptions out in a homuncular functionalist way. But I'm suggesting that if we did do so, we would enable group intentional descriptions to be much more useful than they now are.

In this chapter, then, we've seen the same ambivalence about ascribing beliefs to groups that we see throughout the social sciences, and throughout ordinary and journalistic descriptions. We routinely ascribe beliefs and desires to groups, but we are not really sure how much we mean what we say, or how well such descriptions really enable us to understand the situation. Here, I've suggested that we are not entirely wrong in describing groups using the intentional-sounding language that we do. Indeed, there are many positive features about describing groups this way. But we need to be somewhat cautious—for without more information, such descriptions tell us much less about what is going on than we may think they tell us. We will see that this ambivalence will be the case for just about all the X-do-Y descriptions discussed in this book. Our ordinary idea that these are fairly decent descriptions, but ones that need to be supplemented if we want better understanding, turns out to be quite on the mark. This is true for collective intentional, as well as other interpretations of "the [X] do/believe [Y]."

NOTES

1. I am talking about an agent's internal "mental" representations here. But, of course, these sorts of things aren't the only kinds of things called "representations." Words, pictures, paintings, things "designated" to stand for other things (e.g., "let this penny be the goalie, imagine this nickel is the forward") are all called representations. Finding a definition that encompasses both internal mental representations (in all their variety) and other things called representations (in their even greater variety) is a tough job. Perhaps there is no general definition to be had. But let me try my hand at coming up with one.

In my view, a representation of an X, for an agent is either a) the agent's internal representation of X (as defined in the text), or b) a cluster of features (that is not, itself an X) that, together, in one place, have a robust disposition to cause an internal representation of X to be activated in a certain group of people. Both internal and external representations of X cause dispositions to appropriately interact with X in goal-achieving ways. The internal representations are more proximate to actual interactions and the external ones are more distant.

The requirement that the feature cluster that is the representation of X not itself be an X is needed, or else any actual duck would count as a representation of a duck. The requirement that a cluster of features, together, must cause the internal representation is needed to avoid counting separated distal parts of a causal network that lead to the activation of the inner representation from counting as the cause of the inner representation, and thereby being an external representation.

How robust the disposition to cause internal representations has to be before itself counting as a representation is a judgment call. Suppose a particular backyard fence post tends to cause Tom to activate an internal representation of his mother. Is the post a representation of his mother to him? Well, we probably would say it was if he had had the post mounted in his room as part of a shrine he erected to think about his mother. But if he has fleeting thoughts of her every time he passes it, we probably wouldn't call it a representation of his mother. (Although we might well say that that post represents his mother, or his mother's love of yard work.) On the other hand, a picture of his mother or the words "Anna Mae Brown" so robustly activates an internal representation of his mother that we would almost always call them representations of her.

2. How many steering signals directing an agent's potential interactions with X are required before one really has a representation of X? Well, first, below a certain threshold (e.g., when movements don't usually successfully lead to any goal or subgoal), one would not call it a representation at all. Above that threshold, representations can be more or less thorough. The more goals and subgoals having to do with X that can be achieved vis-à-vis one's stored if-then repertoire of moves regarding it, the more thorough a representation it is. A representation/set-of-coordinated-steering-signals may be good at achieving some goals but bad at achieving others, indicating a less than thorough representation. I can have a pretty decent representation of my desk, one that allows me to know where the pens are kept, but this signal-set may not tell me where the file folders for grade changes are and may not tell me its weight (how much force I would need to move it). A more thorough representation would contain steering signals that allowed me to meet these subgoals.

Note that while saying something is a representation of X tells us a lot about it, there is much that such a label doesn't tell us. Both a thorough and a not very thorough representation of a certain thing might be called "a representation of a vanilla ice cream cone." Our language and folk theories don't have much in them to differentiate between rich thorough representations and minimal ones. Our language is also very rough grained in that we name a set of features a "representation of a vanilla ice cream cone" even though one couldn't distinguish between vanilla ice cream and vanilla sherbet on the basis of this representation. And two radically different sets of steering instructions—both of which enable us to successfully interact with a thing, would both be termed "a representation of a vanilla ice cream cone" even though these representations take radically different forms. Our names for representations are adequate for most purposes, but they give little information about numerous details.

3. Questions about when a goal should be said to be the group's goal and when it is only the goal of individuals in the group are interesting and tricky ones. As we said earlier, it is possible for some peoples' or things' activities to be organized such that they are so dependent on steering signals from something else that we don't think of them as having goals of their own, but instead see them as the organs, tools, or slaves of another system. If, on the other hand, a system as a whole would still use various methods to get to an end state, irrespective of the activities of any particular goal seeker within it, then that system as a whole is a goal seeker. If a corporation was structured to have the robust goal of making money, even if its CEO tried to destroy it from within, then the company has a goal that the CEO doesn't have (and the CEO would likely be replaced). If, by contrast, various routes to seeking that goal would all cease being taken if one unified source of steering signals were removed, then we should say that *that part is the agent that was seeking that goal*—with other parts and people being mere *tools* of that agent. The question of whether there are any interesting boundaries between steering centers, organs, and tools is one we will have to leave for another occasion.

4. This account says how it is possible for groups to have intentional states. Some scholars may well also be interested in the questions of whether and how it is possible for groups to have qualia or consciousness (see Block, 1993). Since I have no general theory about how consciousness is connected to intentionality, or even what consciousness really is, questions concerning the possibility of group consciousness are ones I must leave to others.

5. The view I am expressing here, then, contrasts with the view Gilbert expressed in *On Social Facts* that plural subjects should be at the center of understanding group intentionality. I believe that there are many different ways besides plural subjecthood that groups can come to have intentional states. I also do not think that group intentionality need be the center of social scientific focus. A particular kind of group is or should be thought of as worthy of social scientific focus if there are important generalizations that can be made about that group. I-groups are one class of groups that should be of interest to social scientists. They are groups that have interesting generalizations that are true of them because of the ways they try to bring about certain goal states. But they are certainly not the only sorts of groups that theories of the social should focus on. There are groups as a whole, like the AIDS patients who use up the world's antiviral drugs that I mentioned at the beginning of the chapter, that produce interesting net effects without being an i-group. There might well be interesting social science generalizations about such groups. There might also be interesting generalizations about collections of certain kinds of people who form types of groups that don't, together, necessarily produce any interesting net effect—groups like women born before the baby boom, lepers, first time home buyers, etc. If there are important generalizations true of such groups, then social science should make every effort to explore them, regardless of whether or not such groups might seem, conceptually, "insufficiently social."

6. Such groups, it seems, could be intentional agents. Could they also be moral agents? Well, to begin with, if groups could not be intentional agents, there would be no way for them to be moral agents. What I want to do in this chapter is to show how they could be intentional agents. If they can be, then we can't use their lack of intentionality to rule out any moral evaluation. Now evaluating whether groups can be full-blown moral agents is beyond the scope of this book. Still, some remarks are in order.

One way we can examine whether groups can be moral agents is to look at what our best moral theories say about what additional features intentional agents need in order to be full blown moral agents. We could then look at whether there are any i-groups that possess these additional features. We might, for example, adopt Frankfort's view that moral agency requires our second-order desires to be in harmony with our first-order desires (1971). We would then ask whether and how it is possible for certain groups to have second-order desires.

Given our current lack of consensus about what the requirements for being a morally responsible agent are, I would favor a different type of approach. At our current stage of knowledge, I think it would be useful to simultaneously look at what various theories of moral agency say about problematic borderline cases (including groups) while, at the same time, using these borderline cases to try to help us clarify what counts as moral agency, in a process of reflective equilibrium. One area it would be useful to look at, for example, is animal morality. How complex does animal thinking have to be before we say that they are truly moral agents? Looking at what we learn from these cases could help us develop a theory of moral agency rich enough to tell us what we should believe about intentional groups. Scholars like Bruce Waller (1997) and Frans de Waal (1997) have useful and interesting things to say about animal morality. Another area that could be useful here is looking at the morality of cases in which subagents are involved. If someone with a multiple personality disorder commits a crime, is the whole person guilty? Cases like these could help us develop a theory of moral agency that could tell us something about the moral agency of groups, which are always going to be made up of subagents—subagents that may have different goals from the agent as a whole. Finally, there's a large literature about the morality (if not the moral agency) of corporate actions by scholars like Peter French. Looking at our judgments about the morality of corporate actions is likely to help us develop a theory about the relationship between moral actions and moral agency that's almost certainly going to be relevant to questions about whether groups have moral agency.

Groups, it seems, can be intentional agents. Whether, in addition, they can be moral agents is unclear. But knowing how they can be intentional agents helps give us some promising ways to find that out.

7. Note, however, that there are many scholars who believe that intentional descriptions are not necessarily the most useful ways of describing even individual thinking and behaving (see Churchland 1979; Stich 1983; Ramsey 2007). In this chapter, and in chapters 5 and 6, I discuss some of the problems with giving groups intentional descriptions. Whether there are also additional problems that parallel other problems these scholars point out for individual intentional descriptions is an interesting area for investigation.

8. There's also a different inference-making strategy sometimes used to ascribe beliefs to individuals, which could be used for ascribing intentions to groups. One might try to understand the working of an unobserved "black box" mechanism at a given time, by starting with theories about sets of *earlier initial conditions*, then using dynamic law theories to talk about how forces from within and without will change this set to produce a resulting construction (as in predicting how a satellite will stabilize into an orbit). For individual mental state ascription, versions of this initial-conditions-and-changes strategy have been used at both high and low levels and over large and small time scales. At smaller time scales various researchers have studied how initial mental states are changed by new perceptual information (Marr and Nishihara 1978; Beiderman 1987), operant conditioning (Reynolds 1968), and learning to relax or tighten conditions under which certain behavioral or informational schemas are invoked (Holyoake and Koh, 1987). Over larger time scales, biologists and evolutionary psychologists have been studying how the process of natural selection has shaped and developed probable earlier mental structures (e.g., Barkow, Cosmides, and Tooby 1992).

Where models of individual beliefs should be constrained by theories of which innate beliefs and desires are likely to be there after a long shaping by evolutionary forces, we could also constrain theories of group beliefs and desires by theories of how various group goal-seeking and world-mapping strategies would likely have been shaped by the forces of natural selection. Nelson and Winter (1982) have been developing such principles in order to explain how corporations evolve over time. At a more abstract level, Axelrod and Hamilton (1981) and numerous others have been developing theories about which sorts of behaviors will tend to become stably fixed in groups over time due to the dynamic unfolding. There's no reason to think that these sorts of theories couldn't serve just as well at helping us choose between various behavior-generating models of group inner states as their analogues could in helping us find the best models of individual internal mental states.

9. What is controversial is the stronger thesis of methodological individualism (see Kincaid 1994; Jones 1996; Hodgson 2007). Methodological individualism is that thesis that not only can we always understand what is happening at the group or social level by understanding the thoughts and behaviors of the individuals involved, but that we always ought to. Methodological individualism holds that we never fully understand social behavior unless we understand the behaviors of the individuals involved.

My view is that no one should disagree with the thesis that understanding what's happening at the individual level can sometimes improve our understanding of the social. I hold the stronger thesis that it can usually improve our understanding. I also believe the stronger thesis that we can always explain what's happening at the social level with a full understanding of the individual level. (I argue for this in Jones 2003.) But I don't hold the view that we only understand social phenomena when we know what is happening at the individual level.

Chapter Four

"We Go to the Diner on Fridays"
Norms, Customs, Conventions, and the Like

In the previous chapter, we looked at X-do-Y statements such as "The Boy Scouts built this shelter," where the claim is meant to say something about a group as a whole. In this claim, the speaker is trying to tell listeners that this building was built over time, by the collective labor of a group of Boy Scouts (whose members could change from year to year). In the chapter before that, we discussed X-do-Y statements like "The Boy Scouts in this town know how to start fires without matches," where the speaker is trying to tell listeners that each individual belonging to the local Boy Scout troupe (perhaps with a few exceptions) knows how start a fire without matches. In this chapter we will look at a third major kind of X-do-Y claim. When speakers say things like "The Boy Scouts say the Pledge of Allegiance at the beginning of every meeting," they seem to be describing a somewhat different situation—one in which the Boy Scouts have a norm, custom, or convention of engaging in this practice. A norm is a collective phenomenon in that it is a feature that can be possessed only by a group (Bill or the scoutmaster can't have a norm). At the same time, the presence of a norm seems to be describing what causes individual group members to do what they do (like recite the Pledge of Allegiance). Norms and things like them can be explicitly discussed using terms like *custom, convention, tradition, rule, culture, practice, more, fad*, etc. But X do/believe Y phrases are often used to describe the presence of a norm or custom among a group, even though the words 'norm' or 'custom' are not specifically uttered, as in the Boy Scout case above, or as in cases like, "The students at Ole Miss spend the fall going to tailgate parties." In this chapter we'll examine the concept that seems to be at work here, both when terms like "norm" or "custom" are specifically used and when the notion is alluded to through general X-do-Y locutions.[1]

Invoking norms and customs (whether or not they are called by name) is very common. The *International Encyclopedia of the Social Sciences* begins its article on the study of norms by saying, "No concept is invoked more often by social scientists in the explanations of human behavior than 'norm'" (Gibbs 1968, 212). Yet despite the commonality of such invocations, what terms like "norm" and "convention" refer to is surprisingly unclear. Is a norm a set of attitudes or a set of actions? Geographers know where to find rivers, but where, exactly, is a norm? We speak of French culture, but is this the same sort of thing as corporate culture? (And where does culture in the sense of Mozart and Shakespeare fit in?) How long must people in a society engage in a practice before it is a custom? Is it built into the concept of a custom that one ought to follow it? Absolutely yes, says philosopher Margaret Gilbert in her comprehensive work *On Social Facts* (1989, 404). Not necessarily, says philosopher Raimo Tuomela in his also comprehensive work, *The Philosophy of Social Practices* (2002, 94). Just what sorts of things are norms, customs, traditions, etc.?

THE LACK OF CLARITY OF "NORM" AND "CUSTOM"

It doesn't take long to see that terms like "norm" and "custom" are vague and ambiguous with a bewildering array of different meanings. On the one hand, we can say, "It's the norm to put salt on spaghetti here," to describe something that most in a group do, but few feel any social pressure to do. On the other hand, we can say, "It's the norm to write a thank you note for each birthday gift," to describe something that few in a group do, but most feel social pressure to do. And even if it's clear whether the speaker is talking about regularity rather than pressure, it's not at all clear how many members must engage in a practice before it is a norm. If the speaker is talking about social pressure, it's not clear how many people must apply pressure of some sort before the practice is a norm.

And what sort of thing is a norm? Is it some kind of Hegelian or Durkheimian collective entity, irreducible to individual activity, but with the power to make individuals act in a certain way? By what mechanisms could a collective entity be able to cause individuals to behave in a certain manner? Perhaps "norm" just refers to the existence of a number of individuals who put pressure on other individuals in their group to act a certain way. But what sort of pressure? Praise for doing X, punishment for not doing it, or merely an expectation that X will be done? Or is it possible that all that needs to happen is that others do things such that not doing X will turn out to be very costly for an actor? Or can there be no pressure at all, with a norm still existing merely because a person wants to do what everyone else seems to be doing?

And if norms or customs are behaviors caused by certain kinds of pressures, which sorts of behaviors are *not* governed by norms? On the one hand, we seem to use terms like "norms," "customs," and "conventions" when we want to contrast behavioral rules based on genuine moral considerations from ones that are based on more arbitrary stipulation. A number of psychologists (Turiel, 1979, Blair 1995, Nucci 2001) have written about how people make this distinction. On the other hand, Stephen Stich and his colleagues have recently conducted experiments they interpret as showing that people make no such clear distinctions. According to Stich, people often see behavioral rules with features prototypically associated with conventions (being local, changeable, with violations causing little harm) as proscribing behavior that is, nevertheless, considered to be morally right or wrong. Conversely, they often see the wrongfulness of behavior with features associated with moral values (universal, harm-causing) as variable over time and place, like conventions are thought to be (Kelly, Stich, Haley, Eng, and Fessler 2007).

Terms from this family are also often used to contrast rules and behaviors that are done for rational reasons with rules that are more arbitrary. People often answer questions like "Why do brides wear red in that country?" with answers meant to stress the nonrational nature of such practices: "It's just the custom there," "It's just a practice they have in that culture," "It's just a convention." But if one looks at the literature on these topics, it's not at all clear that these contrast in any way with rational behavior. Ordinary explanation of cultural practices often seems to follow a common social science practice whereby strange activities are accounted for by showing how they are reasonable after all, all things considered. Throughout the twentieth century, giants of social theory like Talcot Parsons in sociology and Bronislaw Malinowski in anthropology would seek to show how various odd seeming cultural practices were actually rational to follow, providing great benefits to practitioners (for example, a seemingly wasteful tribal ceremonial feast was actually a means of distributing food to poorer neighbors). In quite a different way, the philosopher David Lewis and a number of subsequent theorists have developed models of how conventional behavior can be based on strategic rational choice.[2] So does or doesn't conventional behavior contrast with behavior that is rational or moral?

When confronted with the apparent mysteriousness of terms like norm or culture, it's likely that most English speakers would admit that they are not very clear on precisely what these terms refer to and how they should be used. But that needn't mean that these terms are really problematic. Perhaps the reason most people are not completely clear about how they should be used is that they are, first and foremost, social scientific terms. Perhaps such terms have seeped into ordinary language from social science, without speakers really having a full grasp of the precise ways such terms are used in the social sciences. After all, speakers regularly use terms that are prominent in the sciences like "gasses," "waves," and "force" without a full grasp of their technical scientific meanings. Perhaps terms like "culture" and "norm" are only dimly understood by ordinary speakers, but have precise clear meanings when used by social scientists.

A brief look at the social scientific literature, however, shows that the use of some of these terms in the social sciences is anything but clear and consistent. Here's anthropologist Clifford Geertz's attempt to clarify what culture is, for example, in his highly regarded and popular anthropology text, *The Interpretation of Cultures*:

> To say that culture consists of socially established structures of meaning in terms of which people do such things as signal conspiracies and join them or perceive insults and answer them, is no more to say that it is a psychological phenomenon, a characteristic of someone's mind, personality, cognitive structure, or whatever, than to say that Tantrism, genetics, the progressive form of the verb, the classification of wines, the Common Law, or the notion of a "conditional curse" (as Westermark defined the concept of *'ar* in terms of which Cohen pressed his claims to damages) is. (1973, 13)

Readers of Geertz should be forgiven, I think, if they still fail to see how social scientists use the term "culture" to explain behavior after reading that ontological status of culture is similar to the ontological status of Tantrism. If one scans the anthropological literature, one will find other anthropologists giving much clearer characterizations of what culture is. The problem is that many of them differ markedly from one another. When you find a definition that enables you to understand the concept clearly, your confidence is marred by reading another equally authoritative source giving "culture" a different definition. In the 1950s anthropologists Alfred Kroeber and Clyde Kluckholm identified 164 different definitions of culture, and subsequent anthropologists have only added more. The situation only gets more confusing if one moves from looking at definitions of culture to more general theories of what culture consists of. Looking at the different views of culture among anthropologists, one might well wonder if they are studying the same subject matter (see, for example, Harris 2001, Kuper 1999). A similar situation exists in sociology with regards to the definition of "norm." Jack Gibbs (1965), for example, described fifteen different uses of the term in sociology. And when psychologists use the term "norm," they seem to mean something from another family altogether—a mean, median, or modal response (e.g., "some of the subjects gave twos or eights for their answers, but the norm was to write 'five'"; philosophers, meanwhile, often use the term "norm" to mean folk moral beliefs [see Sripada and Stich 2006]). If one wants to get a clear view of what norms and the like are, it does not automatically help to survey the social scientific literature.

If social scientists don't make clear what norms, customs, and culture are, perhaps looking at what philosophers have written on this topic could help. Philosophy, after all, is a discipline in which clarifying disputed concepts is a central aim. And there has been no dearth of philosophers discussing these concepts. But one finds similar problems here. Philosophers have the same disagreements about how to define these terms that social scientists do. Stich, for example, uses the term "norm" as more or less synonymous with "moral value." Philip Pettit (2002), by contrast, emphasizes that a norm (among other things) is a behavioral regularity found in the population. David Lewis (1968), in his definition of "convention" takes care not to use normative terms, whereas Margaret Gilbert writes, "I would expect any acceptable account of social convention to use normative terms" (1989, 352). Meanwhile, as with social scientists, the theories philosophers develop of these entities are even more diverse than the definitions they give. If one wants to get clearer on what we mean by terms like "norm" and "custom," looking at what various philosophers say on the topic may not help much.

CONSTRUCTING A DECENT MODEL
OF WHAT NORMS AND CUSTOMS ARE

One of the things that I want to do in this chapter is sort through the confusion just described and clarify what we mean by terms like "norm" and "custom." But in saying what I think is meant, won't I just be adding to an already crowded confusing cacophony of would-be definers? As I described in the Introduction, I have a couple of assets that should help me in this task. On the one hand, there's my background in the social sciences (MA and ABD in Anthropology). This can hopefully enable me to be a bit more aware of the actual social scientific usage of these terms. On the other hand, unlike social scientists, I'm a professor of analytic philosophy, coming out of a tradition that has a central mission of relentlessly scrutinizing proposed definitions. Analytic philosophers often work to come up with air-tight intuitively acceptable definitions of a term by looking carefully at cases where the term doesn't quite fit or barely fits and trying to discern which features are really sufficient and necessary for applying the term. This, of course, is just what many other analytic philosophers looking at norms or customs are prone to do. I have some reason to hope, however, that the analysis of terms like "norm," and "custom" that I will give in the next section will do a better job at clarifying our common usage of these terms than most philosophical discussions of them. As I will discuss later, most philosophical discussions of terms like "norm," and "custom," etc., have a different emphasis than I do. Where the model of the concept of norm that I will discuss seeks to account for the actual usage and our intuitions regarding "norm" and cognate terms, other theorists often aim to give reforming definitions and theories of norms, customs, and conventions. Not without good reason, many theorists want to provide a clear, consistent, unitary theory of norms, etc. In the social sciences, they are interested in theories of norms that best explain our behavior. In philosophy, they are interested in theories of norms that fit in with our best metaphysical picture of the social world.

It is no mean feat to show how norms fit into the ontology of things existing in the world, and many philosophers struggle mightily to describe how they might do so. But discussions of the place of norms in the world are usually discussions of norms in a truncated, precisified, and systematized sense of the term. Such philosophers are not usually explicating "norms" and "conventions" in the sloppy, everyday, not-very-systematic senses in which we actually use such terms. What I will be doing in the next section, on the other hand, is an instance of what I described in chapter 1. I will be describing a model of our actual social-linguistic rules specifying when we tend to call something a norm or custom—rules that will help enable us to work backwards to find what someone likely means when they call something a norm or custom. This model will describe what it is we tend to label "norms" or "customs. I'll also describe what evidence justifies the claim that this is indeed a model of how we actually think about norms and customs.

One important question concerns why one should care about a model of norms that maps the contours of our folk concepts. Isn't the important thing to know what really exists in the world, regardless of our concepts? Isn't the important thing to be able to explain behavior? I certainly have no objections to refining and precisifying our ordinary concepts in order to help us better understand behavior. Nevertheless, it is still important to know what our commonsense concepts are for at least two reasons. First, we behave the way we do partly because of how we ourselves understand and explain what other people are doing. When we come to believe that a certain behavior is the norm for a group (as opposed to it being there for another reason), that is going to affect the way we behave. What, then, is entailed by people coming to believe something is a norm? What do they understand by this? What do they expect? A refined social scientific or metaphysical theory of norms will answer some questions, but it will not answer these important questions. Second, if a theorist really wants to communicate to others her theory of how behavior is governed, she has to understand how the people she is speaking with have previously defined the terms she is using. To communicate a new theory effectively, we need to understand the prior concepts that need to be rethought. A new theory, to be effective, needs to explicitly state, and in more than one place, something to the effect of "what I mean by 'norm' is X, and this differs from the way it's ordinarily used in ways A, B, and C." Stating this both prevents miscommunication and allows one to introduce a potentially clearer and more useful concept. But one can only make a statement like this if one knows what our ordinary conceptualization of norms and the like are. This, then, is one of the things I hope to accomplish by understanding what we mean by norms. In this, I think the model I discuss in the next section can be helpful in a way that most other models are not.

A MODEL OF OUR SOCIAL-LINGUISTIC RULES REGARDING "NORM," "CUSTOM," AND COGNATE TERMS

As I see it, our social-linguistic rule for using terms like "norms," "customs," "culture," etc., is that one or another of these terms can be used when people conceptualize behavior as belonging to a general category that might be called "what's done" behaviors. The "what's done" behavior category is rather inclusive. Something is a "what's done" behavior if it belongs to any of a disjunctive set of certain behavior types. On the one hand (as we'll discuss further below), almost any behavior that is very widespread in a certain group, whatever the cause of its commonality, can be thought of as a "what's done" behavior. On the other hand, we also conceive of urges to behave in certain ways (even if the behaviors are not always done) that are caused by various conformity mechanisms as "what's done" behaviors. One kind of conforming is wanting to imitate what lots of other people actually do or are assumed to do. Another cause of conforming is social pressure: people wanting to do what others believe they ought to do, or what others are believed to believe they ought to do. Another is social conditioning: people doing what a number of others have praised them for, or avoiding doing what a number of others have punished them for. A disjunction of disjunct classes, then, make up "what's done" behaviors. "What's done" behaviors are either those that are widespread in a group, or the behaviors caused by imitating (real or perceived) behaviors, or caused by social pressure (real or perceived), or caused by social conditioning. Widespread behaviors, no matter what their cause, can be "what's done" behaviors, and conforming behaviors, no matter how widespread, can be "what's done" behaviors. (Note, also, that terms in the "what's done" family like "norm" and "custom" can refer to both the behaviors that result from various conformity mechanisms and to the various conformity methods that tend to cause these behaviors to result.)

But describing this set of disjunctions does not quite capture our "what's done" concept. For the concept of "what's done" behaviors is also a somewhat conjunctive one. While any behavior belonging to these disjunct classes can sometimes count as a "what's done" behavior, the most prototypical "what's done" behaviors are the ones that belong to all these classes, simultaneously. We are most comfortable thinking of something as a "what's done" behavior or calling something a "norm" or "custom," etc., when it is widespread in a group and imitated and done because others believe it should be done. A prototypical "what's done" behavior is one that many group members do because other members are doing it and think they should. Such behaviors are also prototypically assumed to be caused neither by rationally calculating the merits of the behavior, nor because of nonsocial rewards and punishments from nature. Prototypical "what's done" behaviors are those belonging to the conjunction of the aforementioned disjunct classes. We can call prototypical "what's done" behaviors—those belonging to the conjunction of these disjunct classes—"widespread conformity" behaviors. (Behaviors that are both widespread and caused by one or another social conformity mechanism (rather than all of them simultaneously) are also fairly prototypical, though they aren't at the exact center of the prototype.) In ordinary conversation, we use a related family of terms (e.g., "norms," "customs," "conventions," etc.) to describe both the prototypical and non-prototypical behaviors in the "what's done" category.[3] This category can also be invoked when these specific terms are not used, but when people describe situations with a variant of this construction: The X-group does/believes Y, as in "The Lisu build their houses on stilts," or "Joining the military is not an option for Amish people." While terms like "norm" and "custom" all share this common "what's done" core, each term has its own distinct additional features associated with it as well (which we will discuss below). Social scientists, being English speakers, also have this core widespread conformity "what's done" concept in mind when they write (and their "lay" readers surely do). But social scientists use these terms most often in speaking with their professional colleagues, so they are highly prone to also use these terms as they are used in the "dialects" of their disciplines and subdisciplines, where various features may be added or subtracted.

So terms like "norm," "custom," "convention," etc., are prototypically used to describe widespread behavior in a group caused by imitation and social pressure. One of the things that makes understanding these terms difficult, however, is, as we've said, the permissibility of using these terms to describe situations in which there is either widespreadness or conformity. One might say, for example, "Drinking a six-pack a night is the norm for people at this college," without necessarily having in mind that the reason people do this is because others do. The speaker might be using this terminology just to call attention to the fact that this is what lots of people do, whatever their reasons for doing it. English seems to allow this "high frequency" usage of the term "norm," even though it is not how this term is prototypically used. Among social scientists, psychologists and demographers seem to use "norm" in primarily this frequency sense. Shultz et al. 2007, for example, discuss how "Social norms marketing campaigns seek to reduce the occurrence of deleterious behaviors by correcting targets' misperceptions regarding the behaviors' prevalence. The perception of prevalence is commonly referred to as the *descriptive norm* governing a behavior (Cialdini et al. 1991)."

It is also somewhat permissible to use these terms to describe situations in which there are only feelings that one ought to be conforming. We can use terms like "norm" or "custom" to describe a group practice that need not actually be done by large numbers of people (e.g., Americans sitting down for three meals a day). Such practices can be called customs or norms if lots of people believe that lots of others do them or (more importantly) believe they should be done. If speakers think that there is a general belief in a group that behavior Y should be done, then it is not unacceptable to call that a norm for that group. So a listener might hear "drinking a six-pack a night is the norm for people at this college" without thinking that the speaker was speaking falsely, even if she knows that the actual median alcohol consumption for students is only three beers a night—as long as people feel there is a lot of social pressure to drink a six-pack a night. A speaker using these terms this way is using them in what I call the *social pressure* sense. Sociologists and linguists seem to use the term 'norm' in this sense fairly often. When linguist Nessa Wolfson, for example, writes, "This discrepancy between norms and behavior is readily seen in the study of speech acts," (1989, 40) she clearly is speaking of a situation where what people feel like they should do is different from what they actually do. Some philosophers, as well, use the term "norm" to describe behavior that people believe should be done—irrespective of whether the behavior actually is frequently done (see Sripada and Stich 2006).

I have little doubt that one of the things that makes giving explicit definitions (or theories) of each of these concepts so difficult is that these terms are, in fact, ambiguous and polysemous. We call a behavior a "norm" primarily when it is frequent in a population and frequent because of felt social pressure and a desire to imitate. But we can also call something a norm when it is frequent in the absence of social pressure, or when social pressure is present, though a behavior isn't actually frequent. (Surveys indicate speakers seem to differ as to which of these alternative variants is more acceptable.) Such terms, as we will see, are also vague, in that just how many people have to do something or how much pressure there has to be before something is a norm or custom is variable from person to person and situation to situation. We can have difficulties communicating when we make the assumption that these terms are more precisely or more narrowly understood than they actually are. Useful explication of what we mean by terms like "norm," "custom," or "convention," must begin by understanding that these terms have several uses, some quite different from their prototypical ones. Attempts by social scientists (or philosophers) to discuss the nature of norms, etc., are likely to be confusing to people unless we recognize the variable structure of our actual usage of these terms.[4]

EVIDENCE FOR THE MODEL: USAGE AND INTUITIONS

I have suggested that each of the terms in a family that includes "norms," "customs," "conventions," "traditions," etc., expresses a general underlying conceptual category—"what's done" behaviors. I have proposed a model that says that, prototypically, we invoke the "what's done" category for behaviors that are frequent, and caused both by imitation and by beliefs about what others think ought to happen. The "what's done" category and the terms describing it can also be invoked when variants of any of these circumstances are present. Why do I believe the concept underlying these terms is structured this way?

As I described in chapter 1, the method I used for postulating the social-linguistic rules that I do centers around making inferences to the best explanation. I collected a variety of data concerning the use of these terms, and I looked for what best accounted for the data. Assuming a roughly Gricean picture of language, what I needed to find were what beliefs people have (and are trying to get others to have) when they make utterances like "norm," "custom," etc. When I found a model of conceptual structure that best explains all and only the data regarding these terms, I would make an inference to the best explanation, that this conceptual structure was indeed what underlies our use of these terms.[5] Some of the data came from looking carefully at how people seem to use these terms in writing and in conversation. I've looked at lots of books in which people use the terms "norm," "custom," and "convention," looking carefully at the surrounding words and ideas accompanying the phrases. I've paid close attention to when people around me tended to use these terms. I've looked at seemingly similar situations in which they tended not to use these terms. I've looked at listener's reactions to statements. When did people tend to try to correct or argue with another's use of the term "norm" or "custom"?

I've also done for "norm" another thing that I describe in chapter 1 as doing for all the terms for which I'm trying to uncover the social-linguistic rules. I introspectively looked at my own beliefs and intuitions. At those times I felt it was appropriate to use a term like "norm," what did I believe about the world? When I heard someone else use those terms, what did their speaking incline me to believe? If students at Gettysburg College have a food fight in the cafeteria on Labor Day for three years running, does it feel appropriate to call it a custom? How about ten years running? What if they always did it, but had no knowledge of it being done in previous years?

To make sure my own usage of terms like "custom," "convention," or "norm" wasn't idiosyncratic, I tried to gage other people's intuitions about term use as well. I talked to colleagues, friends, and occasionally strangers. As I mentioned earlier, I also administered surveys like the one I described in chapter 1 where I asked students to rank on a 1 to 10 scale their feelings about whether one should describe what is going on by saying a certain behavior is the norm:

Imagine that a group of friends have a dinner party every week. Every week it is held at a different friend's house.

Situation 1

 In the week after each dinner party, each of the friends usually sends the host or hostess a thank-you note for hosting the party. If they don't send it, the host is usually a bit angry with the non-senders. Non-senders tend to feel very guilty about forgetting to send it.

Situation 2

In the week after each dinner party, each of the friends usually *means to* send the host or hostess a thank-you note for hosting the party. But each of them usually gets distracted doing other things, and ends up *forgetting* to do it. The hosts are usually upset with their guests about this. And the non-senders tend to feel very guilty about forgetting to send it.

Situation 3

In the week after each dinner party, each of the friends always send the host or hostess a thank-you note for hosting the party. But none of them feels any obligation to do so. Each sends the note, because he or she feels happy about the party. The hosts are always pleasantly surprised to get all these thank-you notes.

Collecting intuitions like these from others gives you important information that you can't get from merely watching their behaviors. One might never know merely from watching others, for example, if they think a term used by others is used appropriately or inappropriately. Politeness or convenience may dictate that a listener not express disapproval about term usage, even if he feels it. When you are specifically asking for others' intuitions, you remove these factors as an obstacle. You also remove the problem of not knowing exactly what people are referring to when you hear them use these terms. When you ask whether a term can or can't be used to describe this situation, you've directly specified the characteristics of the situation in question in advance.

Looking at my own and others' linguistic behaviors and judgments regarding terms like "norm" in this way, provided me with lots of initial data about how we use this term. I found lots of different sorts of cases in which some or other people found it appropriate to use "norm" or cognate terms. I found cases where hardly anyone felt "norm" was appropriate. I found cases where there was a lot of disagreement about whether norm was appropriate. And I found cases where nearly everyone felt strongly that "norm" was a good way to describe what was going on. I found, for example, that my intuitions are that it is highly appropriate to use the term "norm" to characterize described situations where a behavior is frequent in a group and caused by imitation. If the majority of professors at a university began teaching summer classes in shorts, and most of them (though not the first shorts-wearers) did so because they had seen a number of other professors doing so, then we would clearly count shorts wearing as a norm among professors here. But imitation need not be there to be a norm, however, as we would we would clearly intuitively say that it was a norm to avoid wearing green on Thursdays at a high school (as we actually did in my high school) if students avoided it because they know people would tease them mercilessly if they did. A behavior that is commonly done to avoid the disapproval of others can clearly be called a norm. In his early book on norms, for example the sociologist Ragnar Rommetveit wrote that one of the uses of norms was to describe presence of social pressure or social obligation (1955, 18–26). There are also circumstances, however, where we could still intuitively call a behavior a norm, even if people had no reason to expect that others would scold them for not doing it. If each member of a group of people, for example, felt very strongly that they ought to clean their house before company came because in the past, various people had punished them (perhaps mildly) for not doing that, we'd still call it a norm, even if people have some evidence that scolding or disapproval rarely happened when people visited an uncleaned house nowadays. A behavior that people are inclined to do because of social conditioning, then, also seems to be intuitively considered a norm. In his work, the social theorist Amitai Etzioni stresses this difference between social norms as current external sanctions and social norms as a kind of internal preference formed by conditioning or "cultural imprinting" and other factors (2001, 167).

There seems to be wide agreement that the examples of behavior just discussed count as norms. Being both widespread and caused by one or another type of conformity mechanism, such behaviors seem to be prototypical norms. For other behaviors, it's not completely clear. A number of authors have been willing to call something a norm, simply because it is a widespread behavior in a population, whether or not social pressure or conformity mechanisms are involved. While Rommetveit wrote of the social pressure use of the term "norm," he also wrote that the term could also be used to describe widespread uniform behavior in a group (1955, 18–26). In Jack Gibbs's survey of the use of "norm," he also downplays the importance of the causes of norm behavior, writing, "The origin of a norm is of historical interest only (i.e., it has no necessary relation to any other characteristics of the norm in the present); therefore, the origin of a norm should be treated as a contingent attribute" (1968, 588). And many of our uses of the terms indeed seem to indicate that we are calling something a norm simply because lots of people do it, whether or not there is pressure to do it. We say things like, "If Tom wants to pretend he's French here, he'll have to smoke more—since, if his behavior is too different from the norm, he'll raise suspicions."[6] Similarly, in a number of well-known articles, sociologist H. Wesley Perkins, "the "father of social norms marketing," specifically uses that term "norm" to describe actual frequency in contrast to what people feel it is socially appropriate to do. He and his colleagues describe a recent study of drinking on campus this way:

> First we examined the prevalence of misperceptions of campus drinking norms and the extent to which these misperceptions could be found within individual campus contexts exhibiting differing actual norms. The actual drinking norm for each of the 130 schools represented in the database was estimated by computing the median number of drinks respondents reported consuming the last time they had "partied"/socialized. (2005, 472–73)

At the same time, however, large numbers of my students felt uncomfortable saying that there was a norm of sending thank-you notes when they were sent without there being social pressure to do so.

I, myself, would be uneasy saying that there was a norm to cook pancakes on a large flat skillet, if most of a population did that because they believed cooking that way was the most rationally efficient way to cook pancakes.

It is similarly unclear whether the presence of social pressure (or imitation or conditioning) alone is sufficient to constitute there being a norm, in the absence of widespread instances of the behavior. Sociologist Robert Bierstedt, in his book, *The Social Order*, wrote that a norm was "a standard to which we are expect to conform whether we actually do so or not" (1963, 222). Sociolinguist Wolfson's comment that "speech norms, or community ideals concerning appropriate speech behavior, cannot be equated with speech use which is the behavior itself," (1989, 38) shows she clearly doesn't want to identify norms with frequent behavior alone. We often hear the term "norm" used this way when people talk about norms of beauty that are difficult to live up to. Gibbs also writes that "some laws or norms do not command either popular support or a shared expectation of conformity" (1968, 593). My intuitions, too, are that we can still say that it is a norm to make sure that spoons are placed next to knives at dinner time, even if this is infrequently done. At the same time, however, roughly half my students surveyed did not think there was a norm of sending thank-you notes when there was social pressure to do so, but it wasn't often done (while the other half, as described above, had the opposite inclination). And I must admit that I, too, sometimes feel my intuitions pull in this direction. If there was a great deal of social pressure in a community for parents to spank misbehaving children, but few parents actually did so, I would be somewhat reluctant to say that that community had a norm of punishment by spanking.

A good model of what people mean by "norms" must also account for the variety of ways people use the term in their conversations and their writings. Perhaps the source of the confusion here is that the term "norm" has two clearly distinct meanings. Schultz et al. write that, "A *descriptive* norm refers to people's perceptions of what is commonly done in specific situations. An *injunctive* norm refers to people's perceptions of what is commonly approved or disapproved of within a specific culture" (2007, 429–34). Such a clean division, however, is by no means universally recognized by scholars, and certainly doesn't seem to be there in ordinary English usage. I believe the best way to account for the variety of statements and intuitions about the use of the term "norm" that we see is that most English speakers share a prototypical central norm concept in which a behavior most strongly counts as a norm when it is widespread in a population and got to be that way because of imitation, and past conditioning, and present expectations about social approval.

A variety of things that bear a family resemblance to this prototypical norm concept can also count as norms for people. Different subpopulations differ in the degree to which various different types of things that resemble prototypical norms count as norm-like. For some subpopulations, Schultz's descriptive norms easily count as norms, too, while for others it's only injunctive norms that easily count as norms. My suspicion is that each subpopulation is aware of the way other subpopulations commonly use the term (since such uses are so common), and occasionally use the term this way themselves. But most every subpopulation would agree that the most acceptable uses of the term would be to apply it to prototypical cases where there is widespreadness, and imitation, and social pressure, etc. We need a model that accounts for the array of usages and intuitive judgments about the term "norm" that have been observed. The model that seems to do the best job is one I've proposed.

Over the years, I've used the same techniques I used to examine what people mean by "norm" to look at use of terms such as "custom," "convention," "tradition," and "culture." I've found that while there are some subtle differences between these terms (which I'll describe below), there is a surprising degree of similarity among them regarding usage and intuitions about use. There seems to be a core "what's done" concept (consisting of widespreadness, and imitation, and pressure, etc.) that is present in the most prototypical usages of each of these concepts. Each of the terms in the custom-norm family can be used to describe a "what's done" situation, though there are subtle factors that make one or the other of these terms preferred in particular kinds of situations. The "what's done" category also covers behaviors that are merely frequent, or merely believed to be regarded by others as ought-to-be-done behaviors, although using these terms this way is less common. And speakers don't have firm criteria for how frequent the behaviors must be or how many others must expect it before these terms can be used (though we have some rough criteria that will be discussed below). I think the "what's done" model best explains our usage of these terms. Different models, especially those that assume that these concepts are clearer and less ambiguous than they are, do not adequately account for patterns of actual speaker usage and intuitions.[7]

CAUSES OF SOCIAL CONFORMITY BEHAVIOR

My model suggests that when speakers say that Y is a norm or custom, they are prototypically saying that they think that people in a population do Y in that group because these people believe that lots of others do Y, and they've gotten punishment (or praise) for not doing Y in the past, and they think that others currently think they should do Y. People can also call something a norm if the behavior is caused by any of these different factors which have a family resemblance to each other. I think that, in fact, behavior *is* often caused in these manners, and when people say that a behavior is a norm, etc., they are correctly identifying it as behavior with one or another kind of social cause. Whether we should say the disjunction of factors we label "norm" can itself be the actual cause of a behavior is a question we will explore in the next chapter. What I want to look at now is how each of those different factors that cause the kind of resulting behaviors we label "norm" can come to create these behaviors. How is it that other people's beliefs about what ought to happen can cause a person to behave in a certain way? Why do people behave in a conformist manner? Many scholars in many different fields have views on this subject. To discuss these different views in detail would take another book-length work. Nevertheless, it will be useful to make some remarks on what I think are the most plausible speculations about the roots of conforming behavior.

What makes people inclined toward conformity behavior—inclined to imitate, and to respond to praise and punishment of others? What makes others inclined to praise and punish behavior? Let's assume with Darwin, Skinner, and Decision Theorists that, in general, when agents receive benefits from engaging in a certain type of behavior they tend to continue behaving that way. When a behavior results in obvious harms, it tends to be discontinued (for a variety of reasons, including death of the agent). Explaining why agents respond to punishment and praise (from any source) is straightforward. Punishment, by definition, is harmful to agents, and any mildly rational or even conditionable agent seeks to avoid behaviors they anticipate would likely lead to their being punished by other agents. Punishment can take any form, from killing to avoiding the offending agent. Agents can also reward another agent for his or her behaviors in a similarly large range of ways, from a smile to granting land rights. Some people's behaviors are done to avoid social punishments and to gain social rewards. (And, as we've been saying, we call the behaviors done for this reason "norms," "customs," etc.)

But now the question arises—why will certain behaviors tend to provoke widespread punishment or praise from others in the group? One obvious answer is that if large numbers of group members see that an individual's behavior (e.g., cutting down a valued fruit tree) can be harmful to them, it is in each of their interests to punish the offending agent. It is especially in their interest if doling out the punishment has few costs. (The more people assist in or approve of the punishment, the lower the costs of punishing.)[8]

When you have large numbers of people willing to punish those who do Y because doing Y is harmful to group members, avoiding doing Y becomes widespread and we readily refer to this as a "norm" for the group. Economist Robert Frank (1988) believes that having a tendency to punish harmers is a great asset to a group, since the deterrent effect greatly reduces the amount of harms that group members will suffer from potential harmer's behaviors. He believes that groups where members had an innate tendency to punish would have tremendous advantages over groups that didn't. He suspects that humans have consequently evolved to be genetically predisposed toward vengeful behavior, with a tendency to want to punish harmers, even when the punishing comes with a risk of harm to the punisher. When a large number of people are inclined to punish people for doing Y, a large number of people will be inclined not to do Y, and a norm of not doing Y becomes established. A similar story can be told about rewards. If a small amount of reward (such as praise) greatly increases another's helpful behavior, it's in each group member's interest to reward such behaviors.

It can also be in each group member's interests to punish unusual nonconforming behavior and to praise doing typical expected behavior, even if the unusual behavior isn't causing any obvious direct harm to group members. An agent is best able to make plans when he or she is able to predict what her environment will be like. The most important surrounding environment for any human agent is the behavior of other human beings. One couldn't easily make plans if one were surrounded by people who routinely engage in unusual unexpected behaviors, just as one couldn't if the weather were totally unpredictable. Consequently, agents have an interest in praising others simply for engaging in a certain expected behavior, and punishing them if they do not. When enough people engage in a certain behavior because they hope to avoid the penalties for doing something unexpected, (or because past praise and punishment from many others has made the behavior automatic) the result is the behaviors typically labeled "norms" and "customs."[9]

It is also in people's interests simply to imitate what others are doing, whether or not they are specifically praised or punished for doing so. This is the other main source of social conformity behavior. The social scientific literature is full of complex mathematical models showing why imitating the behaviors of others is generally a rational thing to do (see, for example, Cavalli-Sforza and Feldman 1981). I believe that the usefulness of imitation can be shown by some much more simple considerations as well. To begin with, if an actor can just observe that a particular sort of behavior tends to be correlated with receiving benefits and avoiding harms, it is rational to imitate that same behavior in order to get those benefits for oneself. To take a particularly dramatic example: there is no better guide for how to successfully navigate a mine field than following in the footsteps of others who have made it through unscathed. And not only does observing others for imitation tell us which actions lead to benefits, it does so far more quickly and at less cost than nonobservational trial and error learning (see Bandura 1977), very obviously so in the mine example. When one can see that imitating a certain behavior will lead to a reward, imitating others is clearly the way to go.

Furthermore, even if an agent is in no position to see whether or not a type of behavior immediately brings benefits, imitation is still generally a good strategy. Let's assume that, in general, actors will tend not to repeat behaviors that are similar to those which have brought them harm in similar situations. The class of repeat behaviors, then, will consist mostly of behaviors that are beneficial or neutral (so long as the environment doesn't change too much). This means that if it is repeated behaviors that are being copied, imitators are likely to benefit from the behavior that they imitate. But how can a would-be imitator know whether a candidate for copying is a repeat or a first time behavior? They don't actually need to know. If various factors make the number of neutral/helpful repeat behaviors modeled larger than the number of untested first-time behaviors, copying every behavior automatically means that one is copying more-likely-to-be-beneficial behaviors. One such factor would be the organism's having stronger tendencies toward habit than toward producing novel behaviors. Since producing truly novel behaviors is intrinsically difficult for all agents, we, like all organisms, are invariably creatures of habit. Another factor would be if group members tend to be long-lived. When the number of times an agent faces a certain kind of behavioral choice situation is large, compared to the range of possible behavioral options for this situation, the agent must inevitably repeat what they've done before. (Think of this as analogous to dice throwing; after six throws, all outcomes must be repeats.) The longer-lived that agents tend to be, the greater the likelihood that a given agent is in the mostly repeat stage for that type of behavior. We are a species whose members tend to live long.[10]

A few simple conditions, then, would make imitating a good general strategy. We have every reason to believe those conditions are met in human communities. (For mathematical models showing which other conditions make imitation advantageous, see Boyd and Richerson 1986, 2005.) And if imitating is so advantageous for members of our species, it would be beneficial for natural selection to hardwire a tendency to imitate in us. There is indeed much evidence that such hardwiring for imitation exists. (See, for example, Meltzoff 1996 for a discussion of infants' unlearned tendencies to imitate.) If, for any reason, large numbers of people happen to be doing behavior Y, and people have a tendency to imitate, then large numbers of people will come to do Y because lots of other people are doing Y—and you have what we call "norms," "customs," etc., beginning.

We see then how social conformity behaviors can arise, and where these behaviors fit into the general spectrum of variously caused behaviors. People will often continue to behave in a certain way because of past or anticipated feedback from lots of other people (however the behavior was initiated). When this happens, as we've seen, we tend to call the behavior a "norm" or "custom." We also call a behavior pattern a "norm" or "custom" if it was initiated on the basis of copying others, regardless of whether it continues because of rationality, conditioning, or just force of habit.

One interesting question is why we tend to use the same terms to cover these types of behaviors that can be distinguished from one another. One likely reason is that all of these behaviors have lots in common with the most prototypical norm behaviors which simultaneously have all of these causes. The same name is given to all of them because of this resemblance to the same central prototypical exemplar. Another reason is that they bear a strong family resemblance to each other. "Herding" involves fear of being punished, such that the actions and wants of others make a person do a certain thing. Conditioning happens when someone's mind is remolded by others punishing (or praising) in such a way that the actions and wants of others make a person do a certain thing. With imitation, a person also feels a pressure to act in a certain way, based on the actions and wants of others. When any of these mechanisms with a family resemblance to each other are involved in causing behavior (whatever else is involved in causing), we can talk about a norm causing the behavior.

Furthermore, "what's done" terms are quite informative, even if they are coarse-grained and lump various kinds of behavior together. Knowing a behavior is a norm/custom conformity behavior in any of the senses of conformity still gives an actor important information, even if he or she does not know which type of norm it is. For one thing, if something is a norm because it's socially conditioned, agents know it must be a behavior that is good to engage in while in public, since it's a behavior that's probably been rewarded when publicly performed (and/or punished when not). And, if it's a norm because of imitation, that too, means it's been publicly permitted, for behavior that is socially punished stops being around to be imitated. Behaviors that are norms in either sense, then, are good to engage in in public. For another thing, if we know a behavior is not one from the "what's done" category, we know it is based neither on imitation nor on past or present social feedback. So we know we can't assume any of the things we can assume when a behavior stems from either of these.

There are a number of psychological mechanisms, then, leading to social conformity behaviors. And there are various reasons that it is good for agents to know (and let others know) that a behavior has these types of causes. Our "what's done" terms, then, seem to be an important way of letting people know about the distinguishing causal features of certain behaviors.

NON-PROTOTYPICAL PRESSURE AND
FREQUENCY USES OF NORM-LIKE TERMS

I have argued that the prototypical meaning of saying that a behavior is a norm, custom, convention, etc., is that this behavior is done by a large percentage of group members in a certain situation, and done because a large number of others do it and expect it done. But the model I developed to account for the behavioral and intuitive evidence also suggests that it is acceptable to use these terms to describe situations in which there is widespreadness, or imitation, or social pressure. Let's now discuss, in a bit more detail, less prototypical uses of these terms when there need only be widespreadness or only social pressure.

We sometimes use the term "norm" to mean only the statistically most frequent behavior within a class of behaviors. It can be acceptable to use this term, even if there is no awareness among others of the frequency of this behavior, and no felt social pressure to do it. Demographers and psychologists often use the term "norm" this way. A scholar might speak, for example, of its being the norm among American males to have six sex partners before being married. This need not mean that this is how many partners Americans think they should have, or the number of partners that people would be surprised if someone didn't have. Such scholars simply mean that this is the most common number of partners for people to have, regardless of whether people are aware of this. The pure frequency use of these terms is probably less common than the prototypical "conjunction of conditions" use, because behaviors that become frequent but for which there's little social pressure to continue are fairly rare. The frequency usage is probably more common among academics because they are more prone to study behaviors that lay people might not be prone to pay attention to. Academics also study secretive behaviors that it would be difficult to know about without intensive study. Still, terms like "norm" are sometimes used in this pure frequency sense in ordinary parlance.

And how often must a behavior be done before it is called a "norm" in this frequency sense? It seems to me that people follow a rough rule of thumb specifying that the more frequent the behavior is, the more acceptable it is to call it a "norm" or "custom." It is most permissible to call a behavior "the norm" if it is done by everyone in the group in certain circumstances. It is somewhat less acceptable, if it is done only by a majority.[11] When it is done by less than a majority, the fewer the number of group members who do it, the less acceptable it is to call it a norm. And if there is a behavior X with which behavior Y is mutually exclusive, and behavior X is more frequent in the population than Y (e.g., wearing boxers vs. briefs), it is fairly unacceptable to say Y is a norm, even if done by large numbers of people.

One might, however, say that Y is the norm in a population, even if another behavior is more frequent, if "norm" is being used in the social pressure sense. It is sometimes acceptable to use the words "norm," "custom," etc., when people feel like others think a behavior ought to be done, whether or not it is actually frequent. There are numerous reasons, some discussed above, that others might come to think a behavior ought to be done—e.g., moral or rational reasons. And even a behavior that is merely frequently done can easily come to be thought to be a behavior that should be done. When group members tend to regularly behave in certain ways, observers will generally come to have the simple inductive belief that this is the behavior that will probably happen in these circumstances. This belief can easily come to have normative overtones when people who regularly do Y a) recognize that others know this and plan their own actions around the belief that Y will be done, b) recognize that others will feel thwarted if they are unable to realize their plans, and c) feel that it is not rational or moral to needlessly cause others to feel frustrated. "Others believe I will do Y" can thus turn into a feeling of "I ought to do Y" on Bill's part, and a feeling of "Bill ought to do Y" (in order, at the very least, not to frustrate others) on other people's parts. When group members come to have the belief that others feel a behavior should be done, most actors in the group, hoping to avoid punishment, or to simply avoid resentment for defying expectations, will do the behavior expected of them. With lots of people doing something because of how others will feel if they don't, we get close to what I've called the prototypical sense of "norm" or "custom." Circumstances may arise, however, in which there is an expectation that people do Y, but that few people actually do. New technology, for example, might lead many to abandon an old practice before people realize or approve of its being abandoned. It seems to be somewhat permissible in our language to say that there is a "norm" or "custom" of Y-doing in that group, even if Y isn't done especially frequently.[12] We can still speak, for example, of a custom of handwriting thank-you notes for gifts received, even if a majority of gift-receivers fail to do so. Anthropologists often speak of certain rules of behavior as being part of a particular culture, even though these rules are infrequently followed. There are a couple of likely reasons people still feel free to use these terms. Like prototypical norms, these are situations where groups feel compelled to do certain behaviors. Like prototypical norms, these dispositions do not come from our biological makeup, from nonsocial learning, or from rational self-interest. For one reason or another, however, people sometimes don't act on these dispositions, despite felt social pressure to do so. But situations where people feel social pressure, yet don't act on it, are probably rare enough that we don't feel the need to coin new words to describe them. So the usual terms which describe social pressure situations—"custom," "norm," "tradition," etc.—are pressed into service. It seems permissible to use terms like "norm," "culture," etc., in this social pressure sense when lots of people believe that lots of people believe that Y should be done. How many people? There certainly aren't numerically precise rules. In general, it seems that the more people believe that the more people think Y should be done, the more permissible it is to say that Y is the norm or custom of the group, even if few people are doing Y. For example, in describing a state of affairs in which only a few people in that group believe that large numbers of group members think people should bus their own table at fast food restaurants, it would not be permissible to describe this group as having a custom of bussing their own tables. If the situation were that nearly everyone believes that only a few group members believed this, we couldn't call it a custom then either. But if most people in the group believe that most others thought this should be done, then it is somewhat permissible in our language to speak of that group having a custom of bussing their table at fast food restaurants even if, for one reason or another, few do.

It is this permissibility, I think, that allows people to speak of our society of having a norm of extreme thinness for women. The number of American women who are as thin as fashion models is very small. And research shows that men, at least, do not prefer women to be as thin as typical fashion models (see Buss 1994; Grice 1988). There is neither a majority of women who are that thin, nor does a majority think women should be that thin, but our society is full of books and magazines, even scholarly ones, decrying this "norm" of extreme thinness. One can understand how people can make this claim, if one realizes that there is a social pressure use of these terms. Only a small minority of people expect women to be this thin, but lots of women believe (falsely) that lots of people think that women should be this thin—so a norm does exist in the social pressure sense.[13] If people feel social pressure, they feel social pressure, even if there is not widespread acquiescence to the pressure, and even if there is not really a widespread feeling that the behavior should be engaged in. Our language permits us to use terms like "norm" and "custom" in this non-prototypical sense. Because this sense exists, we need to be cautious about inferring anything about the widespreadness of a behavior when someone speaks of the presence of a norm or custom in the group. And because of the pure "frequency" sense of these terms, and because people need only think that lots of people believe that a behavior ought to be done to call it a norm, we have to be cautious about assuming things about the actual beliefs among group members, when we hear people talk of norms and customs.

DIFFERENCES BETWEEN CONFORMITY TERMS

I have been arguing that terms like "norm," "custom," and the like share some core features. But we should also acknowledge that each of these terms has some especially emphasized or additional features that make it different from others. Let's look briefly at their differences.

The concept of "tradition," like the others, prototypically stresses that lots of people do action Y, and the fact that others do Y is a central reason that people do it. But "tradition" especially emphasizes that the behaviors that people feel compelled to imitate have been in the past. If the idea that Y has been done in the past is considered to make an action more worthy of doing than the mere fact that others do Y, then we tend to speak of Y as a tradition, as opposed to using one of the other terms.

The term "convention" tends to be used when the speaker wants to especially emphasize that the cause of the behavior is that others do or think it should be done, and not due to other factors, especially not the narrow rationality of the behavior. In addition, we are especially apt to use "convention" more than other terms if the behavior initially took the form it did because of arbitrary agreement among group members. If a speaker answers the question "Why does everyone paint their house white here?" by saying, "It's the convention," she is trying to emphasize this is not done primarily for rational reasons. People paint their houses white simply because others do, or think it should be done.

The term "custom" has the special feature of being able to be used to describe the behavior of very small groups—and even, sometimes, of single individuals. We cannot say, "It was Arthur's norm to take a walk every day at 3 o'clock," but we can say, "It was Arthur's custom to take a walk every day at 3 o'clock." As with the other terms, we are saying that the reason Arthur does this is not simply because of rationality, biology, or anything else, but because it is what is frequently done or thought to be what should be done—in this case, by himself. Now, the term "custom," of course, is more often used to describe behavior common in large groups. But we do have, in the term "custom," the ability to describe the behavior of very small groups.[14]

The term "norm" seems to be the generic term we use to describe behavior frequently done because others do or think it should be done. It seems to have few special features of its own. Perhaps the others are more specialized terms that we use when we do want to emphasize more specific things about social pressure. One noteworthy feature that the term "norm" does seem to have is that we seem to be more comfortable using it, rather than the other terms in this family, to discuss features that are merely common in a population. Our ordinary usage of the term "norm" seems to follow certain scientific usage in that it can be used when a trait is merely frequent in a population—no matter what its cause. We can comfortably talk about being shorter than 3'6" as being "the norm" for kindergarteners. But we can't talk about this as being their custom, convention, or tradition. Because "norm" is often used in some sciences in a purely statistical sense, I think that it is commonly used this way in ordinary language, whereas terms like "custom" or "convention" are used in this "pure frequency" way much more rarely.

The term in this family whose usage seems to have the least stringent requirement is "culture." Part of the broadness of the term "culture" comes from the fact that this term is also being used to describe things outside of this family altogether (e.g., the special knowledge produced by and required for understanding certain types of art is also called "culture."). But even when the term is used to describe a type of behavior, our language allows the term to have very broad application. Prototypically, "culture" is used to describe the same core circumstances as the others: frequent behavior in a group, caused by large numbers of others doing it and thinking it should be done. But it is permissible to call various behaviors "cultural" when widespreadness or social pressure is only weakly present. We seem to be comfortable referring to a certain behavior as being done because that it is part of that group's culture, even if group members actually rarely engage in the behavior (e.g., "kilt wearing is a part of Scottish culture"). Now it is somewhat permissible to use any of these terms for behaviors that are not actually frequent. But it seems more permissible to describe infrequent behaviors with "culture" than other terms. More significantly, unlike these other terms, we can use the term "culture" to describe behavior that is not only infrequent, but for which there is only a weak belief that it should be done, or a belief held by small numbers of people. It is permissible in our language to say things like, "Burning cars is a big part of youth culture in France," even if few French youth set fires to cars, or believe other young people really should spend their time doing this.

And as with the term "norm," we are also pretty comfortable using "culture" even when there aren't social conformity mechanisms at work. A practice that is present in a group because it is rationally efficient, or because of the way a biological disposition is manifested in that particular environment can be said to be a part of that group's culture, even without the intervening mechanisms of social conformity. We use the word "culture" to describe situations where a particular behavior is both relatively distinctive to that group, yet is relatively widespread within that group. Most of the time this combination happens because people are copying or responding to pressure from other group members (as opposed to acting on a panhuman disposition). But sometimes, the environment and various other psychological mechanisms can also cause behavior that is both group-distinctive and widespread within it. The family resemblance of behaviors with these surface traits to behaviors caused by social conformity mechanisms, leads us to label all such behaviors "part of a group's culture" despite their not all being caused by social conformity mechanisms.[15]

The term "culture" then, while prototypically describing, "what's done" behaviors, can be used very broadly. It can describe common behaviors and not-so-common behaviors, expected and not-so-expected behaviors, and behaviors caused by conformity mechanisms, along with behaviors not so caused. This broadness of the concept of culture is one of the reasons that scholars with such diverse interests in types and causes of human behavior can all be housed comfortably within the discipline of cultural anthropology. But it also means that when anthropologists describe a behavior as part of a group's culture, much supplemental description is needed to give readers a clear picture of exactly how common and how expected the behavior is, as well as what its causes are.

OTHERS' MODELS OF THESE CONCEPTS

I believe the model I've described of how we think of norms, customs, certain X-do-Y statements, and other things we label with "what's done" terms is a more well-supported theory of what we tend to mean when we are using terms like "norm" than other models. (This is not to say that an even better supported model would not emerge with much more empirical work on using data from a larger sample than I was able to use here.) It would be surprising if a complicated term like "norm," used to describe a number of different sorts of situations by practitioners in a number of different disciplines, were not a radial category with a central prototypical usage, and various other usages with a family resemblance to the prototype getting less acceptable the further they get from the prototypical one. The model of these concepts that I've proposed is one of just such a radial category—with the behavioral commonality, imitation, and past and present social pressure being the features present at the prototypical center. These terms can also be used (somewhat less acceptably) to describe similar situations where only some of these features are present. Yet numerous other models of norm do not describe a family resemblance–based concept. It is very common for other scholars to give a much more restrictive and unitary model of what terms like "norm" mean. Why have there been so many social scientific and philosophical explications of "norms" and "conventions" that are different from this one? What can I say to those who object to my explication and favor their own?

It is often difficult to say anything general about why one thinks one's own model is preferable to all others—each rival model is usually thought to suffer from a particular mistake that your own model avoids (though a different mistake from ones other rival models make). In this case, however, there is something general that can be said about what makes other models different from mine. The reason I think that my model of our use of terms like "norm" is better than others, is that a great many theorists tend not to actually be interested in our use of these terms. As I said above, where my model seeks to account for the actual usage and our intuitions regarding these terms, other theorists often aim to give reforming definitions and theories of norms, customs, and conventions. Philosophers and social scientists often want to provide a clear, consistent, unitary theory of norms, etc. But, if what I've been saying is correct, the concept of "norm" is just not clear or unitary.[16] Let's consider how this can create complications and problems.

It is easy to see why social scientific explications of norms and customs are likely to be aiming at something different than uncovering our common sense conceptualization. To begin with, scientists in most fields see it as their job to use certain concepts to explain things. They can often use concepts to try to give explanations, without ever having to delve into the details of what the concept means. Computer scientists, for example, can talk about rules every day without ever stopping to think what "rule" really means. Now there certainly are times when some social scientists devote some effort to giving explicit definitions or theories about what norms or conventions are (rather than just explaining with the assumption that their audience already understands these notions). When they do so, however, they tend not to be looking at what people ordinarily mean by these terms. They are more prone to look at what their colleagues mean, but even this is not the primary focus. When social scientists explicate a term like "norm" or "culture," they do so in hopes of defining a concept that can be used to help people better understand why people behave as they do. If a term is polysemous, ambiguous, or vague, labeling something with that term provides less than clear information about the thing labeled. Social scientists, then, tend to want to define norms or customs or conventions in ways that make such terms clear and precise.

But much confusion can result from the fact that there are numerous different ways one can reformulate and redefine a vague term more clearly, while still staying close to its original (sloppier) meaning. A theorist can make the term more exclusive and restrictive by reducing the number of sufficient conditions for counting as an instance of it. Norms, for example, could be redefined as only those behaviors acquired by imitation. One could also make a term more exclusive and restrictive by increasing the number of its necessary conditions (e.g., there must be felt social pressure for something to count as a norm). Alternatively, one could simplify (and broaden) the concept by reducing the number of necessary conditions to an easily remembered set (e.g., any behavior that becomes frequent in a group for any reason is a norm of the group). One might also assign the concept more crisply defined boundaries (e.g., say that a behavior doesn't count as a norm unless more than sixty percent of the group engages in it). Social scientists will likely choose the reconceptualization that they find most useful in their particular subspecialization.

Each of these ways of producing a reforming definition clarifies and improves our commonsense concepts in some respects. Yet social scientists operating with an improved conception of norm are likely to have some trouble communicating with other social scientists who have concocted different improved conceptualizations. They'll also have some trouble communicating with nonspecialist readers. A reader who has come to have certain meanings of "norm" engrained in her mind from a lifetime of use is not going to change her views about what is meant by "norm," after spending a few seconds reading a scholar's new definition. She is likely to be confused about what to expect upon reading that a certain behavior is the norm in a group. Would that be "norm" in Professor X's new sense, Professor Y's new sense, or in her previously understood sense?

If social science expositions of these concepts are problematic in these respects, one might think that philosophical expositions of norms, customs, conventions, etc., are less so. After all, philosophy in general and "ordinary language philosophy" in particular have a long history of trying to carefully explicate our commonsense concepts. And there has been no dearth of philosophers discussing these concepts. But many philosophical discussions, I find, suffer from similar problems to those of social scientists. Philosophers, while a bit more constrained to give explications that adhere to the contours of our commonsense concepts, nevertheless are primarily interested in giving good theories of what norms, customs, conventions, etc., are. Good philosophical theories, at a minimum, try to be coherent and systematic. Philosophical theories of things also try to provide explanations that are consistent with our best overall metaphysical pictures. Philosophers who discuss norms, etc., are usually aiming at developing a more useful systematic theory, using such terms in a reformed sense, rather than explicating our sloppy everyday senses. Cristina Bicchieri's comprehensive work on norms is typical in this respect. Says Bicchieri: "The definition of social norm I am proposing should be taken as a rational reconstruction of what a social norm is, not a faithful descriptive account of the real beliefs and preferences people have or of the way in which they in fact deliberate" (2006, 3).

But as we just described, these terms can be precisified in many different ways. When philosophers reformulate these concepts, they, like social scientists, tend to "customize" them according to the needs of the particular subproblems they are working on. Quite often when philosophers discuss norms and conventions (or the kindred notion, rules), they are interested in explicating what it means to be a norm or rule of language. This is unsurprising. Understanding how language works is a central part of philosophy (*the* central part, according to many twentieth-century philosophers; see Rorty 1991). Yet it's quite possible that norms of language have different properties than other kinds of social norms. Many philosophical theories about the entities of this realm, then, are not necessarily theories of norms, rules, and conventions that describe a range of social behavior. These philosophical explications, then, will be different from mine, and cannot be expected to tell us how people use the terms.

Overlapping with this emphasis on language is a special focus on the nature of convention. Much philosophical discussion on convention tends to focus on conventions as a way to solve social coordination problems. This, no doubt, is due to the extensive influence of David Lewis's masterful 1967 book, *Convention* (which was written, largely, to make sense of the notion of convention in language). Numerous philosophers have responded to Lewis's views with criticisms and theories of their own (see, for example, Cabaco 2002; Jackman 1999; Gilbert 1996). Most of these theories try to provide an improved picture of the metaphysics of convention. In doing so, however, they carve out a concept more refined and precise than our ordinary one. Lewis, trying to give a naturalistic theory, tries to define convention without using any normative terms. This, it seems to me, ignores a feature of our ordinary notion of convention—we call a behavior a convention if we think that others feel this is the behavior we ought to do. Margaret Gilbert, meanwhile, who has a theory that tries to spell out the metaphysics of obligation, takes Lewis to task for ignoring the normative aspect of conventions. Gilbert herself, however, overlooks the fact that we can say things like "the convention here in Green Island is to put cinnamon, not sugar, in tea," even when no one necessarily feels like they ought to do this. In a similar respect, Stich and his coworkers, in their work on folk morality, give an elaborate theory of norms that ignores the "frequency" sense in which we use the term. "Norms," write Sripada and Stich "are rules which specify behaviors that are required or forbidden independently of any legal or social institution or authority though of course some norms are also enforced by laws or other social institutions" (2006). Now Stich and Sripada explicitly state that they are using the term "norm" to describe a metaphysically interesting "natural kind," rather than giving an analysis of our common conceptualization. I think this is usually the case with philosophical explications of norms, and this is why few philosophical analyses are likely to agree with mine, which is based on modeling our ordinary language and intuitions. This is not to say that philosophical and social scientific precisification is not an important task. It is only that understanding our existing concepts, as I explained earlier, is also important. It may be useful to clarify the meanings of old terms this way, even when one is not reforming old terms, but introducing new terms, like "joint action." This is because it's not unlikely that people will be initially conceptualizing the behavior being discussed by the new terms, through using their old concepts. A good way of making the meaning of the new terms clear is by specifying how they do and don't relate to prior concepts of what is happening in certain situations.

Terms like "norm," "custom," "convention," "tradition," and "culture" are used throughout the social sciences and throughout everyday conversation to describe certain types of behaviors. We also make use of these concepts when these words are not specifically used. I believe that one of the things we sometimes mean when we use X-do-Y phrases is that the X group has a norm of doing Y. But despite the ubiquity of "what's done" phrases and terms, it is not very clear what people mean by them. In this chapter, I have tried to explain what we ordinarily mean by such terms. I have argued that the primary, most accepted sense of these terms is to describe behavior that is frequent in a group, and frequent because of imitation and because of the belief that others think this behavior should be done. I have discussed how there are, indeed, behaviors that are caused in these conformity-oriented ways, and that these terms are useful for letting people know that the behaviors in question have these particular features. Still, these terms can be confusing. The confusion is partly due to the fact that behavior that is merely frequent, and behavior for which there is social pressure but which may or may not be frequent, can also be described by these terms. Confusion also stems from the fact that ordinary language does not put strict conditions on how frequent a behavior must be, or how much pressure for a behavior must exist before it qualifies as a norm or custom. A final source of confusion is that in order to try to reduce confusion, various scholars have tried to give explications of these terms that assign meanings to them that are clearer and more precise than the ones the terms actually have in everyday discourse. I think we can do a much better job clarifying these terms, if we are clearer about our ordinary thinking about what they entail. I hope this chapter has helped make clearer what we mean when we use terms like "norm" or "custom." Getting clear about our ideas about customs, etc., helps us better understand sentences like "We go to the diner on Fridays"—the third major way of using X-do-Y statements.

NOTES

1. Why should we think that the concept of a norm or custom is being invoked when people are not using the word "norm"? This is essentially asking "How do we know what 'the X people do Y' means?" or "How do we know that 'the X people do Y' means 'the X people have a norm of doing Y'?" We figure this out the same way we figure out what any unknown words or phrases mean: We use an inference to the best explanation to posit that P or Q was what the speaker seemed to be trying to get us to believe. We look at the context in which a person said that the X do Y, and we try to figure out what she believed and was trying to get us to believe. What situation was prevailing at the time of utterance? What other inferences did the speaker seem to be making? When we look at our own intuitions about when it would be appropriate to use such terms to try to communicate, we look at numerous other uses of the phrase to see if other speakers seem to be using it in the same or different ways. We then make some guesses about what it seems that the speakers uttering such phrases were trying to say. Then we look at numerous other uses of the phrase to see if other speakers seem to be using it in the ways we hypothesized or in different ways. Ultimately we arrive at the model that best seems to explain the usage of the phrase.

In the groups that anthropologists study, it is not at all uncommon for group members to say things like "We X marry our mother's brother's daughters," only for the anthropologist to find that this is not a practice that is followed at all. Clearly the speakers using such phrases are not talking about a particular endeavor that the group as a collective whole is all working toward. But neither are they reporting on the behaviors of individuals—since this is not how individuals behave. They seem, instead, to be describing the kinds of situations we typically describe with terms like "norm" or "custom." Similarly when we say things like "Americans eat three meals a day, but Nepalis eat only two" it seems to be clearly describing a norm situation. As before, we aren't describing a collective endeavor. And given that the practice is often not done, the phrase is not clearly interpreted as one of the 'all or most of the individuals do' (or the exceptions) described in chapter 2. Sometimes, then, the best interpretation of the X-do-Y utterance, is that the speakers are talking about members of the X group feeling pressure to do what their peers do or want done—the same kind of thing they describe with terms like "norm."

2. The relationship between norms and rationality is indeed a vexed and confusing one. As mentioned above, some scholars stress the rationality of norms, while other scholars seem to use "convention," "norm," and other "what's done" terms specifically to highlight the lack of rationality in the behavior in question (see Hechter 1994). So do norm accounts really contrast with rationality ones? There are a number of things that make it difficult for norm accounts to be even the sort of thing that can contrast with rationality accounts. First, while "norm" and the like are often used to inform us about the cause of a behavior, "rational" is most often used as an honorific evaluative term describing the success of a behavior in satisfying goals. Contrasting norm-based behavior with rational behavior, then, looks like apples and oranges. Even if what was being compared was evaluatively rational behavior and evaluatively non-rational behavior, it's hard to know what is meant when someone claims a behavior is rational.

To a rough approximation, a behavior is rational if, were the world to be as the agent believed it was, the behavior would help meet the agent's goals. But are we talking about long term goals or short term goals? Global goals or local goals? And even if we are clearly talking about global goals, is the rational behavior the one that tends, in general, to satisfy these goals, or is it the behavior that would satisfy these goals in these particular circumstances? It's not easy to identify which type behavior is the kind of rational behavior that a norm-based behavior is supposed to contrast with.

Perhaps what those who aim to contrast norm-based behaviors with rational behaviors have in mind is contrasting norm-caused behaviors with ones caused by sets of mechanisms which tend to produce behavior which is evaluatively rational. But even when people are clearly talking about mechanisms (and not evaluations), there are lots of different sets of mechanisms that regularly are termed "rational." Sometimes economists speak of behaviors caused by rationality as if rationality were a large impersonal force akin to natural selection. Physical anthropologists, on the other hand, might speak of human rationality to talk about the mechanisms our brains use for making deductively valid inferences. And even if it were clear which sorts of causal mechanism were being described as the rational ones, every behavior is caused by a long complex causal chain involving scores of different mechanisms. Most norm-caused actions consist of scores of smaller sub-actions, many of which make use of mechanism that work rationally. (In the process of painting one's house green, because that's what's conventionally done in this neighborhood, one may well rationally infer that Glidden brand is the most efficient paint for the money.) And many rational actions consist of a set of subtasks, many of which might be the way they are because of norms or conventions. (One might purchase a can of Glidden paint because that would rationally satisfy one's goals, and one might pay for it in cash because that's the convention in one's family.) With rational action being subparts of norm-based action and vice versa, how can norm-behavior contrast with rational behavior?

Yet, while there are many things that can keep norm-based behavior from clearly contrasting with rational behavior, there are some circumstances in which it is possible for them to contrast and compete. In order to avoid an apples and oranges problem, one must start by making sure one is comparing different types of causal mechanisms (not causal mechanisms and evaluations of performances). Then, in order to clearly contrast a rational causal mechanism with a norm-based mechanism, we need to be clear about which kind of rational mechanism we are talking about that contrasts with the norm based ones (e.g., rationality as a general natural selection-like force.) We need to make sure we are talking about a mechanism set that is competing with norms as opposed to one that is a part of norm-based activity. (See Jones 2011 for a discussion of which kinds of explanations compete with other ones.) We then have to specify how these mechanisms producing the behavior are evalutively rational in one or another senses of the term (e.g., locally and in general), while norm-based behavior is not rational in this same sense.

In the following chapter, we will discuss a way a certain type of high-level rationality could, indeed, compete with a norm explanation. One might claim that the real reason a certain behavior was done the way it was done was because this was a rational response to environmental pressures. The fact that the behavior also happened to be a custom, the argument could go, is superfluous because the rationality of the behavior would ensure that it is done, whether doing it was the custom or not. Claiming that a behavior is a norm or custom or convention might sometimes be a way of calling attention to the fact that the speaker does not think that these kinds of high-level rational forces were what made the behavior happen—the norm was. But, as we've just seen, a norm-based behavior being nonrational in this sense doesn't mean that it was nonrational in the sense of it not serving one's short term goals to avoid social punishment.

3. Readers of Saul Kripke's *Wittgenstein on Rules and Private Language* may wonder how people could possibly infer that something was a norm from observations of others' behaviors, for Kripke's work suggests that there are many puzzles concerning how inferring rules from observing behavior is possible. In this book, Kripke wonders how it is that an individual person adding 6 plus 7 and getting 13 can be said to be following the addition rule, rather than following the rules of an infinite number of other mathematical functions that are all consistent with a person's behavior here. (For example, following a rule that says "+" means add two numbers together unless their sum is over 57 (call this "quus") would also yield the "13" answer.)

In my view, Kripke's work points to at least three puzzles. There is a metaphysical puzzle regarding how an individual could really have a mental rule at all. There is an epistemic puzzle concerning how an individual could justify their self-attribution of following the "plus" rule rather than the behaviorally equivalent "quus" rule. And there is a psychological puzzle regarding how individuals could come to see behaviors as instantiating certain rules.

Worrisome as these problems may be, I don't think any of them pose insurmountable difficulties for the project I am engaged in here. Kripke's metaphysical puzzle posed no problems for my project. Kripke is interested in the underlying metaphysics of meanings and rules regarding internal mental symbols. I am looking at other people's beliefs about certain behaviors. I am not, here, looking at the correct metaphysics of any entity. And it is beliefs about the norms and customs causing behavior that I am focusing on (even if "rules" may be related). I am also not looking at how people justify their claims about internal rules, epistemically.

But the puzzles Kripke discusses do raise interesting psychological questions. How do potential actors know which are the norms of how to behave, given all that they've seen are others' behaviors (or others' dispositions to punish) that are compatible with a number of different norms? Well, to begin with, an observer herself doesn't need to think of what she is doing as following a norm or rule in order to imitate a behavior and be part of a set of behaviors that others see as the norm. But there is still the question of how an actor knows how to classify the behavior they've seen in order to imitate it, given that any behavior can be classified as an instance of numerous different behavioral patterns. This is a general under-determination problem; one discussed by Quine, Duhem, Goodman, and many others besides Kripke. As with any under-determination problem, observers need to try to figure out which of many possible accounts of something is the best, all things considered. When many different candidates are rationally equivalent, various psychological factors may limit which ones are actually salient for observers (this is what Chomsky's (1986) work on people's grammatical hypotheses focuses on). In seeing certain people solve mathematical problems, for example, most observers will decide their subjects are adding, even though it is logically possible they are "quadding." If the observers imitate their subjects' behaviors, they, too, will add.

Much the same answer can be given to the question of how observers see behavior as an instance of a certain general behavioral pattern, a norm that everyone is following. Observers categorize certain behavior (or the pressure for behavior) as an instance of behavior type X, rather than Y (which it is indistinguishable from on the surface) because this is the best or most salient account of what is happening, all things considered. They combine this classification with a general (and I think accurate) idea that people are inclined to imitate the behaviors of others, or to keep doing the behaviors that they are rewarded for. If the behavior is seen as behavior X (rather than Y) and it is assumed that X is caused by imitation and social pressure, then behavior X will be seen by observers as a prototypical norm or custom. And it can be seen as a non-prototypical "frequency" norm, just by being classified as the commonly done X behavior. The question of what is the best social scientific explanation for conformist behavior is another one entirely—one explored later in the chapter.

4. One might think of me as describing the norms for when we can use the term "norm." I'm not doing exactly that here (see below), but if I was, this need not be viciously circular. It would not be viciously circular to define what a norm is, and then describe norms for various word usage behaviors—including the use of the word "norm." To fully understand what I am saying about norms, then, one could first understand my proposed definition, and then see how one can use this definition to understand the commonality and acceptability of the term.

Since the term "norm" is so polysemous and vague, however, I want to try to be a bit clearer about what I am saying about this model. My view is that the term "norm," as well as each of these other terms, is both most commonly and most acceptably used to describe a behavior that is both frequent and caused by imitation and others' pressure. (When I say "prototypical use," I am talking about the use of the term that a plurality of speakers intuitively feel is most acceptable. This, unsurprisingly, is also the way in which people will actually use the term the most). It is both less acceptable and less common to use these terms to describe pure frequency or pure social pressure situations. Still, the terms are sometimes used this way (and speakers seem to differ on which of these two uses is the more acceptable one). It's possible that "what's done" is a concept with what linguist George Lakoff calls a "radial" structure, with a prototypical core meaning, surrounded by less typical "extended" meanings (1987). It seems plausible that "what's done" is a radial concept with the complex core meaning: "common behavior caused by seeing what others do and expect us to do." We have come to extend the usage of terms that are prototypically used to describe this core to also describe common behavior and conformity behavior alone.

It is also possible, however, that there is no general "what's done" concept. Perhaps what we have are just separate "norm," "custom," "convention," etc., concepts. If so, my model is not much affected. If what we have are separate concepts, these would still be concepts where each of these notions had its own unique features, but each also had a large set of features that it shared with others that are similar. In this case, the "what's done" notion is not a separate concept but rather a description of a large subset of features that the concepts of norms, customs, etc. all share, in addition to having unique features.

My model, then, says that the prototypical meaning for terms like "norm" is a situation that is widespread *and* imitated *and* one feels pressure to do. A group of English speakers will also tolerate people calling a behavior that is widespread, *or* imitated, *or* for which there is social pressure a norm. What is less clear is whether the same individuals tend to use "norm" to describe each of these disjuncts, or whether it is different members of the group who each finds one of the uses acceptable—leaving the group as a whole to have a disjunctive set of uses for the term. My preliminary research suggests the latter.

5. For those theorists who are skeptical about underlying concepts (e.g., for Quinean or Wittgensteinian reasons), I think it's possible to give a theory of the usages of these terms that stresses similar rules of word use to the ones that I discuss here, but without using mentalistic concepts. In such descriptions, "rules of use" would be cashed out in terms of dispositions to make certain sounds in certain situations, and to praise and punish others for making or not making such sounds in the right situations.

6. The use of intuitions and thought experiments is especially important for figuring out which properties are the essential ones for being a norm. One of the things that makes it hard to know what counts as a norm is that the behaviors that are most strongly considered to be norm have numerous different features associated with norms. They are widespread in a group, *and* they got that way because of imitation, past condition, *and* present intimidation, etc. But could a behavior lack some of these traits and still be considered a norm? Actual situations where we have some of these traits without lots of the others are rare. Consequently it is important to imagine circumstances in which one set of traits is present and the others are not, and see if we would intuitively consider such a situation one that feels appropriate to say that a norm is present. My intuitions, for example, are that we would still consider it to be a norm to clean up one's house for company, even if it was neither widely done, nor punished when it was not done, if a number of people in the past, were punished by people for not doing it. This is an indication that social conditioning alone can be sufficient for enabling something to count as a norm.

7. The contention here, then, is that speakers of English prototypically understand words like "custom" and "norm" this way. This means that when we are translating alien words into our language, we should not use our word "custom" as a translation for alien terms that do not have the connotation of being caused by imitating or pressure from others for alien speakers. (Just as we should not properly translate one of their terms as "ball" if their term is used to denote objects that are round but are not played with.) Similarly, we may see certain behavioral practices in alien societies as being what we would call, "customs" without their being conceptualized in that way at all in the alien society. This doesn't mean it is any less appropriate for us to call such behaviors "customs," than it is to call their clothes maroon, even if they don't have a word for that color in their vocabulary. When we use the word "custom" to our fellow English speakers, we are describing behavior we think was caused in a

certain way (irrespective of how the aliens see the behavior). The issue of how aliens themselves conceptualize their behavior (an issue Peter Winch 1990 focused on) is an interesting one. But I am not focusing on this question, here.

8. A continual puzzle for decision theorists is why agents will punish at all, rather than "free ride" and hope that others will bear the costs of punishing. There are various proposals in the literature. The most common is some kind of group selection in which groups whose members had hardwired proclivities to punish were much more successful than groups that did not, with the result that many of us now have hardwired genetic proclivities to punish, even at great costs to ourselves (see Boyd and Richerson 2005; Frank 1988). Another suggestion is that those who fail to punish, are themselves punished, as are those who fail to punish punishers, in a continuous iteration (see Binmore 1998, and see Cinyaguguma, Page, and Putterman 2004 for a mixture of both methods). I suspect that a common type of situation is one where the benefits of punishing are high but one cannot expect others to punish—so people readily take on the burden of punishment. One can't expect others to do the punishing when they didn't see the transgression, when they aren't affected as much, or their esteem isn't as important to the harmers. In these cases, free riding is not possible. Punishing ones offspring provides good examples of these sorts of cases.

9. This gives us some clues about which "grain size" of behavior are considered candidates for being customs or norms. If a group of kids at a summer camp all began running in the morning, would the custom be "morning running," "morning exercise," or "morning running with a long stride"? If the group is indifferent to anyones particular running form, then running with a certain form is not part of the custom. If, on the other hand, someone who went swimming in the morning instead of running was scorned by the group, then we would say the custom was a custom of morning running, nor merely morning exercise. Similar things can be said about customs and norms, and the "grain size" of the activity people feel disposed to imitate.

10. Thorny questions of how similar behaviors have to be before they count as repeat behaviors, how similar to choice situations they have to be before they count as the same, and how we can distinguish and count possible behavioral variants need not be answered in order to roughly determine the rough relative sizes of these behavioral class ranges vis-à-vis each other.

11. This means that a large percentage of the behaviors described in chapter 2, where "the X do Y" means that many individuals in the X group do Y, can be described as "norms" in this frequency sense.

12. Some scholars miss this social pressure sense in their discussions of norms (e.g., Pettit 2002). But such terms are used in this "believed people should" way quite often in the social sciences, as well as in ordinary language (see Flores 1990; Nagel 2000).

13. Psychologist Floyd Allport, in 1924, described a related type of situation in which people try to conform to a behavior that is thought to be common but isn't, and termed it "pluralistic ignorance" (1924a). Pluralistic ignorance is widely discussed in the social science literature (see, for example, Lambert et. al. 2003).

14. But it does seem that we can also use the term "norm" in a pure frequency sense for single individuals. We can say things like "Getting up at 11 is the norm for

Bill." We can also speak of a single individual doing something because there is a collective social norm. But it would be highly unusual to talk about a single person having a norm based on his own social pressure.

15. Interestingly, while the "culture" seems the most appropriate of any of the "what's done" terms for behaviors that are widespread within a group, but rare outside it, each of the what's done terms seem more strongly appropriate and prototypical for this situation than for others. It feels more intuitively appropriate to say, "There's a custom of putting powered sugar on pancakes in Longston," for example, than it does to say, "There's a custom of syrup on pancakes in Longston [and everywhere else]." Perhaps this is because of situations in which a behavior is widespread in a particular locale and not elsewhere and is likely to have gotten there through the mechanisms that make something prototypically a "what's done" behavior—imitation, conditioning, and "herding." Behavior that is more universally widespread is as likely to have gotten there by other means, such as nonsocial conditioning, or rationally inferring that this is a useful way to behave.

16. There are, of course, many scholars who recognize our usage of the term is multifaceted and confusing. Gibb's (1965) classic discussion of the term was all about how varied the use of this term was. And Hechter and Opp, in a comprehensive volume aiming to summarize recent thinking about norms, write, "To begin with the concept of social norm clearly means different things to different scholars" (2005, xii.) But a common reaction of scholars is to try to give a reforming definition that creates a clearer concept, rather than trying to model the actual complexity of our usage as I do here. When scholars try to emphasize a unitary concept, I suspect that the concepts they emphasize tend to be skewed toward ones close to our most prototypical ordinary "what's done" concepts.

Chapter Five

Can X-Do-Y Statements Explain?

What has emerged in our study of X-do-Y statements so far is that, while such statements contain a degree of vagueness and ambiguity, they are not the false, uninformative, or unconstrained statements they might seem to be. We may have to squint a little to get good information out of X-do-Y statements. But such descriptions do contain some good information about what is happening with the groups of people described. In this chapter, we will consider another function of X-do-Y statements besides describing what groups do—explaining what they do. Can such statements really tell us why we have certain social circumstances, as well as what they are?

To examine the issue of how well these explain, we need to remember that an X-do-Y statement can be interpreted as trying to say one (or more) of three different things:

1. That there are a number of individuals in group X that do (or believe, etc.) Y.
2. That the group as a whole has a net effect of making Y happen.
3. That the X group has a norm or custom of doing Y.

Now there is no reason to think that the explanatory powers of each of these kinds of statements would automatically tend to be the same as the other. Statements about groups as a whole might tend to produce rather poor explanations, while custom accounts might tend to be good explanations. In this chapter then, we'll look separately at the explanatory potential of each of these different kinds of X-do-Y statements.

EXPLANATION WITH NORM/CUSTOM ACCOUNTS

I will begin by taking a long look at norm/custom explanations (as distinct from the norm/custom descriptions we looked at in the previous chapter). These seem to be the type of X-do-Y statements that scholars, at least, are most inclined to use in an explanatory way. While journalists and people in everyday conversation might speak about "what France is really interested in" one sees this less often in scholarly publications. Norms, on the other hand, are ubiquitous in scholarly publications. Indeed, as we saw in the previous chapter, the *International Encyclopedia of the Social Sciences* begins its article on the study of norms by saying, "No concept is invoked more often by social scientists in the explanations of human behavior than 'norm'" (Gibbs 1968). And as we have seen, there are numerous other concepts such as custom, convention, tradition, and culture that are similar to norm. Now social scientists and others, in their use of terms like "norm," often seem to use the terms in an explanatory way. It is not uncommon to see social scientists explain things by saying things like "social norms (such as the norm of internality) lead them to seek other values and thus to reason and infer differently" (Le Fosh and Somat 2003, 150). Scholars like Triandis (1977), Kerr (1995), and Ajzen and Fishbein (2000) all find the concept to be centrally important in explaining human behavior. But can norms and related concepts really explain social behavior? Let us turn now to this question.

One reason to be concerned about whether norms/customs can really provide explanations of behavior is that quite often, for the kinds of situations norms are invoked to explain, one can see other plausible explanations of the behaviors as well. Picture the following (not unusual) scenario: A group of friends is sitting around a table in the lounge of their college dormitory, talking. A young stranger walks into the lounge.

"Hi," says the stranger, "I'm looking for Bill Tavy. I'm an old friend of his from high school. I was in the area and heard that Bill lives here in Dunham Dorm, but he wasn't in his room. Do any of you know him, or where he might be?"

"Oh yeah, we know Bill," says one, "but you'll never find him around here. He spends every night these days studying in the basement of the College Union." The stranger looks surprised.

"Say what? Why would Bill be studying in the Union basement on a Friday night?" Each of the friends now answers at once, while the stranger waves his hands, motioning for them to slow down so he can catch their various answers.

"Everyone's being sick a lot these days makes doctors the top of the social heap. Bill lives for prestige, so he's making sure he becomes one," Tom is saying. At the same time Dave is remarking, "Well, if you were in high school with Bill, you know how his dad was always grounding him whenever he got even a B." Tina, meanwhile, explains, "Well, med school applicants are way up this year, so all the med school geeks are studying harder to compete." Margaret also chimes in saying, "Everyone bothers you when you try to study in the library." Over the din of everyone else's talking, the stranger thinks he hears Roger saying "It's a custom here for students who really want to cram to study in the basement of the Union."

Note that there are a number of explanations of Bill's behavior given here. Now if all of these explanations are complimentary, the fact that other explanations besides norm/custom ones are often given doesn't pose any problem for norm/custom accounts. But if norm/custom explanations compete with these other types of accounts in the sense that both explanations can't be true at the same time, and if there are good reasons to think that these other accounts are more plausible, then norm/custom explanations are in trouble.[1] I will argue that there are, in fact, good reasons to think that other sorts of accounts are usually more correct explanations than norm accounts, and that norm accounts are not really explaining the phenomena they purport to explain. But we should note first that there are lots of circumstances in which norm/custom explanations don't actually compete with other explanations. Let's get clear about these noncompeting circumstances first before discussing cases in which norm accounts cannot be true if other accounts are.

Competing and Noncompeting Explanations—
A General Overview

If by "competing" accounts, one means accounts whose truth is mutually exclusive, there will be numerous kinds of pairs of accounts that don't really compete, but may look like they do. As I see it, there are two main families of accounts that appear to compete but don't really. The first family consists of explanations that appear to give different accounts of the same facts, but really give different accounts of different facts. This is often caused by different (explanandum) facts sharing the same (ambiguous) descriptive label. The second family consists of explanations that appear to give different (explanans) accounts of the same states of affairs, but which really describe different portions of the same (presumed) explanatory elements, or give different descriptions of the same portions. When people give apparently contrasting accounts belonging to either of these two groups, it is perfectly possible for both accounts to be true. Below, I will discuss various important subtypes of each of these groups, in general and in the particular case of norms. This should give us a better understanding of why we often get numerous different accounts of various social circumstances, even when speakers don't necessarily disagree with one another about why what happens, happens.

In looking at when explanations do and don't compete, in the strong sense, one immediate difficulty is that there are numerous different theories of what an explanation is. For the purpose of discussing which explanations compete, it will help to simplify things and focus, for the moment, on one particular theory of explanation. In what follows, I will be assuming that explaining is largely a matter of finding causes. I will also try to remain largely neutral on many hotly debated philosophical disputes concerning what causes are. I believe that much can be said about the issues of whether it was W or X (or both, or either) that really caused Y, even if we don't resolve various issues about what a cause is. Still, of course, we need to make some assumptions about what we are dealing with when we talk about causes. Since I will be discussing whether causes can explain, I will be looking at causes in the sense of causal explanation, where the focus will be on causal facts. (Note, though, that along with Hall (2008), and Bennett (1988), I'm assuming that some facts are facts about events.) I'll assume that a causal fact must be a necessary part of a sufficient condition of whether the effect obtains (see Mackie 1974, Bennett 1988)). Whatever we think causes, explanations, or competition is, an account of human origins that says that humans are distant descendents of chimpanzees strongly competes with an explanation that says that humans and chimps shared common ancestry up to Nakalitpithecus in the Pliocene and then diverged. A social explanation that says that Bill put the baking soda in the refrigerator because it is the custom competes with one that says he never heard of anyone else doing it, but figured out on his own that it would reduce odors. The custom explanation implies an awareness of others doing this as part of set of facts leading to Bill's doing this with the baking soda, whereas the ingenuity explanation implies such awareness was absent.[2]

Just as I believe that the issues addressed here do not require that I focus much on different ideas about causation, I also believe that there is no need, here, to distinguish between behaviors that are *actions* done for reasons and behaviors that are not. There are philosophical issues for which it is important to make this distinction, just as there are contexts in which we need to distinguish between a murder, an assassination, and a mercy killing. A forensic scientist investigating the cause of death, however, can leave the classification of different types of killing up to the lawyers. Likewise, most social scientists and ordinary language speakers interested in whether W or X is the cause of a behavior can leave further questions about whether a behavior caused this way should be considered to be an *action* to scholars whose goals require them to make this distinction. As far as I can see, none of the issues discussed in this paper depends on such distinctions being made, so I shall not be making them here.

In my view, then, an account that says C is part of the cause of E clearly competes with an account that says it is not. In the following sections I will look in more detail at some of the main ways that two explanations may look like they are competing when they aren't.

Different Accounts of Different (but Same-Seeming) Social Facts

One of the main reasons why there are different explanations of the kinds of things customs explain is that the different explanations are explaining different facts. As different facts, they naturally have different explanations. But the idea that two different things are being explained can be obscured when the facts being explained share the same ambiguous description. It appears as if there are two different explanations of the same fact, rather than two different explanations of quite different facts (which happen to have a similar description).

There are a number of different reasons that different facts can be given the same description. Sometimes there are just idiosyncratic ambiguities in the language. Terms are sometimes mere homographs of one another. Why do most of the citizens of Glens Falls have glasses? Paul says it's because they are concerned about the environment and don't want to use disposable cups. James says it's because it's the custom to wear frames instead of contact lenses. Here, "glasses" refers to two different things, and the explanations of the two different phenomena don't compete at all. In the social realm, confusion can be caused by something called *group ambiguity*—when the language uses the same word or phrase for 1) properties belonging to each of the individuals in a group, but also for 2) properties of the whole collection. Sally can say that the increase in the amount of money paid to public defenders came because the legislature has a custom of trying to pay public and private workers similarly. Susan can say that the increase in the amount of money paid to public defenders came because the state had to add ten new defenders to keep up with the increase in crime. The custom explanation doesn't really compete with the increased population one because they explain different facts. Sally is explaining why individual public defenders got a pay raise, while Susan is explaining why the total expenditure on public defense increased (which could have happened even if individual defenders hadn't been paid more). The potential confusion here is caused by English not distinguishing between individual and group properties in the phrase "the increase in the amount of money paid to public defenders." But the two accounts are explaining different situations.

Same-Seeming "Horizontal" Facts

A major sub-family, in this general family of accounts that merely seem to compete due to different explananda sharing the same description, includes those accounts where different subtypes or subparts are described by the same superordinate description. This could be called the problem of same-seeming horizontal (or parallel) facts. In the natural sciences, for example, members of the category jade can be members of the mineral classes jadite or nephrite. Mark might say that jade is formed through the high-pressure metamorphosis of sodium and aluminum-rich albite. Bill might say that jade is formed through a recrystalization of magnesium-rich limestone through temperature or pressure. Both processes do produce jade, but one produces nephrite-jade, while the other produces jadite-jade. In social circumstances, one might get similar apparently competing explanations when two different subgroups can be called by the same superordinate name. Why did the high school students of Snyder County reduce their smoking? Mark says they feared what it would do to their looks. Bill says it's because they feared what it would do their lungs. Such explanations need not compete if the north Snyder County high school students that Mark is talking about attended a speech by a wrinkled old actress talking about what smoking did to her skin, while the students of south Snyder County that Bill is speaking about went to a different assembly where they saw a disturbing presentation by a man with emphysema.

There are different types of horizontal subordinate problems because of different bases on which things can be grouped together into a unified class. In other works (Jones 2008), I have discussed there being two types of unification. One I called subtype and similarity (SS) unification; the other I called conjunction and coordination (CC) unification. SS unification involves putting things into the same superordinate class because class members seem to share some or other dimension of similarity—cars, boats, and trains, are all "vehicles." CC unification puts various items into a single class because they connect with one another in some way—engines, spark plugs, tires, etc., can all be part of a unified "car." The jadite-nephrite horizontal subordinate problem occurs when there are different yet similar subtypes of the same general type. We have a somewhat different horizontal problem if people try to explain different parts of a larger particular whole, but each refers to what they explain with the name of the same larger whole. Suppose two people give accounts of how a Tsunami came to destroy a section of forest along the coast. One person might emphasize the earthquake-based cause of the giant wave. Another might emphasize how the forest improbably came to be there along in the Tsunami's path (e.g., seeds dropped by birds). What's going on here is not two competing explanations for the event, but independent explanations of different facts coupled together to form the event as a whole. Each of these facts co-occurs and is described by the same set of sentences. The fact that we could use the same phrases to describe what was being explained by three different accounts was part of the point Bengt Hansson was making years ago when he noted that one might tell different stories about why *Adam* (rather than Eve) ate the apple, why Adam ate the *apple* (rather than a pear), why Adam *ate* the apple (rather than burying it in the ground) (1975).

One of the reasons we likely give different explanations for the same social event is that different people are inclined to try to explain different facts that each form a part of the total event. Some of these facts within this combined fact-set may involve norms or customs in that they were caused by social pressure, etc., while others do not. For the same reasons that some might explain why Adam ate the apple with an account of why Adam (rather than Eve) did, while others look at why it was an apple (rather than a pear), some might seek to explain why Majid was sitting on the floor eating with a rival politician by saying why they were eating on the floor (custom), while others focus on why the rivals were consorting (exploring an alliance against a mutual enemy). Here the fact that there are two different foci is obscured because both are described by the same superordinate phrases that describe the larger event as a whole.

This "looking at different horizontal subparts" is one of the causes of confusion in the story we started out with. When we are trying to explain Bill's sitting in College Union studying an anatomy text, we are tying to explain an event with innumerable properties. The event described here consists of Bill, in a building, at a college, moving his eyes over a textbook, with various activities happening in his brain. A full understanding of this event involves understanding how Bill (with his body, mind, and current mindset), the building, and the book came to be present there at that time. One might seek or give an explanation of how any of these properties came to be there at that time, without such accounts competing with each other in any way. Explanations of Bill's studying in the Union might center on trying to explain why Bill, of all people, would tend to be studious. Or they could focus on why Bill, with all his traits, would suddenly begin emphasizing studiousness, or why Bill's studiousness would manifest itself by poring over texts in the Union (for example, social pressure to go there). These different accounts are attempting to explain different properties, which co-occur. They do not compete with each other. If a custom/norm account helps explain where the studiousness takes place, that doesn't compete with an account of how Bill came to be studious. It only appears to compete because the co-occurring facts are described by the same sentence.

Same-Seeming "Vertical" Facts

If different "horizontal" subtypes or subparts labeled with the same superordinate class name create one type of problem, problems the fact that superordinate and subordinate classes can also share the same name, creates another type. We could call this the vertical (or nesting) subclass problem. The can of Pepsi sitting beside me, for example, is also a piece of aluminum, and a piece of metal. What's the explanation for the Pepsi can's existence? Some of its properties came to be for the reasons that all bits of metal exist—the cooling that occurs in the particles in the far-from-the-center portions of nuclear fusion stars. It also has the property of being made of aluminum, which we get when we refine bauxite ore. This particular can came into existence when some people rolled and pressed processed aluminum. A person explaining the existence of this object might give an explanation of how things with metallic properties came to be (if they hadn't, this can wouldn't exist). She might explain how we obtain things with the more narrow property of being made of aluminum. Or she might talk about what goes on at the Pepsi factory. When we refer to things in English, we can do it in all kinds of ways, including naming the superordinate classes they belong to (e.g., "this metal object"). When asked to explain something's existence, we sometimes give explanations of the existence of a top-level superordinate class. This is not inappropriate, for the particular thing would not exist in this state, were it not for the factors that created the more general property the thing may share with many other things. But we might also give an explanation of the very particular detailed state of affairs that someone is pointing to, even if he draws attention to it by its superordinate name. A teenager walking in the woods with a pair of biologist uncles might ask them why a pair of lizards he saw were mating like that. His paleontologist uncle might tell him about all the advantages of sexual reproduction and how creatures that came to reproduce this way became common on earth. His herpetologist uncle give might give him a detailed description of how pheromones from the female lizard activate certain neurotransmitters in the male lizard's brain, causing him to behave in a certain way. The first account is an explanation of the general category of "mating." Lizard mating is a specific instance of mating which could not exist, had not certain factors created the existence of the property of sexual reproduction. On the other hand, "mating" can also refer to the specific kind of act those lizards were doing. This is partly explained by neurotransmitters causing certain kinds of brain and behavior activity. One account explains the existence of the more general activity; the other explains the more specific activity that is referred to by the same description. These explanations are of different things. Both can be true and they don't compete.

The same kind of "vertical" superordinate-subordinate confusion can happen with social explanations in terms of customs. "Why is Aunt Hawa eating a sweet after dinner?" a recent immigrant from Africa wants to know. "In America, there's a custom of eating sweet things after supper called dessert," says Hawa's older daughter, explaining the existence of the general practice of which this act is an instance. "Mommy's been obsessed with pie today, after she saw that Sara Lee billboard," says the younger daughter, explaining what made Hawa want the particular kind of sweet food she does, at the particular time she wanted and expected to eat sweet foods. Such accounts are really explaining different things (the development of a widespread state of affairs and the development of a very specific one). But since both states can both be described by the same superordinate description ("wanting dessert") it can look as though we have competing explanations of the same things.[3]

Different-Seeming (but Largely the Same) Accounts of Social Facts

The other major family of different accounts that only apparently compete consists of cases when speakers give different descriptions of the same causes. The simplest way this can happen is when different speakers make statements with highly similar truth conditions, but they use different combinations of terms or concepts. If Tammy says the plastic camera melted because the temperature in the parked car rose to 214 degrees Fahrenheit, she doesn't envision a different process then Collette who says that it melted because the temperature in the car was 101 Celsius. What the English call "custom," the French call "coutome." What many anthropologists call following "cultural rules" seems to be what many sociologists would call following "social norms." When a sociologist says that Bill was willing to wait in a long line for food because he was following the social norm, she doesn't have a different conception of what is happening than the teenager who said that Bill was just doing what everyone else does and making sure he didn't get in trouble. Different descriptions of what is believed to be the same causal process do not really compete.

The Different Parts Family

One prominent subfamily of ways in which different accounts of the same facts do not really compete is when different explainers are looking at different parts of the total set of circumstances involved in causing something. Most events are caused by a number of antecedent conditions, which were individually necessary and jointly sufficient for the event's happening. Few explanation-givers ever bother to specify all of these different necessary conditions, and that means that most explainers will be giving only part of the story about why this event has to happen. People focusing on different antecedent conditions need not be giving accounts that compete. Suppose that for Bill to be drinking a cup of coffee it had to be the case that a) he was feeling cold, b) he was feeling tired, c) he was wanting to be more alert, d) others around him have a habit of drinking coffee. Without all of these conditions, he wouldn't be drinking coffee. In this case, when Margaret saying he is drinking coffee because he wants to pass his chemistry test, and Jane saying he is because it's the custom to do it here, they need not be giving competing explanations. They could just be naming different parts of what both would agree is the same more complete explanation.

Now just as Bill's drinking coffee had four individually necessary and jointly sufficient antecedent conditions, each of these four conditions might itself have four or more causal antecedent conditions, and each of these have four of their own, extending backwards through time in a giant branching progressing causal network. Different people, for various reasons, are interested in focusing on different branches. Why is Bill drinking coffee now? His fatigue is part of the cause of this, but John may talk about Bill's being up late (one of the causes of his fatigue and subsequently of his drinking coffee) while Jim talks about his getting up very early to study (a parallel cause of his fatigue and subsequently of his drinking coffee). Ellen, meanwhile, may talk about the early winter as the cause of his being cold (which helps cause the coffee drinking), while Matt talks about the defective heater in the dorm. Besides looking at different branches, or different branches of branches, some people may be interested in looking far back into something's causal history, while others look at more recent history. Why was coffee popular among Bill's peers? Arthur might talk about coffee first starting to become popular in America after the British cut off tea imports during the War of 1812. David could talk about how a legendary coffeehouse on campus in the sixties made coffee de rigueur for cramming seniors. Neither David, nor Arthur, nor Ellen, nor John would in any way be giving competing explanations of Bill's coffee drinking. All are giving different branches or parts of the total causal explanation.

The Nesting Family

Another set of ways in which different descriptions of causes can easily be confused with different causal explanations is when one explainer uses a more general "nesting" (superordinate, subsumptive) terms to describe the causes, while another explainer describes the same causes using more particular subordinate descriptions. Such explanations seem to compete because a superordinate term can refer to different entities and processes than subordinate ones. Indeed, as we'll see below, they often do refer to different processes and when they do so, such accounts really do compete. But there are other times in which people use superordinate terms (like red) and subordinate terms (like scarlet) to refer to the same things. So the different verbal descriptions of what's happening need not mean different underlying models of the properties and processes involved.

Imagine that, as in popular mythology, the color red actually does anger bulls and cause them to charge. Imagine further that it is only the scarlet shade of red that causes bulls to charge. Now imagine that Ned the neighbor walks on a well-trodden path across Fred the farmer's pasture, wearing his favorite scarlet hat. Benny the bull sees him and charges, and Ned barely escapes by leaping over a fence. At the corner store, people are abuzz, talking about what caused all the commotion. Fred says that he'll have to tell Ned not to wear that red hat again, since seeing *red made the bull furious*. Ned's wife Nelly says she warned Ned that *scarlet makes bulls charge* and he got attacked, just as she'd predicted. While the speakers are using different terms, they aren't giving different explanations, here. When Fred uses the superordinate term "red," he is attempting to refer to the same causal condition that Nelly calls "scarlet." The color scarlet is what the linguistic philosopher Paul Grice would call the "speaker meaning" of Fred's term "red" (the particular thing he has in mind and intends to communicate about using the term). Fred and Nelly may well have identical mental pictures of the exact shade of offending color that generally causes the bull to react. The difference is that one person refers to the color using a *term* that allows one to differentiate the particular offending shade of hat from others that are close to it. The other person, while intending to refer to exactly the same shade, uses a broader term that doesn't make such fine-grained distinctions. The people in this example are not giving different explanations; they are giving the same explanations using different terminology.

We can get apparently competing social explanations through this same process of one speaker using a superordinate term and a second speaker using a different subordinate term to refer to the same causal process. Why was Ned walking across the field to get to the store? Barry says that Ned watched people walk across the field for years to get to the store. He was just trying to get there by doing the same thing they did. Marty, on the other hand, says that Ned walked across the field because it was the custom to do so. Now Marty, as a native English speaker, knows (at least implicitly) that the word "custom" can refer to more than imitation causing someone to do something. A custom can cause someone to do something through their having been often punished (perhaps mildly) when they didn't do something. A custom can also cause behavior through someone's fear of punishment if they don't do it this way (whether or not there's been any past punishment), or by his or her belief that others think they should do it this way (whether or not there would be any punishment). Marty is quite well aware that in this case, Ned wasn't worried about punishment, he was just imitating. But using the superordinate term (custom) is just as easy, indeed easier, than using a more precise one, so he explains Ned walking across the field by saying that that is the custom in these parts. Here, too, Barry and Marty shouldn't be thought of as giving slightly competing accounts of why Ned walked across the field. One speaker uses more precise terminology while the other uses looser terminology to describe the same underlying causal picture they both have.

Competing Superordinate-Subordinate Accounts

The previous section describes circumstances in which different ways of describing an event (one using superordinate and one using subordinate terms) apparently compete, yet don't really. There are other times, however, when such accounts do compete, but can appear as though they don't. Figuring out when superordinate explanations compete with subordinate ones and when they don't can be very difficult. Determining which kind of explanation is correct when they compete is difficult as well. The next several sections, then, will focus on when superordinate and subordinate accounts compete and what this competition means for the plausibility of norm/custom explanations.

The most straightforward way in which an account which describes causes by referring to more general superordinate kinds can compete with accounts describing causes in terms of more specific subordinate kinds is when the use of these different sorts of terms indicates a difference of opinion as to whether any member of the broader kind could be causally efficacious in the case described, or whether only a member of a narrower subkind could serve as the causal factor in question. In the case of the bull chasing the neighbor described above, Fred and Nelly, while using the terms "red" and "scarlet" respectively, still had the same beliefs about what caused the bull's behavior, and need not be thought of as giving rival accounts. But one can easily imagine circumstances in which it is not the case that these different statements express roughly the same beliefs about what causes what. One can easily imagine circumstances in which Nelly utters her sentence about scarlet while believing that bulls are really only irked by that particular scarlet shade of red. Fred, on the other hand, might believe that scarlet, crimson, rose, burgundy, or any other shade of red is sufficient to infuriate bulls. Here, the two do not really agree about what caused the bull to charge. In this scenario, Fred believes that the particular shade of red was irrelevant to the bull's charging; any shade of red would have done it. The reason that the bull charged was because he saw something from the red category and that enraged him, not because he saw something scarlet. Nelly, however, believes that bulls actually make fine-grained discriminations here. She believes that most shades of red affect bulls very little, but something about scarlet makes their bovine blood boil. The notion that bulls are angered by redness and that is what made the bull charge in this case is mistaken, in her view. The bull's charge, according to Nelly, was caused by the sight of scarlet enraging him. In this scenario, there are many things that Fred and Nelly agree on but there are ways in which they disagree about the underlying causal facts. Nelly may agree with Fred about what happened in the antecedent event and that the thing that caused the bull to charge was colored red. But she believes, unlike Fred, that in counterfactual situations in which the hat was a different shade of red, the bull would not have charged. She disagrees, then that the fact of the hat's redness was sufficient, in these conditions, to explain the bull's charging. Unlike Fred, Nelly does not believe that an instantiation of redness was the cause of the bull's charging. Fred, on the other hand, might well agree with Nelly that the thing that made the bull charge was scarlet colored. He agrees that the hat's color was sufficient to cause a charge in these conditions. But he also believes that any shade of red would have been sufficient, so that being scarlet was unnecessary. For Fred, being scarlet was not what caused the bull to charge, merely being red was.[4]

Similar disagreements about whether all members or only particular subordinate members of a superordinate category can be causally responsible can arise with regard to norm-custom explanations. Suppose that members of the Wahiri tribe were inclined to kill on sight any member of the Calumi tribe that they come across. One can imagine some social psychologist studying the tribe and coming to the conclusion that what makes such bloodthirsty behavior possible is extensive conditioning whereby Wahiris are punished throughout their youth whenever an opportunity to kill a Calumi tribe member arises and they don't do it. Suppose now that a sociologist studying the Calumi tribe explains that an unusual social norm among the Wahiri makes them try to kill any Calumis they see. Saying that there's a social norm, recall, is saying that members of the X group are inclined to do Y because they've been conditioned by their peers to do Y, or they fear their peers will punish them for not doing Y, or they believe their peers think they should do Y, or they are imitating the behavior of their peers, etc. What can make these truly rival accounts is the sociologist thinking that any of these factors is sufficient to make members of the Wahiri tribe kill Calumis (no specific conformity condition is necessary). The social psychologist's claim is that only extreme conditioning enables the Wahiris to overcome their natural caution or empathy and become unthinking killers (the extreme conditioning *is* necessary). Here, too, the two scholars may agree about many facts, but they disagree about the counterfactual and causal facts. They disagree about what explains the Wahiris' propensity to kill Calumis. The norm explanation here is a competitor of the psychological explanation, even though the psychological mechanisms involved are subsumed by the superordinate norm category.

Scholars can be giving rival superordinate and subordinate accounts when they disagree about what's necessary or sufficient for causing a result. But there is a more subtle way they can disagree as well. Scholars can also disagree about which explanation is right when the accounts proposed represent different views about whether it's possible for disjunctions to really cause or explain something. A person who believes that a disjunction of different facts is the cause of Y believes something different than someone who believes that Y cannot be caused by a disjunction, but only by one or another of the disjuncts described. Consider our psychologist and our sociologist. In the previous example, the dispute was about whether each of the disjuncts that constitutes something's being a social norm were *all* capable of causing Wahiri tribe members to kill any Calumi tribe members, or whether *only* the particular disjunct of extreme social conditioning was sufficient. Suppose, however, that both the sociologist and the psychologist come to agree that the presence of *any* of these disjuncts (being conditioned by their peers to do Y, or fearing their peers will punish them for not doing Y, or believing their peers think they should do Y, or imitating the behavior of their peers, etc.) is itself sufficient to incite Wahiri members to kill Calumis. They might, nevertheless, disagree about what causes a given Wahiri killing. The sociologist and the psychologist could both believe that Wahiri society is structured such that people sometimes imitate others killing Calumis and they sometimes kill out of fear of ridicule if they don't. They could both believe that the presence of any of these disjuncts constitutes the Wahiri having a norm of Calumi killing. The psychologist, however, could hold that what actually causes any particular Calumi killing is not the set of disjunctive facts making up the norm, but only the particular disjunct (e.g., fear of punishment) that actually moved a Wahiri man to kill in that case. The sociologist, on the other hand, could hold that the proper culprit here is the set of disjunctive facts making up the social norm. Saying that fear of punishment caused the killing of Mr. Cato Calumi is unnecessarily specific. In the set of conditions existing there, all that needed to happen for that Calumi to die was for some or other tokening of the idea that Calumi killing is "what's done around here" to arise in the head of a Calumi-spotting Wahiri. In Wahiri society, says the sociologist, a disjunction of different factors leading Wahiris to try to kill Calumis (a norm of Calumi-killing) exists. When a Wahiri feels the pull of the norm of Calumi-killing, he kills one, and that (along with the weaponry, the Wahiri being faster, etc.) is why the Calumi dies. It doesn't matter if that norm is felt as the pressure to imitate others or as fear of punishment. To explain the death, it doesn't matter which manifestation of the disjunctive fact of the norm was occurring at a given time. The disjunctive fact of a norm of wanting, for various reasons, to kill Calumis is the proper description of the cause of the Calumi death.

The difference between the hypothetical psychological and sociological explanation, here, is an example of a disagreement that is due to different beliefs about whether disjunctive facts can cause anything. The accounts here are true rivals and not just apparent ones. They differ in beliefs about what is really causing what here. A sociologist who says that the existence of a norm is the true causal explanation of the Calumi killing, with particular motivations being irrelevant, has a different explanation than a psychologist who claims that Wally Wahiri killed Cato Calumi because he feared his friends would laugh at him if he didn't. This is true even if the sociologist doesn't disagree that that was a motivator, and even if the psychologist believes that imitation, etc., often regularly serves as a motivator in such circumstances.

While disjunctive explanations are sometimes given in conversation and scholarly papers, the intuition that disjunctions can't really cause anything is a very strong one. The philosophical literature is full of arguments and examples aiming to show that there really are no disjunctive causes (see, for example, Armstrong 1980; Lewis 1986; Kim 2000; Audi 2009). One of the most prominent anti-disjunctive arguments is given by Jaegwon Kim. Kim asks us to consider this "explanation" of Mary's pain (2000, 108):

Rheumatoid arthritis causes painful joints.
So does lupus.
Mary has either rheumatoid arthritis or lupus.
Therefore Mary has painful joints.

Says Kim:

> Do we have here an explanation of why Mary is experiencing pain in her joints? Do we know what is causing her pains? I think there is a perfectly clear and intelligible sense in which we don't as yet have an explanation: what we have is a disjunction of two explanations, not a single explanation. What I mean is this: we have two possible explanations, and we know that one or the other is the correct one but not which it is. What we have, I claim, is not an explanation with a disjunctive cause, "having rheumatoid arthritis or lupus." There are no such "disjunctive diseases." (2000, 108)

If the arguments against the possibility of disjunctive causes and explanations are correct, and if culture, norm, or custom explanations really are attempts to give disjunctive explanations, then a large class of attempted social scientific explanations are in deep trouble. If there are no disjunctive explanations, it simply can't be the case that the correct explanation of Cato Calumi's death is Wahiris being conditioned by their peers to do Y, or fearing their peers will punish them for not doing Y, or believing their peers think they should do Y, or imitating the behavior of their peers, etc.

Now, as we have seen, it can sometimes be the case that when someone says, "Wally Wahiri killed Cato because of the norm of Calumi killing," she might be thinking that Wally killed Cato because he worried about the punishments he'd receive if he didn't—and just uses the term "norm" as a quick way to express that. Giving an explanation that uses the term "norm" in this sense may be a vague unspecific explanation—but it is not a false one. Even if instantiating a disjunctive property like "pilot error" is not sufficient to cause a plane to crash, it's not false to say that what made a particular plan crash was an instance of pilot error. What would be wrong, however, would be to claim that all that was needed for this plane to crash was to have an instantiation of the general property pilot error in the right circumstances. Similarly, if what is meant by "because of the norm of Calumi killing," is that the whole set of disjunctive facts caused the killing, then the claimer believes something false if there are no true disjunctive causes. The killing could be caused by fear of punishment, or it could be caused by imitating others (a related point is made in Henderson 2005). But it can't really be caused by [fear of punishment or imitating others]. If the anti-disjunction arguments are right, it could still be that any of the low level explanations based on any of the particular disjuncts are right. But the explanation in terms of the high-level disjunctive class as a whole must be wrong. Any account using terms like "culture," "norm," or "custom" that tries to give a causal explanation of an event in this way is on the wrong track. Further, if the anti-disjunctive arguments are right, it doesn't matter if, as we've said in the previous sections, norm/custom explanations don't really compete with lots of other kinds of accounts. Even if a norm/custom explanation doesn't compete with, say, an earlier part of a causal chain, it will compete with (and lose to) an account using lower level disjuncts. For "what's done" accounts to work at all, there must be an effective response to the charge that disjunctions don't work.

Responding to Anti-Disjunction Arguments

Disjunctive Explanations Are Fine

The most straightforward response to the charge that disjunctions can't really cause anything is to argue that they can. Disjunctions, one might argue, are perfectly fine portions of explanations. They are even preferable, in certain circumstances. A number of philosophers have recently held that in certain cases, disjunctions really can be causes (Bennett 1988, Mackie 1993, Mellor 1995, and Sartorio 2006). An extremely broad defense of disjunctive explanations would be to argue that if, in specific conditions C, the addition of any one of a number of different factors F could have caused Y, then we should say the true cause of Y is the appearance of some or other member of F. Anything else is overkill. In his classic antireductionist article, "1953 and All That: A Tale of Two Sciences," Philip Kitcher (1984) argues against giving various particular low-level accounts of cellular meiosis. He writes:

> Yet simply plugging a molecular account into the [high-level] narratives offered at previous stages would decrease the explanatory power of those narratives. What is relevant to answering our original question is the fact that nonhomologous chromosomes assort independently. What is relevant to the issue of why nonhomologous chromosomes assort independently is the fact that the chromosomes are not selectively oriented toward the poles of the spindle. . . . In neither case are the molecular details relevant. Indeed, adding those details would only disguise the relevant factor. (1984, 348)

One can imagine using Kitcher's injunctions against irrelevant detail as part of the defense of a disjunctive causation. Naming particular disjuncts as causes in some cases is to be guilty of giving irrelevant detail since just being any one of the members of the disjunctive class is sufficient to cause the result. Using a general term (like norm), on the other hand, that covers a range of disjuncts can correctly specify the set of factors necessary for making that effect happen in those conditions. Naming the disjunction, on this view, gives us a better explanation than providing particular antecedent conditions.[5]

A less ambitious defense of disjunctive explanations is to argue that there are certain kinds of narrow conditions for which disjunctive explanations are the appropriate ones. A disjunction of factors is the best explanation for an event having redundant causation when, if one factor didn't trigger an event, other ones would. Imagine Jim faces death by firing squad and that soldier number four is first to shoot a bullet that stops Jim's heart. One could argue that that wasn't really the cause of his death because, even if four's bullet hadn't killed him, Jim still would have died then from bullets of soldiers one, two, or three. It is more accurate to say that his death was caused by the firing squad. Counterfactual analyses of causation say that X is the cause of Y when if X hadn't happened, Y wouldn't have happened. One might argue that in redundant cases where there's over determination or preemption, one must cite all the disjuncts as causes to satisfy the counterfactual analysis. Remove soldier number four, and you would still get Jim's death, so soldier four's shooting did not cause the death, even if his bullet pierced Jim's heart first. Remove the whole firing squad, on the other hand, and Jim lives on—so the firing squad (soldier one *or* two *or* three shooting) is really the cause of his death. Perhaps "what's done" explanations are true when you have circumstances such that if Cato Calumi had not been killed because of Wally Wahiri's conditioning as a Calumi killer, he would have been killed because of Wally worrying about ridicule for not killing. When there are redundant causes of Y, it can be argued, it is best to cite their disjunction as the causal explanation of Y.

One could also argue that even if disjunctions cannot cause single events, they are the best explanation for a general result. Whenever a Calumi is spotted by a Wahiri, you always have an attempted Calumi killing. Why? The norm of Calumi killing ensures this. Any time a Calumi is sighted by a Wahiri, the Wahiri either wants to imitate his Calumi-killing uncles, or worries about how his friends will treat him if he doesn't kill, or has a reflex brought on by a lifetime of Calumi killing conditioning. Even if you don't need a disjunction to explain a particular case, you need the disjunction to explain why there is a generalization about Calumi killing in these parts.

It is well beyond the scope of this book to say whether these are adequate responses to worries about disjunctive causes. It is fair to say that opponents of disjunction will not likely find them persuasive. Opponents of disjunctive explanation would likely say that the demand that we name all of the things that could lead to result Y in those conditions (thus insuring the cause is necessary for result Y) is a wildly implausible constraint on counting as an event's cause. And they would likely reply to the claim that you can only explain a general result with a disjunction, by saying that there is no reason to think we really have a counterfactual-supporting generalization here. What we have, the objection goes, are lots of particular cases of Wahiris killing Calumis for lots of different reasons. For some or other reason we sometimes give a common name to the various different sets of motivations involved in Calumi killing. But that doesn't mean that we really have a general fact about a common underlying property. What we really have here is a set of different acts of killing, each of which has a different causal explanation. We sometimes only bother to refer to these various causes with a vague subsuming name. But we don't really have a generalization about a disjunctive kind here.

Norm/Custom Explanations Are Not Disjunctive

Another way of responding to the challenge that disjunctive properties can't be causal is to argue that the property of being a norm (or a custom) isn't a disjunctive property after all. If by "norm" we were talking about a unitary property and not a lot of different things, we wouldn't have the disjunction problem and we'd be in a much better position to know what to expect, knowing a norm is in place. There are several different ways one could argue that norms are not disjunctive. Let's look at them, in turn.

Norms as Reducible to a Non-Disjunctive Low-Level Property

One way to argue that norms are not disjunctive is to claim that a norm is reductively identifiable with some perfectly respectable unified low-level property. If a norm turns out to be, say, a type of psychological disposition in enactors, then we don't have to worry about the possibly problematic status of disjunctive properties because the property of being a norm just isn't really a disjunctive one. But, given the number of different social forces discussed above that could be involved in a norm causing various Calumis to be killed, how could one claim that a norm is actually a unified low-level property? There are various ways this might work. One way would be to claim that, however many different forces might be involved during various stages of the Calami-killing process, all these Calami-killings involve, at some point in the process, some nondisjunctive common factor that we can identify as a norm. But what, exactly, would the common element be? Some Wahiris likely kill Calamis because they have seen other Wahiris do it and want to imitate them. Others, while never having seen a killing, believe that their peers will tell heroic stories about them if they ever kill a Calami. Still others have been punished for not killing Wahiris when they had the chance. All of these things have the same effect (trying to kill Calamis). And all can be called by the same name ("norm"). But what really constitutes the common property that is the norm, instantiated in these various cases? I see no evidence of any common property of this sort that's sufficient, given background, to cause the effects in question.

The problem is not that there aren't some commonalities in these different causal processes that lead to attempted Calami-killing. Even in a class as diverse as "norm" there will invariably be many commonalities (e.g., norms all have the property of being possessed by people and not animals, being possessed by groups and not individuals, existing over a range of time and not just for a moment, etc.). The problem is that none of these commonalities can plausibly be identified as a "norm" which, when combined with other known background features, is sufficient to cause the effect in question.

In our Calami-killing case, each causal process leading to attempting Calami-killing involves Wahiris coming to have a psychological disposition to kill any Calamis they saw. Could we identify the norm of Calami-killing among the Wahiris with a psychological disposition to kill Calamis? While explaining the Calami-killing with a norm identified this way has the virtue of appealing to what might be a genuine shared property, that property isn't giving people sufficient useful information to explain the behavior in question. It is like saying, as the old joke goes, that various sleeping pills put people to sleep because they all have the property of "dormitive virtue." In this case, we already knew that Wahiris had the disposition to kill Calamis. What the norm explanation was supposed to do was give more information about the causal chain that produced the killing. Identifying the norm with this shared psychological disposition clearly doesn't give us that additional information.

And this problem is not due simply to picking out the common property lying at the end of a causal chain. The problem is that it looks like any non-disjunctive truly common low-level property we could identify as the norm would not be sufficient, even with the addition of basic background knowledge, to say why the behavior ensued. Consider an analogous situation. Imagine a psychologist who wants to avoid the disjunction problem inherent in giving an account of why Willy Sutton robbed banks. A disjunction problem would arise if he said "it was either because of his extreme poverty as a youth or his hanging out with future criminals as a youth." Such a disjunction could be avoided if he switched his explanation to saying "he robbed banks because that's where the money is." As a neat joke, this is an oldie but goodie. But it's a poor explanation of Sutton's behavior because knowing that "that's where the money is," along with standard background conditions, is not sufficient to cause bank robbery. We still need to know what else it was in Sutton's history or psychological profile that made him inclined to thievery. Avoiding the disjunction problem this way creates a bigger problem of trading a rather complete explanation for a small piece of an explanation. We would be doing the same thing if we tried to identify "norm" to mean one small common element in various different not-well-understood causal chains leading to a behavior like Calami-killing. We might try to say, for example, that the common feature of the norm of Calami-killing is lots of Wahiris' extreme hatred of Calamis. But the presence of this feature is not enough to cause (or explain) lots of Calamis dying at the hands of Wahiris. The problem is that to find a property that's truly common to all or most of the diverse alleged instances of the norm of Calami-killing, we must locate a property with few features (since every extra "property-of-the-property" possessed makes it more difficult for it to be common to a diverse set of cases.) But such stripped-down, common-to-all-cases properties will tend not to be sufficient to give a causal explanation of the behavior in question.

A related way of solving the disjunction problem has related problems. We might try to say that what we call a norm isn't defined by being a complex shared feature-set, but rather by having a simple shared property. Perhaps there are some common features that all things called norms share. They might all, for example, develop by way of some kind of "culture acquisition device." This, however, gets us back to the problem just discussed. There is no difficulty finding properties that are common to all things called norms. (Norms all have the property of existing on Planet Earth, for example.) The problem is that merely knowing that this shared feature is present, along with some or other undefined features that a norm is composed of, isn't sufficient for knowing why a certain behavior ensues. We might know that the various structures making up the Wahiri norm of Calami-killing all have the general feature of people worrying about what others think. In other words, a general (perhaps innate) disposition to worry about others' thoughts about you might be involved in all cases of norm-caused Calami-killing. Such cases might all even have the more specific feature of worrying about what others think about Calamis not being killed. But knowing that *that* property is present is certainly not sufficient to tell us that Calami-killing will be attempted, even along with lots of other background information. The causal factors sufficient to make Wahiris try to kill Calamis must involve more than this. But what do they involve? If we know only that [worrying about what others will think about non-killing] is present, we don't know which set of structures was there that, along with background conditions, actually ensure that a Wahiri will try to kill a Calami that he sees. We won't know what set of factors were present in any of the particular cases of the norm of Calami-killing causing Calami-killing behavior. And we don't know what set caused things in the collective set of past (or past and future) Calami-killings. We will know that certain features (like worry) are present, but these features are insufficient to explain the Calami-killing. Knowing that a norm is causing things (even with additional background information) does not tell you enough about what is causing what, if knowing the norm is present only involves knowing that certain watered-down general features are present. And when, on the other hand, we try to name more substantive, less watered-down set of features, we will invariably find that these more content-rich feature sets are only present in some of the cases we consider norm-caused.

Now a slightly different strategy for finding a common property, perhaps a property with more content, is to restrict the number of cases that we consider as candidates for being caused by a norm. We might say, for example, that we really have a norm causing things only when a person actually sees lots of other people performing the behavior and that seeing, along with various psychological mechanisms, causes the person to want to do what the others do. Now, such a sense of norm has the virtue (like the cases above) that it can't fail to be causal because it refers to a disjunction of different properties. But there are big disadvantages to construing statements about norms in this way. A very large number of explanations given in terms of norms will turn out to be false on this construal, since actions done because of mechanisms other than imitation (for example, ones done because of social conditioning) are wrongly being termed "norm explanations." Only actions done because of imitation would be true norm-caused ones. A related problem is that the true norm explanations (the imitation-based ones on this construal) will be able to explain far fewer kinds of cases than norms are currently thought to be able to explain (we can't explain actions done because others want them done in terms of norms). If one's worry is that accounts of norms are not really providing us with true explanations of behavior because they refer to disjunctive properties, one is unlikely to be satisfied by a "cure" for this problem that entails a large percentage of existing norm explanations actually being false.

It seems unlikely, then, that we can solve the problem of there being a disjunction of different things called norms by claiming that underneath this apparent diversity, we can find a nondisjunctive unifying low-level property. The properties that are most plausibly common to a very large number of norm cases are generally ones that are insufficient for explaining the behavior in question. And the property-combinations more specific to certain things called "norms," tend not to be shared by all or most cases of norms.

Irreducible High-Level Norms
But perhaps we can avoid the disjunction problem by saying that beneath the apparent diversity of norms, there is a nondisjunctive unifying irreducible high-level property. The move here is to suggest that norms or customs could exist as a type of irreducible dualistic force, perhaps at the social level, that's analogous to the non-physically-reducible dualism of one kind or another that many people believe exists for mental phenomena. Just as some proponents of autonomous mental powers claim that there is high-level mental causation distinct from any physical base, perhaps there are high-level normative or cultural laws that exert "downward causation" pressures on the individuals in a society. Or one could advocate for irreducible high-level cultural or normative factors without having to go all the way to an analogue of substance dualism. Perhaps, as functionalists (like Fodor 1993) have claimed about the mental, there is a general "what's done" property that supervenes on various individual motivations without being reducible to any of them. It is the higher-level property, not merely the lower-level multiple "realizers," that really explains why people act as they do. Throughout the history of the social sciences and throughout contemporary social science, there are claims that there are high-level social properties that have causal powers that are autonomous from those of individual actors. Norms and culture are among the factors sometimes claimed to be these kinds of unified high-level autonomous properties (e.g., Durkheim 2001 [1923] and Schneider 1985).

But none of these "customs are a high-level nondisjunctive property" moves is any more plausible than "customs are low-level nondisjunctive property" responses just discussed. To begin with, a full-blown downward-causing social dualism of independent Hegelian norms that control individuals is even more implausible than a Cartesian mentalistic dualism (see Jackson and Pettit 1992 for arguments to that effect). The idea that norms could be analogous to the "non reductive physical" properties that functionalists propose for the mental realm is more plausible. To be analogously structured, there would have to be "normative laws" or causes (though this is already less plausible than mental laws), which are enacted by various lower-level realizers but which are nevertheless not identifiable with these realizers.

The issue of whether or not any kind of individually realized but nonindividualistic forces can cause anyone to do anything is one of the many issues that have been discussed under the general rubric of the debates about "methodological individualism," which I mentioned in chapter 3. While the issues about whether social properties can reduce to individualistic ones has been debated for decades in various forms, it is my view that these debates very often parallel debates in the philosophy of mind about whether mental properties reduce to physical neurological ones. In that realm, it should be clear to all participants that within the last decade there has been a dramatic turn from a general consensus about the correctness of a non-reductive physicalism to a situation where non-reductive physicalism is on the defensive from numerous fronts. A growing body of criticism (e.g., Churchland 2005, Jones 2004a, Kim 2000, 2005, Bechtel and Mundale 1999, Sober 1999, Melnyk 1995) argues that the lower-level physical factors that functionalists concede directly cause behavior to be explained are what behavior should be explained in terms of. In the philosophy of mind, many now hold (and I agree) that the position that mental states are physical states but are not reducible to them is an unstable one. I want to suggest here that, for exactly parallel reasons, it is implausible to claim that norms and customs supervene on the psychological or behavioral dispositions of individuals but are not reducible to them. While the anti- anti-reductionist view is now well known in the philosophy of mind, few scholars seem to have seen that the same arguments are general enough to apply to claims about norms, customs, and culture as high-level irreducible properties. Below, I will discuss how the same considerations apply to both cases, with similar anti-high-level autonomy morals. While the arguments of Kim (2000, 2005) about the problems of non-reductive physicalism are perhaps the most well known, I am best able to discuss my own arguments in this realm. Let me explain why I think both the instability of non-reductive physicalism, in and of itself, and a parallel implausibility for anti-individualism cause problems for the view that norms are high-level irreducible nondisjunctive properties.

The anti-high-level autonomous property arguments that I've laid out in various places (2003, 2004a, 2004b) regarding the mental realm go like this: If a certain plausible physicalism is true, then when a finite disjunction of Xs causes a finite disjunction of Ys, physicalism dictates that we can always just list the physical laws and particular conditions that make each case possible. If there is an infinite number of Xs or Ys, however, the causal closure of physics still ensures that there can't be any nonphysical forces that ensure that only Ys result from Xs. And since any action can only result from physical forces (as physicalists who believe in the causal closure of physics hold), there can't be any super/meta forces that make sure that some or other combination of contingencies and physical forces will always be on hand to guarantee that Xs always result in Ys. If some combination of facts and forces always does guarantee it, then this must be because the laws of physics alone are such that nothing else could happen in these circumstances. Physicalism and causal closure allow there to be no mechanisms making multiple realizable generalizations true besides systematic physical forces operating on certain possible physical arrangements.

Now this argument alone, if correct, means that there can't be autonomous forces involving norms or customs that are not reducible to physics, in principle. Customs can't be autonomous controlling high-level properties that make what happens happen—unless we can, in principle, redescribe them in physical terms. Earlier, however, we saw that there didn't seem to be any low-level unitary way to describe them that didn't involve disjunction. So for customs to be nondisjunctive properties, it seems that they must be irreducible high-level properties. But the argument I've just given concludes there are no irreducible nonphysical properties, if physicalism is true.

But suppose, as is possible, that physicalism is untrue. Suppose there are nonphysical souls. This wouldn't really help the advocate of irreducible customs. An exactly parallel anti-autonomy argument can be made if one adopts a plausible view of social action, widely held by all but the most Hegelian of social scholars—the causal closure of individual agency. The causal closure of individual agency holds that every event that happens in the social world is caused by no forces other than the actions of some or other set of individuals. Social antireductionists might want to try, like their psychofunctionalist counterparts, to avoid the extravagant metaphysics of "social dualism" while at the same time believing that generalizations about what must happen can't always be reduced to these purely individualistic activities. On this view, while there are no spooky higher-level entities controlling individuals, there are, nevertheless, irreducibly social properties. But the causal closure of individual agency, bars this possibility in an exactly parallel way to how the seemingly innocent causal closure of physics causes problems for autonomous high-level mental causes. Included in these autonomous social properties we really can't have are irreducible high-level customs and norms. If there are a finite number of individualistic psychological factors that make people act like their neighbors, we can just list them. If there are an infinite number of ways that some or other combination of facts guarantees that norm X always makes behavior Y happen, then causal closure allows there to be no mechanisms to force these multiply realizable generalizations to be true besides individualistically describable psychological factors.

If customs or norms really do causally explain things, on this argument, this must be because they are ultimately identifiable as lower-level psychological dispositions. But, as was discussed earlier, psychological dispositions we identify as norms seem to be disjunctive ones.

Even Worse Problems for Norm/Custom Accounts

But there is a worse problem for custom and norm accounts. Suppose it turns out that there can be autonomous high-level properties after all. Or suppose that, contrary to the current consensus in philosophy, disjunctions of properties can be causal. Both of these possibilities leave custom explanations vulnerable to being undermined from above. Let me explain.

If disjunctions can be causal, there is nothing wrong with an explanation that cites the presence of a custom in Wahiri society as the cause of a given Calami member's death. The problem is that the same considerations suggesting we should attribute cause to the larger disjunctive set (custom) rather than one of the disjuncts, would also suggest we should attribute the cause to an even larger set of disjuncts: a set like [custom or fear]. Imagine, as is likely, that in addition to conditioning and/or imitation, fear of Calumis makes Wahiris try to kill their rivals. A counterfactual-oriented notion of causation, along with the requirement not to give more specificity than is required for the effect, could mandate that "custom" [imitation or conditioning or herding] provides a better explanation for Calami-killing than imitation. It didn't need to be imitation that killed Cato, since any way the custom of Calami-killing was implemented would do it. But this also mandates that [custom or fear] (call this the "kill-on-sight disposition") is a better causal explanation than the custom one. Opponents of disjunction often hold that disjunctive explanations are undermined "from below," with lower-level accounts being the real explanations for various results. But if disjunctive explanation advocates are correct and disjunctive accounts are legitimate, then norm/custom accounts can also easily be undermined from above this way. If there can be disjunctive causes, then there are often good reasons to consider a larger disjunctive set the cause of something, rather than the smaller one.

Note that this is not merely the logical worry that if A or B causes X, then A or B or C must as well. The only disjunctions we should consider as being good candidates for disjunctive causes should be disjunctions that are counterfactual supporting. Conditioning, imitation (or any other form of custom) would also have produced a certain result in these circumstances, so we name the general property (custom) rather than something unnecessarily specific. So we are not saying that if we are able to say "[imitation or conditioning] killed Cato Calami" then we are just as able to say"[imitation or conditioning or praying to a monkey-god] killed Cato Calumi." We are saying merely that in the case of the custom, here, if [imitating killers or being conditioned-to-kill] is a more accurate description of the cause of Cato's death than [imitating killers] alone, then [killing out of custom or killing out of fear] is a more accurate description of the cause of Cato's death than [killing out of custom] alone. The disjunction can only grow larger while still being a true cause so long as each disjunct would have the same effect in those circumstances. I am not claiming, then, that any large disjunct will "undermine from above" all subvening subset disjuncts. But it is plausible that, for most cases where what could cause an effect are the disjuncts making up a custom, other variables could cause the same effect as well. This makes the larger disjunct consisting of the custom factors along with these other factors a better cause, thus "undermining from above" the narrower custom cause. The idea that disjunctive causes can be "undermined from above" in this manner has not been well noticed at all. But it is a problem that advocates for explanation with customs or norms would do well to be aware of.

There are very similar worries about undermining from above if high-level autonomous properties could turn out to be causal after all. If high level autonomous properties can exist, and customs are among them, it seems likely that claims about the causal power of customs will often be "undermined from above" by the presence of even higher-level properties in the same way that causal disjunctions could be undermined from above by wider disjunctions. Suppose someone could demonstrate that, in cases like the Calumi killing, it's really the presence of the high-level property of having this social custom, and not the low-level mechanism "realizing" the social custom (e.g., fear of ridicule), that explains the ensuing behavior. The problem is that in the majority of circumstances where one can give this kind of norm explanation, one can also give an even higher-level rationality or optimality explanation that by rights should "screen off" the lower-level norm account. Since ancient Greek times, numerous scholars have sought to explain things with variants of rationality or optimality accounts: organisms do Y because Y is a very good way of conferring important benefits on the organism. (See Bueno de Mesquita 2009 for good examples of style of explanation.) It's easy to envision someone arguing that the Calumi-killing cases that others explain with a custom account should really be explained this way: In the forests where the Wahiri and the Calumi live, there are not enough resources to support both tribes. There are even fewer resources in nearby regions. Tribes that have survived in this region are ones who have been able systematically to eliminate their rivals. Developing a strategy of killing all Calumis is, thus, a rational strategy for Wahiri survival. For this reason, Calumi killing has been socially selected. Sometimes Wahiris kill Calumis after thinking about what can be done about resource scarcity. Other times they act because of the social pressure that has developed. As in most rationality or optimality explanations, the exact low-level mechanism leading to the action is held to be irrelevant. Biological adaptationist versions of optimality generally pay little attention to questions of how mutations arise and create the mechanism for doing some task. In the case of "social adaptationism" (or what used to be called "functionalism"), it is similarly taken for granted that useful structures will arise over time by some means or other, and then be selected for their usefulness. Whatever lower-level psychological mechanisms lead any individual Wahiri to kill a Calumi, the right explanation for the killing, this argument goes, is that it is highly rational for a Wahiri to do so.[6] Advocates for higher-level explanations might be right that we have good reasons for thinking that "custom" explanations "screen off" lower-level accounts like those in terms of imitation. But it looks like those same considerations should suggest that custom accounts are themselves often screened off by accounts at an even higher-level. Arguments advocating the more general account as being the truly causal one end up undermining customs "from above" with regards to both higher-level and disjunctive accounts.

Why Can't Higher- and Lower-Level Accounts Be Correct at the Same Time?

Now one way that advocates of norm or custom explanations could try to avoid the worry that norm accounts are "undermined from above," either by an even higher-level account (like one in terms of rationality) or by a wider disjunction (like [custom or fear]), would be to argue that norm/custom accounts aren't undermined by more general accounts because customs and more general properties can both be causal at the same time. Customs could be causing things to happen, while at the same time rationality or [custom-or-fear] could also be causing at a higher-level. At the same time, conditioning, and certain neurological states could be causing at lower levels. But defending customs this way requires that one specifically deny a widely held idea about causation known as the "Causal Exclusion Principle." One of the simplest versions of the principle is described by Kim this way: "If an event e has a sufficient cause c at t, no event at t distinct from c can be a cause of e (unless this is a genuine case of causal overdetermination)" (2005). If one wants to claim that norms or customs are not undermined from above because customs can be causal at the same time as these higher-level factors, then it must be the case that the causal exclusion principle is false.

But there are two worries about trying to get around the "undermining from above" by denying the causal exclusion principle. The first is that this principle is a very plausible one. The second is that even if we deny it, it's not clear that this helps the likelihood of causation by norms very much. The plausibility of the principle is straightforward. Indeed, some believe it is simply an analytic truth that (without overdetermination) nothing can have two different sets of sufficient causes. The intuitive pull of causal exclusion is certainly very strong. If something expands when heated due to its property of being made of metal, then it seems that it cannot be true that it also has an additional cause of expanding due to its being made of copper. The causal power of the property of being metallic here screens off the causal power of being copper, rendering it superfluous. Exclusionary screening off seems to occur in the other direction as well. If something is giving off light due to its releasing black body radiation after being heated to a certain temperature, there can be no additional higher-source also producing that same light. Even a critic of the causal exclusion principle, Thomas Bontly, writes, "Many find Kim's principle plausible; few have questioned it directly. Kim himself in a recent discussion calls the exclusion principle 'a general metaphysical constraint' one he thinks cannot be successfully challenged . . . I should say at the outset that I do not think it possible at this point to prove the exclusion principle incorrect" (2005, 263). If something other than a custom provides (along with background) a sufficient cause for something, it's hard to see how the exclusion principle is false and a custom can cause it too, at the same time. (Unless, we are talking about one of the noncompeting situations referred to above.)

Furthermore, while one must hold the implausible view that the causal exclusion principle cannot be true, in order to claim that customs and something distinct from them can both be sufficient for causing, it's not clear that taking this position really even helps the causal customs advocate. Even with no causal exclusion principle, norms and customs still are problematic if there are no disjunctions and no autonomous high-level causes. And even allowing higher-level or disjunctive causes, customs could still be undermined from above by rationality, etc., because the lower-level isn't counterfactually necessary—whether or not there is causal exclusion. (Or they could be undermined from below if just instancing one or another kind of custom is insufficient for the result). All these considerations suggest that customs and conditioning explanations are mutually incompatible, even if there were no general causal exclusion saying only one could be right. Norms/customs and lower-level explanations like those in terms of imitation or conditioning look to be in competition—and it doesn't look like the outcome could be a draw.

Norms as Explanatory: Concluding Remarks

We've seen then, that although it is not impossible that norms could turn out to be able to explain behavior, it seems very implausible that they could do so. One could retain a belief in the causal power of norms, but only at the cost of giving up things that norm-advocates should want to retain (e.g., the wide scope of things explainable by norms). Or norms could turn out to be causal if a number of difficult-to-meet conditions are met simultaneously. Norms could be causal if (numerous philosophical arguments to the contrary) there can be disjunctive causes and, at the same time, there turn out to be no more general higher-level disjuncts that screen off the causal efficacy of the lower levels. Norms could also be causal if (numerous philosophical arguments to the contrary) there can be autonomous high level causes and, at the same time, there turn out to be no more general higher level causes that screen off the causal efficacy of the lower levels. It is possible that norms can cause behavior, but it would be very difficult for all those conditions to be met, and there is little evidence that they are met. Surprisingly then, the evidence suggests that, despite their widespread use, norms can't really cause behaviors. There may well be a custom of the X people doing Y, but that's unlikely to be a good explanation of why the X do Y.

GROUP INTENTIONAL EXPLANATIONS

Let's turn now to the question of how well statements about the thoughts or activities of groups as a whole can work as explanations. In chapter 3, we saw that talking about how a group acts or even how it thinks can be a perfectly adequate description of what a group tends to do. The question we're considering now is whether such talk about what the group as a whole is inclined to think or do can be a good explanation of some set of circumstances.[7]

To begin with, there are certainly some senses in which the activities of a group as a whole can be part of an explanation of states of affairs. If a pond goes dry largely because many different citizens of Bendersville together extract lots of water from it for various purposes, then the activities of Bendersville citizens as a whole is clearly part of the explanation of what happened to the pond. There is no doubt that the collective activities of many people are often part of a causal chain determining what happens. But one of the really interesting questions about how explanatory group activity can be is whether intentional descriptions of groups (e.g., "France was afraid of what Italy would do") tend to give us good explanations. We saw in chapter 3 that, surprisingly, we do not have to think of our common practice of ascribing intentional states to groups as completely metaphorical. Groups may well be able to possess something like rudimentary goals and representations. The question we face now is whether such ascriptions can really provide good explanations of what those groups do.

In asking about the explanatory potential of group intentional activities, we should note from the outset that such attempted explanations will often have to confront the same worries that bedevil high-level norm/custom accounts. Whenever we are talking about high-level explanatory variables above the level of the individual (or even above the level of physics), the number of potential ways such accounts can be undermined is vast. Suppose someone says "Microsoft's fear of losing market share to Safari led it to try to increase the speed of its own browser. But at the same time, that goal of increased speed caused it to lose focus on search specificity." Here, as in the norm case, we are confronted with numerous potential problems. If by "Microsoft's fear" we mean a finite number of different disjunctive forms of internal organizations ("Microsoft's fear" could refer to worried projections by the accounting department, OR envious employee chatter about the sleekness of Safari, OR anxious feedback from sales reps, etc.) then we have to confront all of the arguments that there are no real disjunctive causes. But if, on the other hand, high-level disjunctive causes do exist, do we know that there are not even higher-level disjunctive causes (e.g., more general market forces) that "screen off" the causal efficacy of "Microsoft's fear" as unnecessarily specific? As with the norm case, it's possible that there could be cases that can escape being tripped up by one or another of these problems. But the defender of high-level group intentions, like the defender of high-level explanatory norms, is going to have to do some fancy footwork to show this escape is possible. Now seeing whether or how the group intentional claims can escape the worries that bedevil norm accounts would take us into a long detour. Among the reasons it's not worth taking this detour is the fact that even if group intentional accounts were able to escape these problems, there is another family of even more worrisome problems regarding intentional explanation that would have to be confronted. Let's turn to these now.

Not Enough Information in Group Intentionality Claims

In typical ordinary intentional explanations, we rely on the assumption that the mind generally operates according to principles like these:

For any agent X, if

1. X wants D and
2. X believes that A is a means to attain D, under the circumstances,
3. there is no action believed by X to be a way of bringing about D that under the circumstances is more preferred by X
4. X has no wants that override D
5. X knows how to do A
6. X is able to do A
7. X does A. (adapted from Rosenburg 1988)

When we give intentional explanations, as with most accounts, we rarely explicitly mention all parts—just the parts we think our audience doesn't know because they aren't able to automatically fill them in with background information. Why is Dave digging a trench in his yard with a shovel? We understand why he is doing what he does when we are told that, "He needed to put in a new pipe to reach a sprinkler head at the end of his lawn." In giving this account, the speaker doesn't feel he needs to spell out for the listener that Dave believes that a shovel is the right tool for the job and that certain movements by his arms will lift and move the dirt. He doesn't have to explain why Dave had no other overriding desires or plans. He doesn't have to explain how it is that Dave's muscles and tools respond to his wishes, nor how dirt responds to his thrusts. A typical speaker can assume that a typical listener knows all this. According to many philosophers, the speaker can make this assumption because he can fairly safely assume that the listener, being much like the speaker, can be expected to know the same unsaid things the speaker would know if he was in the listener's circumstances. Because the listener knows so many of the causal variables involved in the production of everyday behavior—what mental factors are and aren't involved and how the familiar world responds to the muscle movements the mental factors cause—an explanation need only involve discovering and supplying the few details the listener is unlikely to already know.

When giving an intentional explanation of the behavior of a group to someone, however, we are explaining the behavior of an exotic alien actor that obviously thinks and behaves somewhat differently from ourselves and interacts with much less familiar kinds of obstacles. Suppose that Apple cancels a scheduled advertising campaign and we are told that this is because Apple "wants to lower expectations about capacities of its new iPhone." Can that tell you why Apple did what it did, in the ways that knowing Dave's desire told you why he was shoveling? In the individual case we know something about what other desires are likely present or absent which could interfere

with acting on the desire for D. But even if we know about a group's desire
for D, we are unlikely to know what sets of other desires are swirling about
its inner states, which may or may not interfere with the desire for a given D
outcome. Whatever we know about the beliefs and desires of the Apple Corporation, it is not clear we will know which "desires" have the most strength,
and command the most resources and attention. In the ditch digging case, we
understand which sequence of moves with a shovel in his hand Dave knows
how to do in order to get the ditch dug. With the company, we don't antecedently know what analogues of muscles and tools the company even has at
its disposal in order to create plans of action. We don't antecedently know
much about the procedures by which a particular "plan of attack" is designed
and selected, or what would lead to the selection of this or that plan of action
when different ones would meet the goal. We easily understand the effect
that making digging movements with a shovel has on the earth, but we likely
have only the most hazy understanding of the giant environment (here, net-
works of retail agents and potential customers) the group is trying to interact
with, and how that environment will respond. In general, while we tend to
know a fair amount about the environmental obstacles our fellow individual
humans will be trying to interact with, the muscles and tools they have at
their disposal for doing so, and the knowledge of how to use them, we won't
know this for groups that act as agents without a great deal of further study.
Being told about a set of some belief and desire-like states that a company
has will generally not enable us to predict in much detail what the company
will be able to achieve—and such knowledge will not enable us to give the
corresponding retroactive explanation of why certain activity results. Indeed,
even when we are discussing individuals, it's hard to predict and explain
what people will do when the person we are talking about is a person unlike
ourselves or is in a situation unlike those we have been in. A group agent is
automatically an exotic, alien agent, very different from us. Trying to give an
intentional explanation of its behavior is more like explaining the behavior
of a Martian robot than the behavior of another person. Now Martian robot
behavior could certainly be given some sort of intentional agent explanations
if Martian robots were intention agents. But we can't give explanations of
their behavior without learning much more about their inner states, their tools
for interacting with their environments, and the environmental situations
they find themselves in. By contrast, our familiarity with the typical inner
and outer states of agents like ourselves enables us to give explanations of
behavior by finding out only a little more information. Saying that X believes
B and desires D often provides us with the information needed to explain the
activity that ensues when we are talking about non-alien individuals. But giving a group an intentional characterization does not allow us to explain the

group's activities in the same way we can an individual's (without having to gather a great deal more information). It is not wrong to say that the X thinks Y to describe the situation of a group. But one generally needs to do far more to explain how this makes social scenarios occur as they do.

MANY-INDIVIDUALS-DO-Y EXPLANATIONS

We've seen that while Y is what the X do (as a custom/norm) can be a good description of what is going on in a group, this does not necessarily provide one with a good explanation of what makes Y happen. We've just seen that saying that the X group (as a whole) believes or desires Y is unlikely to provide a good explanation of social circumstances (though it might well be an adequate description of the state of the X group). Suppose, however, that the speaker is trying to tell us that a lot of X do Y (the speaker is making a "many individuals" family claim), and that that is why certain things happen. I'll now discuss why saying that the X do Y in the sense that many members of the X group do Y is also unlikely to provide us with good explanations of what behavior will ensue. Claims about many members of the X group doing or thinking Y will suffer from many of the same shortcomings of the other two X-do-Y interpretations and some other ones as well.

The first problem is that even within the "many individuals" family, X-do-Y statements are somewhat ambiguous. Recall from chapter 2 that the rules of our language allow us to say that the X do Y when most of the X do, when a plurality do, when it's surprising that some of the X do, when the X and no other groups do to that extent, when a particular subgroup of the X do, and when one wants to caricature the activities of the X group. If we want to know what social state affairs will happen or why a certain state did happen, we will often need to know if it was a majority, a plurality, or just some of the X that previously did Y. Different things could well result from each of these different antecedents. Just knowing that Romanians wished the longtime leader Ceauşescu to be gone cannot begin to tell us why he was overthrown without our knowing whether this fact referred to a majority of Romanians feeling this, a majority of certain subset of Romanians wishing for this, the surprising (to some) fact that there were some Romanians that felt like this, or whether there were more Romanians, as opposed to neighboring Bulgarians who wished Ceauşescu to be gone. Because X-do-Y statements are so vague, they can truthfully describe a very large range of situations. But because such statements can describe so many different antecedent situations, knowing merely that we have one of the X-do-Y situations doesn't give us enough information about which antecedent circumstances we have to enable us to explain how the antecedent helped cause the subsequent social situation we want to account for.

But suppose however we were lucky enough to be able to tell from the context that a speaker making an X-do-Y statement was indicating that, say, a plurality of the X do Y. Some of the problems we discussed in the previous section might well still be with us.

Coming to know certain of the beliefs, desires, and even actions of every member of the X group needs to be supplemented by more information if we want to use that to predict or explain even what a typical X member will cause to happen in his or her local environment. For knowing what an X member will do, because of a desire or belief requires knowing a) the other beliefs, desires, and actions of the X member, b) the tools he or she has at his or her disposal, and c), the kind of environment the X member is interacting with. If the X members are like ourselves, and the circumstances each is in are typical ones that we are familiar with, we may well know these things. If they are different from us and in very different circumstances from us, then we won't. Knowing the beliefs and desires of typical Xs by itself is not enough.

And even if we know what local effects a typical X member will produce when she believes or acts a certain way, that will not tell us what the global net effect of many Xs acting this way will be unless we know how many X members are acting, and how each person and his or her immediate environment are organized vis-à-vis the other X-members and their environments. If a plurality of the town of Oceanview fishes on Sundays, we won't know how many fish are likely to be caught unless we know (among other things) how many fishermen there are. Not only that, it matters whether these fishermen bunch together or spread out when they fish. If they bunch together, it matters whether they are organized in a circle, making it hard for fish to escape, or whether they are arranged in a random way. We won't know these things, however, if we know only what a plurality of individual X members tend to do.

Now suppose, though, that we know that so long as any percentage larger than 20 percent of the X do some Y, then Z will happen (e.g., at least 20 percent of the Puska tribe are herders, so when they move into a region the grass gets overgrazed). Wouldn't it be the case, here, that we would be able to explain why that result happens simply on the basis knowing that the X do Y?

I think that if, whenever over 20 percent of the X does Y, you get Z, then you could indeed explain why Z happens by saying that the X did Y—causing Z to happen. Still, you can only explain this way if you somehow are able to know that the statement that the X do Y can really be taken as providing the information that at least 20 percent of the X do Y—rather than one of the other possible X-do-Y interpretations: say, the Pushka are herders as an entertaining caricature, or that it's only a percentage of a prominent subgroup of Pushka that are herders, or that it's a surprising fact that some Pushka's herd cattle, or that the Pushka herd more cattle than comparable groups do. The existence of these other possible interpretations means that you can't even interpret an X-do-Y statement as saying that at least 20 percent of the X do Y.

But what if, finally, someone claims that one could explain Z on the basis of any of the X-do-Y claims being true. I doubt this claim could be explanatory for several reasons. First, some X-do-Y statements are just not in the business of saying what the Xs Y-doing achieves. One class of X-do-Y statements, for example, is just aiming to call attention to the fact that there are, surprisingly some Xs that do Y (Burmese women who wear a tower of rings to elongate their neck). It doesn't give enough information about the amount of Y-doing to make almost any causal claims. And a caricature claim is just aiming to amuse. Next, the different kinds of X-do-Y statements have such different meanings that it is very unlikely that we are likely to have any uniform effect Z, as the result of X doing Y, in the different senses of X doing Y. If they all really did have the same effect, then that same effect is more likely the result of something else continually being the case in the different X-do-Y situations at hand, rather than it having to be the result of one or another kind of X-do-Y situation. Finally, if it really was the case that either the X do Y (surprise class), or the X do Y (distinctiveness class) or the X do Y (plurality class), etc. that is causally responsible for Z, then we are back to the disjunction problem we saw earlier. It's unclear that a disjunction can really cause, as opposed to one or another of the particular disjuncts really being the cause in a given case.

As with the norm and the group-as-agent interpretations, then, it seems that interpreting an X-do-Y statement in the many-individuals-do-Y way may provide us with adequate descriptive knowledge of something, but is unlikely to provide us information that takes us very far toward explaining social phenomena.

X-do-Y statements can be used for many purposes. Among those purposes is telling people that the X people do Y, in order to explain why some social state of affairs occurs. In this chapter, I have tried to show that whatever else such statements can accomplish, they tend to be very poor at helping to explain why a given part of the social world is as it is. If social scientists and others really want to explain why certain social states of affairs exist, they are generally going to have to say much more than that it is because the Xs do Y.

NOTES

1. There are numerous different ways in which different explanations can be thought of as competing with each other in some sense. For example, some might say one explanation competes favorably with another if it is simpler. Others claim that we should prefer explanations that best cohere with other well-established theories (see Sklar 1985; Leiter 2007). In this chapter, I will be using a much more stringent conception of competition. I am most interested here in explanations that compete in the strong sense such that they can't both be true at the same time.

If one is suspicious of truth, many of the same arguments I give here can work with the closest analog ones favors (e.g., being highly globally warranted). So two different accounts don't compete, on this view, if they can both be highly warranted.

2. The permissiveness of terms like "norm" or "custom" makes things a little tricky here. We might well say Bill's solitary rational behavior was still an example of something that was a custom because that behavior is widespread in a population. But we wouldn't say it was done "out of custom" or caused or explained by custom. And it would not be caused in the way that custom behaviors prototypically are, by imitation or perceived social pressure. In this chapter, I am focusing on behaviors that are explained to be as they are on the basis of there being a custom or norm to behave a certain way. Behaviors that can be classified as being instances of a norm merely because they are widespread in a population can sometimes be called norms or customs, but they are not considered prototypical norms, and they will not be the type of norm explanation we are discussing here.

3. With accounts like this, what is being given by one of the speakers is a salient subset of the (much larger) total set of causal facts accounting for a general kind of situation, Y.

The speaker with that focus is concentrating on explaining only why we have this general type of situation. She may not be interested in explaining the more particular subtype of situation that discussants have mentioned, or she may think that the additional facts that could be added to explain the more particular subtype are already well known to the listener. But what we have, at any rate, is a situation where, in addition to giving an explanation of the general kind of situation Y, we are also giving an explanation of part of the more particular subkind of situation Y_1, and we are also giving part of the explanation of the subkind, situation Y_1. It's little surprise that it is difficult to be clear about exactly what is being accounted for.

4. There are, however, ways in which Fred and Nelly could hold views close to these, which we could nevertheless view as having noncompeting accounts. Similar to the dessert case described above, Nelly might hold that scarlet was responsible for the charging, but this need not compete with Fred's belief that merely being red was responsible, since Nelly could be explaining the cause of that exact act of bull charging, while Fred is explaining only why some or other type of charging had to take place.

A more subtle way of noncompeting is for Fred and Nelly to differ only in the range of counterfactual possibilities they are interested in countenancing. Fred could believe that what had to happen for the bull to charge was for there to be an instancing of some or other member of the set of possible things that could have made the bull charge in those circumstances—with this set consisting of all kinds of shades of red. Nelly could agree with Fred that instancing any member of a certain large set of possible effectors is what we should label as "the cause" of the charging in these circumstances. Nelly and Fred, however, might be thinking of narrower and wider senses, respectively of "possible effectors in these circumstances." Nelly could be thinking of the set of properties whose instancing could cause the charging in a narrow set of possible worlds (ones in which Ned's hat was scarlet, as it is in the actual world). In Nelly's view, it might well be the case that any shade of red would have caused a bull to charge, but the only shade that the hat could have been, in worlds with pasts like ours, is scarlet. In the circumstances being discussed, thinks Nelly, the only thing that could have made the bull charge was seeing an instance of scarlet. No other potential causers could have been instanced in these circumstances, so we can't talk about it being an instancing of a larger set (like those with other shades of red) that caused that charging. Fred could agree with all this, but say that he wants to describe what would counterfactually (and causally) happen, given a larger set of possible worlds. Fred and Nelly could agree that neither's decision about the range of possible worlds they are considering is privileged. So they need have no disagreement about what the counterfactual and causal facts are, regarding various different sets of possibilities.

5. Other ambitious defenses of disjunctive causes include:

- The possibility that we are better off using an epistemic notion of explanation or cause, where we still have a pretty good explanation if we've narrowed the cause down to either A or B, even if we can't narrow it any further.
- The possibility that it's a brute fact about nature that disjunctive natural kinds exist.
- The idea that the arguments against disjunctive causes tend to presuppose there can't be disjunctive effects—a presupposition without support that unfairly biases people against disjunctive causes. If we think there can be a "P or Q" event, then we're more likely to think that "L or M" can cause it.

6. A good real life example of someone making an argument like this can be found in economist Tim Harford's (2008) book, *The Logic of Life*:

But "black culture" doesn't explain why the single moms are disproportionately in the states where lots of young black men are in prison. Economics does: women's bargaining power is badly dented by the imprisonment of potential husbands. The better-educated guys stay out of jail, and they are smart enough to realize that with the competition locked up, they don't have to get married to enjoy themselves. "Culture" is no explanation; that women respond rationally to a tough situation is a much better one. (73)

7. Of course, the circumstances we'd need to explain, here, are circumstances besides the group as a whole tending to do Y. It would be circular to explain why the group tends to do Y by saying the group tends to do Y.

Chapter Six

Final Thoughts: Statements about Groups and Stereotyping

In this book we've looked at various claims that are described using the general form, *the X [people] do Y*. Such statements are ubiquitous in our conversations and even in specialized social science. People make important decisions on the basis of such statements. Yet such statements are undeniably vague and in many quarters they are regarded with suspicion and/or seen as likely instances of unjustified stereotyping. In this book we've looked at ways in which such statements are and aren't able to provide us with useful information. Over the course of these chapters, I've delivered a somewhat mixed verdict about what statements of this sort can tell us. Here is a quick listing of the main findings of this book thus far:

1. X-do-Y statements (e.g., "Bolivians run up debt"), whether they are about individuals in the X group doing Y, a group as a whole doing Y, or a custom of Y-doing existing, tend not to be very useful for explaining why things happen. Without a lot of additional knowledge, such statements tend not to enable us to know enough about the makeup of the X group being discussed or about the group's environment to understand why a certain result occurs. If social scientists and others really want to explain why certain social states of affairs exists, they are generally going to have to say much more than that it is because the X do Y.

2. Even if such statements are not very good at explaining, they need not be untrue descriptions. X-do-Y phrases have truth conditions that are not difficult to satisfy. Even statements about the goals and representations of groups could be literally true and not merely metaphorical.

3. Despite the truthfulness of X-do-Y statements, their vagueness and ambiguity make it hard to know what is being described.

4. Despite this vagueness and ambiguity, there are, nevertheless, many social/linguistic rules regarding when such phrases can be used. We can

179

use these rules and various contextual information to help determine more precisely what a speaker really has in mind when uttering an X-do-Y phrase.

Such phrases, in other words, are neither as useless nor as useful as they may seem at first blush. We shouldn't rely on them to really give us good explanations of much. But they are not merely unjustified or metaphorical generalizations either. We looked at how groups really could have goals and representations in certain conditions. We found that people claim that the X do Y in a norm/custom sense when they think that people in the X do Y because these group members think that other group members do Y. We found that it tends not to be permissible to say that the X do Y if there are merely some X members who do Y, but it is permissible if a plurality do Y. Knowing what is permissible to say in various circumstances can help us work backwards to what people tend to be believing when they make certain utterances, and then back further still to what is likely true.

Yet it's not unlikely that some readers will find it hard to shake the belief that such statements have very little value. Of what use are statements about groups if you can't explain behavior with such statements? And isn't there just something wrong with making sweeping general statements about a group that gloss over differences between individuals in this group? Let's finish by saying something about these concerns.

THE EPISTEMIC VALUE OF X-DO-Y STATEMENTS

If X-do-Y statements can't be used to explain behavior, what good are these phrases? We need to start by remembering that there's a number of ways in which we can improve our knowledge. When someone tells us truthfully that the X do Y (and this, as we've seen, can easily be a true statement), and we didn't know this previously, then our knowledge is improved. Our knowledge is also improved when the facts we learn are better justified. And phrasing claims a certain way can enable the information contained to be very efficiently stored (and communicated). Even though these phrases are vague and ambiguous our knowledge really can sometimes be improved in one or another of these ways when we hear X-do-Y statements. I'll now discuss how.

When we hear someone say that the X do Y, some new beliefs are created in us or some old beliefs are confirmed. If the person is speaking sincerely, we know some things about what the speaker believes. If we have good reasons to believe that speaker has beliefs that are true, we probably know some things about the world. What do we likely know? Well, whatever else we know, we know that people in the X group are disposed to engage in a Y-doing activity. We might not know whether it's people collectively or individually who are so disposed, and we may not know if this disposition is there because of what others are doing. But we do know that, among this group of people, there is at least the minimal property of a likely disposition toward Y-doing. If we know that, we are ahead of the game compared to people who don't know that. Furthermore, while vague general facts can contain less information than more specific facts, they do have the advantage of being more easily justified, since they have less stringent truth conditions. Having better-justified beliefs is one aspect of having better knowledge.

But, in addition to coming to have a justified true belief about this minimal general property, learning that the X do Y can help us come to know some things with more specificity as well. When we come to know that the X do Y, we also know implicitly that it is very likely that either a number of individuals in the X group do Y, or that the members of the X group collectively do Y, or the X group has a custom of doing Y. We may not be able to explain anything with a disjunctive fact like this. But anytime we know that what we have lies within a relatively small range of possibility (three likely options), we know much more than we do if we know only that it's within a much larger range of comparable options. Furthermore, knowing the minimal fact of Xs doing Y can easily serve as a base that more knowledge can be *added to* to give us a more thorough representation of what is there. Perhaps we start off knowing people in the X group are Y-doing, but then we come to know that the Y-doing is a collective activity—something achieved by each individual doing some other activity. We might add to this information about how many X people we are talking about and how they are organized. We might add information about the tools they have at their disposal and about what kind of environment they are embedded in. This extra information added to the X-do-Y base could enable us to have a more thorough representation of what is going on. With sufficient information added to the base, we might even come to have a good explanation of why what happens, happens. The original information may be minimal, but it could be structured such that information can potentially be added to it to create a thorough, maybe even explanatory, account of resulting events.

And, indeed, not only are X-do-Y claims such that additional information could easily be added to them. They are often made in the context of certain assumed background knowledge and additional conversational cues, such that additional information often is provided, implicitly or explicitly, to create more thorough representations of the social facts. When someone says "Las Vegans are into belly dancing these days," the "these days" shows we are probably not talking about a tradition or custom. And formulating the name Las Vegans in this way signals that one is unlikely to be talking about a group as a holistic agent. Furthermore, as we discussed in chapter 2, common background knowledge and the context of the conversation likely indicate that what the person was talking about was not large percentages of the total population of the city, but large numbers of the subgroup of Las Vegans who take exercise classes in gyms. X-do-Y statements by themselves may be vague and ambiguous, but they are often accompanied by additional information or given in a context that enables a listener to understand that the speaker is making a much more precise claim—one that may provide a great deal of useful information.

Epistemic Value through Subsumption

One other way that using X-do-Y phrases, along with background and contextual information, can help us understand and represent the world is that the use of subsumption in these phrases can provide a relatively efficient means of storing and sharing information. Let's assume that, as we've described above, X-do-Y phrases, in context, can give us important information—either of minimal features, disjunctive sets, or more specific scenarios. As beings that need to have a great deal of social information, our fundamental epistemic challenge is to gather as much information like this as we can and to store it and share it as efficiently as possible. Using general subsumptive representational schemes—like X do Y—descriptions, enables us to communicate more quickly, access information more quickly, save computational time and energy, and save memory space by keeping us from having to separately record similar information over and over again. Such subsumptive representations can also save memory space by avoiding storing certain details.

"Subsumption" is a general term for what happens when an information processor takes a larger set of signals (sensory perceptions, motor procedure signals, symbols, etc.) and converts it to a smaller set of signals. "Cluster subsumption" is what we can call a large number of different items, connected to each other in space or time, represented by a single concept. "Type subsumption" is what we call a number of discernibly different properties (wherever they may be in space and time) that are represented by the same concept. These sorts of subsumption are often combined, and both can save a great many resources for agents. A cluster concept can save time, for example, when agents communicate using a label that represents a concatenated cluster, rather than explicitly naming each detail of the cluster. Consider the amount of time saved when an agent makes use of "cluster subsumption" to communicate to an agent that a particular snake, Sammy, is present. Without a subsumptive concept it might take hours for a speaker to describe and the listener to hear about the entire array of basic physical properties that compose Sammy the snake's body. Using a subsumptive label, however, Agent

#1 could take a detailed representation of Sammy, utter the words "Sammy the snake" and enable Agent #2 to create the same representation using some type of "decoding" device. This act of communication takes a fraction of the resources that would have been required to create the representation in the listener by describing one physical bit at a time. We get the same sort of savings when, instead of naming each member of the Boston Philharmonic Orchestra and describing the color of their clothes we use an X-do-Y phrase and say "The Boston Philharmonic dresses in black for every concert."

Subsumptive representations also save storage space, in that the agent can represent things in memory by using only that concept, rather than the entire array of entities and properties that that concept represents. A person acquires a "type subsumptive" concept by utilizing a symbol or signal that can be used to mark the presence, not only of a particular entity or arrangement, but also of other arrangements identical or highly similar to the first. Memory is saved because the complicated arrangement represented by the concept need only be stored in a single place in memory and referred back to, instead of having to represent that whole space-hogging representation over and over again in memory. For example, an agent can represent where carbon is present by noting that fact with some sort of carbon symbol instead of storing information about the complex arrangement of electrons, protons, and neutrons that make up the carbon atoms in each particular place. An agent can compactly store all the instances of the presence of the subatomic arrangement with a subsuming carbon symbol, and extract the details that this subsuming symbol represents only when she needs them. One could do the same thing with a representation of the type, orchestra.

One especially good way to save representational resources is by having very general subsumptive terms, and combining them together in layers to provide more specific information. To begin with, we can increase memory savings by allowing type concepts to be less stringent regarding the range of things to which the concept applies. The stringent label "glucose," for example, refers to a certain arrangement of carbon, hydrogen and oxygen molecules. The less stringent label "sugar" refers to both monosaccharides like glucose and disaccharides like sucrose and lactose. The even more tolerant "type of type" concept "carbohydrate" refers to sugars, starches, or any molecular arrangement that follows the general $Cx(H20)x$ schematic arrangement. Using less stringent terms can save memory space in a number of different ways. Take a concept mentally defined as applying to those things that possess a large set of features (e.g., a dog has four legs, fur, a snout, etc.). Each of those features in turn might possess its own large set of features (a snout is a protuberance from the face, with a nose on the end and a mouth running its length . . .). One can make a concept less stringent by removing some of its satisfaction conditions—or removing some of the conditions of the conditions. The less stringent "rectangle" concept, for example, can be made by removing the "equal side-length" requirement from the "square" concept. A concept that is less stringent in this way takes up less memory space in its original definition storage. A less stringent concept can also take up less initial memory storage space, if the agent simply does not store the lower-level defining features of defining features. An agent, for example, might have a less stringent concept of "brick wall" by defining "brick" as a rectangular cube of burned clay but store very little information about what it means to be a unit of clay. By making "definition trees" of smaller width or depth, an agent can save a lot of memory space.

Now a less stringent concept needn't always take up less storage space with an initial definition than a more stringent one (e.g., why should we suppose the mental mechanisms for representing "blue" must take up less space than those for representing "indigo"?). But even though it may take no less memory space to initially define a less stringent type, less stringent types (including types of types) can still ultimately enable agents to represent things in the world using far less storage space than reductive or more stringent subsumptive representations do. All type concepts save memory space by enabling an agent to avoid having to create a new description "from scratch" of every arrangement we might want to represent. But the more stringently an agent defines her type concepts, the more memory space she has to take up defining different type concepts for slightly different arrangements of properties. (An agent, for example, could conceivably have different concepts for five different subtypes of fructose). The use of less stringent types, on the other hand, means more things can be described using fewer concepts.

We use less memory space by not taking up the space to define new concepts. Consider the less stringent type "hammer." This concept is such that numerous different arrangements count as examples of a hammer. The less stringent the concept is, the more things we can store in memory, with the description "hammer there," (referring back to a singly-stored hammer definition), and the fewer hammer-resembling arrangements we have to describe by naming the piece-by-piece arrangements of component parts. A piece-by-piece description not only takes up lots of memory space, but also takes up more memory space each time it must be given. Now another way we could take up less memory space than using piece-by-piece descriptions is to create lots of different stringent concepts for different types of hammers. But we can use even less memory space by not creating these new concepts, and making do with the more generic, less stringent concept "hammer." And if an agent seeks to be more specific about the exact types of hammers that are in various places (ballpeen hammer, claw hammer, rubber hammer), she can do it at a minimal cost in space by adding features to an already-defined, less-stringent concept, rather than having to create numerous new definitions from scratch.

Regarding the case at hand: we can save representational resources by having a non-stringent subsumptive X-do-Y representation that tells us merely that either a number of the individuals in the X group do Y, that the members of the X group collectively do Y, or that the X group has a custom of doing Y. For various purposes, we may only need to know that one or another of these scenarios is the case. Representing (or communicating) more details than this may be more than what's needed for the task at hand. So representing only that one or the other of these scenarios is true is an excellent way not to be using more resources than needed. And if the task does require that we know more detail, this can be represented, like our ballpeen hammer, by adding features to the more general representation. We can use our generic X-do-Y representation, along with implicit or explicit background cues which tell us which of the three X-do-Y situations it is. Other background information could be used to help make still clearer how many Xs are doing Y and how often. A speaker could even provide enough information in the total of what is said to enable listeners to explain what is happening—this while using only the minimalist resources of X-do-Y representations. Storing beliefs and creating beliefs in others with these phrases, then, while leaving much to be desired in many ways, can also play an important useful role in helping us understand the social world.

THE RIGHTNESS AND WRONGNESS OF X-DO-Y PHRASES

Over the years, as I've talked to people about this book, they very often jump to the conclusion that what this book is all about is coming up with a clear rationale for condemning stereotyping. There's often a feeling that there is something wrong with making sweeping generalizations about groups, and people I talk to can only imagine that any book about such generalizations must be a laundry list of reasons why this must be a bad practice. In the past, I have frequently protested that I'm not looking at normative issues in the sense of saying what speakers ought to say. I tell them that I have been studying the semantics of certain kinds of statements and the underlying metaphysics of certain kinds of social situations, but that I haven't really been looking at the rightness or wrongness of anything. But, given the interest people have in the normative issues regarding generalizations about groups, and given that people will likely try to draw normative conclusions about what I say whether I want them to or not, it's probably wise for me to make some remarks about the normative issues involved here. It's also true that any good normative judgment about the rightness or wrongness of something should be based on a good understanding of what is happening. In that way, the issues discussed in this book are not irrelevant to the normative issues that people often want to focus on. So while normative issues have not been a central focus of this book, I will say a few things about how normative issues regarding statements about groups interface with the kinds of issues I have been talking about.

The prototypical normative issue that people focus on, regarding statements about groups, is stereotyping. Now, a stereotype is, among other things, a belief that all or most of the individual members of some group X have some characteristic Y. The first way in which the semantic and metaphysics issues we have been discussing have a bearing on the issue of stereotyping is that we've seen that when someone makes an X-do-Y statement, that needn't mean that he or she holds a stereotype at all. Our language allows people to sincerely claim that the X do Y when they are not interested in saying anything about individual X members. While the X-do-Y claims from the "many individuals" subfamily of such statements often do say something about the majority of the individuals in the X group, claims in the group-as-agent family and claims in the norm/custom family are usually not about the characteristics of individuals. When an X group as a whole does some Y, this might be accomplished by each individual doing a different task than every other individual. So speakers need not be envisioning each of the X group members doing the same Y. And having a norm, custom, convention, tradition, etc. is something typically done by a group, not an individual. A person making X-do-Y statements, then, may not believe something about the individuals in X, so we can't automatically accuse such speakers of holding a harmful stereotype.

If we want to examine problems with stereotyping, then, we need to look at people making X-do-Y claims that belong mainly to the "many individuals" family. Even in this family, however, note that the idea of all or most of the X doing Y is just one of the six main circumstances in which many individual X-do-Y statements are permissible in our language. In the other five circumstances, people can sincerely claim that the X do Y without believing that all or most of the X do. Recall that people can say that "That football team's members spend more time in jail than on the field," as an entertaining caricature, rather than describing a characteristic that is true of most players. A person can say "Las Vegans are really into belly dancing these days" with it being clear from context that the person is only talking about women taking exercise classes in gyms, rather than most Las Vegans. Speakers will say things like "Burmese women elongate their necks with rings" when they merely find it surprising that a number do, even if they don't believe that most do. Our language allows speakers to say that English soccer fans are hooligans, even as they believe that most English fans are well behaved, as long as they think there is more hooliganism among English fans than other fans. Even when they say that Adams County residents drive pickup trucks with the idea that a plurality does so, there's no implicit commitment to any number doing so. It's just that the residents who drive pickup trucks outnumber residents who drive other types of vehicles. Making an X-do-Y statement, then, need not be indicative of a speaker holding a stereotypical belief about what most X members do. She may mean something else entirely, according to our social/linguistic rules. We should be cautious about condemning a speaker for holding stereotypical beliefs then, merely because she has made an X-do-Y statement. Still, making X-do-Y statements with any of these circumstances in mind (or with norm or group-agent circumstances in mind) could well contribute to listeners coming to believe stereotypes—since the listeners may have trouble disambiguating which of the circumstances the speakers are describing. And if holding stereotypes is problematic, then saying things that cause people to hold stereotypes is potentially problematic as well. Keeping in mind that when someone makes X-do-Y statements, that needn't mean they are stereotyping, let us look at what may be problematic about stereotyping when it does occur.

The notion that stereotypes are inherently problematic is widespread. "The idea that stereotypes are inaccurate and unjustified pervades the social sciences, many educational and business communities, and the everyday discourse of pundits and politicians. . . . It is a common theme in everyday cultural discourse," writes psychologist Yueh-Ting Lee (1995, 4). If one thinks about it, however, it's easy to find the disesteem in which stereotypes are held somewhat baffling. After all, stereotyping is just a type of inductive generalization—making an inference about what a larger group is probably like, based on examining a smaller sample that is usually easier to observe. Making inductive generalizations is a fundamental building block of knowing almost anything about the world. So how can there be anything inherently wrong with making inductive generalizations about people? One thing that makes discussions of these issues problematic is that the term "stereotype" is generally used in a pejorative way. This means that we build into the concept of stereotype the idea that someone holding them is doing something epistemically or morally wrong. If we think of stereotypes as wrongly held by definition, then we have already decided before doing any investigation that there must be something wrong with them. This isn't very conducive to freely investigating, what, if anything, is wrong with stereotypes. So as not to prejudge the issues this way, I'll avoid, when necessary, using the inherently pejorative "stereotype" in favor of looking for possible problems regarding the more neutrally described "generalizations about group members."

When thinking about what might be wrong with making generalizations about group members, we should start by separating *epistemic* normative judgments from *moral* normative judgments. Questions about epistemic normative matters concern when we have enough evidence to justify our belief in something. Questions about moral norms look at whether something is the ethically wrong thing to do, say, or think. Let's consider epistemic matters here first.

Epistemic Issues Regarding Stereotyping

A central way in which people come to hold stereotypes is that they informally make what is formally called an inductive generalization. An inductive generalization is made when someone reasons that, because some percentage of an observed group of Xs have property Y, then that same percentage of the group of Xs as a whole have Y. The first point that should be made about inductive generalizations is that there's nothing inherently epistemically wrong about making them about people. Indeed, doing so is a near necessity. If we didn't routinely make inductive generalizations about people, toddlers wouldn't be able to learn that humans can usually speak while other things do not, that children are consistently smaller than adults, or even that that woman with certain characteristics will consistently be the thing that can nurse me. Making inductive generalizations about the world around us is as natural and necessary as eating. What's problematic, as we saw in chapter 2, is that it's easy to do inductive generalizing badly: Psychologists and journalists alike have documented how common it is for people to make a bad hasty generalization, based on a small unrepresentative sample. And even a large sample is an unreliable guide to understanding a larger group if it is a biased sample. But it's easy for people to miss that the sampled group is unrepresentative, as the pollsters who mistakenly called the 1948 election for Dewey eventually realized. (The pollsters missed the fact that Dewey supporters owned telephones more often so were more frequently called than Truman supporters.) People also have a tendency to look for confirming instances of a claim, rather than look for random samples. And they exhibit belief perseverance where they continue to maintain their initial beliefs, even in the face of contrary evidence.

Now none of these cases show that there is anything inherently epistemically wrong with forming generalizations about X-group members on the basis of some X-group members. If the observed X-group members form a large random sample of the group as a whole, the inferences one makes about the group as a whole based on observed members are likely to be true. But we do have to remember that people have strong predispositions to make poor inductive generalizations in various circumstances. When someone makes a general statement about a group, we should remember that a high percent of inferences about groups are made in error. Given this, while we should not automatically assume the claim is likely untrue, we should also not automatically assume the claim is likely true. Claims about what most X members are likely to do are not automatically on epistemically poor grounds. But if we want to trust them, we are better off going the extra mile to make sure that they are on epistemically good grounds. Given how error-prone people are, we shouldn't automatically take a person's belief that most of the X do Y (or even lots of people's beliefs that the X do Y) as being good evidence that most of the X indeed do Y. Epistemically, there's nothing inherently wrong with generalizations about groups. Given human cognitive foibles, however, we are justified in being cautious and skeptical about accepting stereotypical claims without independently verifying them.

A similar cautious stance should be taken regarding beliefs about individuals that people come to have based on general, possibly stereotypical, beliefs about characteristics of the group. Reasoning about individuals on the basis of beliefs about most of a group is an instance of a formal category called statistical syllogism. We reason with statistical syllogisms when we infer that if a high percentage of the F group have or are property G, and if a P is an F, then P is probably a G. If 80 percent of the items at the Seven-Eleven are usually more expensive than things at Mighty Mart, then hot dog buns are likely to be more expensive at the Seven-Eleven. If 80 percent of the UNLV international students club are not American citizens, odds are good that Amir, a club member, is not an American citizen. Like inductive generalizations, there is nothing inherently epistemically wrong with using statistical syllogisms in reasoning. Indeed, such reasoning is a central, necessary, and often accurate part of everyday thinking. And there is nothing inherently epistemically unjustified in making such syllogistic inferences about people like Amir. We must remember, however, that, like inductive generalizations, it's easy to make errors regarding statistical syllogisms. We need to remember that our confidence about individual cases should wane as the percentage of the group having a trait becomes smaller. (We can be much less confident that Amir is not an American citizen if only 60 percent rather than 80 percent of the group are not citizens.) The most common way errors are made is by neglecting what is called the "requirement of total evidence" (see Salmon 2001). When we are reasoning using statistical syllogisms, we must use whatever statistical information we have about any of the classes that the individual we are reasoning about is in. If we know that Amir was born in the United States and that nearly all people born in the United States hold U.S. citizenship, we can't ignore that fact and reason that he must not be an

American citizen based on the high percentage of non-citizens in the UNLV International Students Club. Because neglecting the requirement of total evidence can cause people to make epistemic errors about individuals, we need to be cautious about making inferences about individuals based on what we know about the groups they belong to. But from a pure epistemic standpoint, it is not inherently unjustified to make an inference about an individual based on general information about the group she is in. If there is something wrong with doing so, the problem is more likely to be moral than epistemic. Let's now say something about moral matters here.

Stereotyping and Morality

We saw in the last section that stereotyping is a form of inductive generalization, and that there is nothing inherently wrong, epistemically, with making inductive generalizations, as long as it is done carefully. But is there something morally wrong with generalizations about groups? Let me begin by saying that, while I want to say a few things about moral matters here, this book is not a work of moral philosophy. Questions about the morality of stereotyping are very complex and likely require a book length treatment of their own. What I'll do in what follows is to lay out what some of the main moral issues regarding stereotyping might be. I'll try to make moral judgments only when I think there are clear commonsensical judgments to be made. Questions about what is the morally right thing to do regarding murky complex questions about stereotyping I'll leave to others. For simplicity and clarity's sake, I'll also concentrate on negative stereotypes, even though there are interesting moral questions regarding positive stereotypes as well (e.g., is there something morally questionable about saying that Asian kids are smart?).

The first thing to say about negative stereotypes is something quite straightforward. Except in extraordinary circumstances, it is epistemically and morally wrong to make negative generalizations about groups that you have good reason to believe are probably untrue. A basic moral principle that most of us share is that it is usually wrong to knowingly say untrue statements about people. One shouldn't say things like "Mexicans are thieves" if one knows that most Mexicans are not.

The next most important thing to point out about negative generalizations about groups is that, whether they are untrue or true, people believing them raises the probability of various harms coming to group members. Harms can come to the group as a whole, but also to individual group members when people combine negative beliefs about the group with syllogistic reasoning that leads them to believe those bad things are likely true about the individual members of that group. What harms? Well, at one extreme, there is just the psychological harm done to a person simply by being looked at with suspicion or scorn. People usually want the respect and esteem of their fellows. A person likely feels some psychological pain that is every bit as bad as a cut or scrape (and maybe quite a bit worse) if he is looked at suspiciously because he is of Hispanic descent and a certain set of people believes "Mexicans are thieves."[1] At the other extreme, we sometimes have wars or massacres partly as a result of people holding stereotypes like "Jews want to control the financial world." In between these extremes are the harms that come from things like discrimination in employment and schooling. If group A members widely believe that group B members are lazy, then group A members are simply less likely to offer jobs to group B members than to members of other groups. While we may want to think that "sticks and stones may break my bones but words will never hurt me," it's a simple truth that people making derogatory statements about another group will raise the probability of group members being harmed in one way or another.

Now the fact that making negative generalizations can harm people is a strong reason not to do so. But, by itself, it is not yet a definitive reason not to do so. Giving someone an automobile raises the probability of their getting into an accident, but that doesn't mean that no one should ever do it. One might well hold the position that, however costly negative generalizations are in the harms they can cause people, it's worth it to pay those costs in order to avoid the costs of having to condemn all negative generalizations as immoral. One extreme version of this view would be the position that, whatever harms negative generalizations cause (and perhaps however false they may be), a person should be able to say whatever one wants and no one should condemn her for saying it. In a recent *New York Times* article, a well known blogger expressed a version of this sentiment: "At some point I'd grown accustomed to the idea that there was a public place where I would always be allowed to write, without supervision, about how I felt. Even having to take into account someone else's feelings about being written about felt like being stifled in some essential way. As Henry and I fought, I kept coming back to the idea that I had a right to say whatever I wanted" (Gould 2008). When stated so baldly, it's easy to see what's wrong with the idea (as even this blogger eventually realized). While in the United States we grant people the legal right to say whatever they wish within certain limits (e.g., people are still sued for libel), that doesn't mean we should feel no moral qualms for saying certain things. It is rude and offensive to say to a coworker, "Wow, you are really looking old and ugly these days," or "Jeez, your breasts look terrific." We would not accept someone's proclaiming, "Saying such things was the right thing to do because I believed they were true." Nor would we usually think anyone was doing the wrong thing by saying, "You know, talking like that is really uncalled for." We tend to believe that it is sometimes more moral to condemn people for saying offensive things than to avoid being at all censorious. And we often feel it is more important to protect people's feelings (or avoid other harms) than to make sure we volunteer honest statements about anything we believe. If we want to defend making derogatory generalizations about groups, we will need a stronger defense than "I should be able to say whatever I think, whatever harms it may cause."[2] That view violates a number of moral principles that nearly every group holds dear.

At the other extreme from "I should be able to make any stereotypical statement regardless of who it harms," is the claim "People should never make derogatory generalizations about groups, regardless of how true they are believed to be, or what social good could come of making such statements." There are many good reasons for disagreeing with such a view. But this view is actually much less implausible than the other extreme just discussed. As we noted above, most of us tend to think making certain statements would be wrong, almost regardless of the circumstances. It's hard to think of a situation, for example, where we would think it was morally unproblematic to say to a coworker he looks old and ugly. We tend to think that certain statements are likely to cause too much harm to justify making them. Now some people believe that most derogatory statements about groups should be in this forbidden class. Derogatory statements can not only give rise to negative beliefs about the group, but also to harms that stem simply from thinking about another group as different from your own. For decades, psychologists have been documenting that people begin to discriminate against out-group members and in favor of their own groups, even for group membership that is randomly assigned (see Tajfel 1970). One of the early studies of this was Sherif's (1966) notorious Robber's Cave State Park experiment in which two groups of twelve-year-old boys in a Boy Scout camp became very hostile toward each other, on the basis of little more than being randomly assigned to different camping groups. The idea that emphasizing certain group difference in and of itself can be morally problematic is inherent in a set of official policies adopted in France. Despite widespread unemployment and other problems, French citizens of African or Arab decent cannot receive anything like American-style affirmative action. In fact, in France, the government and private companies are constitutionally prohibited from even gathering statistical data on ethnic groups. This is perhaps unsurprising in a country where people still remember how, under the Vichy regime, police statistics were used to strip Jews of their citizenship and deport them. The idea that making derogatory statements about groups is a moral wrong, then, is an idea that has a lot of support in various quarters, and has decent arguments in favor of it.[3]

But there are also a number of good arguments, in favor of permitting derogatory statements about groups, if there's good evidence that such claims are true. Perhaps the strongest argument is that statements can sometimes help a group to make changes regarding traits that they themselves regard as negative. A speaker might say, "20 percent of French Muslims are underemployed," not to denigrate such groups, but in order to start exploring ways to change that unemployment rate. Someone might comment that "black children tend to score 15 points lower on standardized tests than white children" not to disparage the intelligence of African Americans, but as part of a discussion about how to improve the education system or to improve testing. If all negative generalizations about groups must be considered morally off-limits, then it will be much harder to work on concrete plans to benefit groups that have various disadvantages and problems.

Another argument for not avoiding negative generalizations about groups, one that often goes along with the first, is that socially stigmatizing certain traits can sometimes benefit society as a whole. Pointing out that certain groups tend to have certain traits widely regarded as undesirable can play a big role in getting people to rid themselves of these traits. While few beyond the most bigoted believe, in their considered judgments, that it would be just and fair to condemn people for traits they can't help but have (e.g., physical slowness in the aged), most believe that condemnation is socially appropriate for behaviors and attitudes we, as a society, hope to change. If it were really true that nearly all of the members of the Golden Hill Country Club were anti-Semitic for example, would it be wrong to say, "The GHCC is full of anti-Semites"? Calling attention to a trait that most group members genuinely have by making a generalization about the prevalence of that trait in the group can be an important step toward creating pressures on that group to change. (Of course, the principle of honesty requires one qualify that not all group members have this trait if all don't share it.) It would be more difficult to create such social pressures if we adopted a blanket moral prohibition on making negative generalizations about groups. Now, of course, the benefits of such social pressures have to be weighed against the possible harms or rights violations of labeling people and of causing there to be pressures on the group to change when they may not want to. But it does not seem reasonable to assume at the outset that labeling this way is never worth the possible benefits.

One might also argue that, regardless of whether a group benefits in any way from other groups saying negative things about them, other groups benefit just from knowing that a negatively regarded feature is truly present among most members of certain groups. Indeed, one might go even further and argue that, regardless of whether there is any benefit to anyone, knowledge is intrinsically valuable. It's important for people to know the truth about what is out there in the social world. And if it takes people making negative statements about groups to produce more knowledge, then so be it.

I think that, together, these three arguments make a strong case for the moral permissibility of sometimes making negative statements about groups, if such statements are true. I've said little about what kinds of groups, what kind of traits, and in what conversational contexts such statements should be considered most permissible. Here there is lots of room for more exploration and debate. Indeed, while I think a strong case should be made for not saying never regarding such statements, even here, the existence of plausible arguments against making any such statements means that this issue, too, should be vigorously debated.

We've been discussing whether it's morally permissible to make negative generalizations about groups when such statements are likely true. What about when it's unclear whether such statements are true or not? Here, I think it's reasonable to take a similar approach to that taken in law regarding "reasonable doubt." In a criminal trial, the burden of proof is on the prosecutor to prove it is "beyond reasonable doubt" that the accused is indeed guilty of what they are accused of. The idea is that, since punishment causes harm, we must be careful to make very sure that the people being punished deserve it. And we must make it somewhat difficult to establish guilt, for if we made it easy do to so without substantial evidence, then odds are that a fair number of innocent people would end up being falsely convicted on the basis of flimsy evidence. Our desire to avoid this is often summed up in the dictum of the eighteenth century jurist, William Blackstone: "Better that ten guilty persons escape than that one innocent suffers." Before a guilty verdict can be reached, then, a prosecutor must do more than show that the preponderance of evidence suggests that the accused is guilty. She must establish guilt "beyond a reasonable doubt." It seems to me that we should think of negative statements about groups somewhat analogously. Claiming that group members are guilty of having a trait widely regarded as negative can easily result in the harms discussed above. It seems a reasonable moral requirement, then, to ask of people that, if they are going to make negative statements about groups that expose members to various harms, speakers should try to make sure that the truth of such statements is beyond reasonable doubt. We should try to refrain from making negative generalizations about groups unless we are reasonably sure they are true. (And even if we are reasonably sure they are true, what we should do then is debatable, as we have just described.) The same moral instincts that give rise to Blackstone's dictum should lead people to think that it is better to let many negative traits of groups go unremarked upon, than to make negative statements about groups (exposing them to scorn and much worse) when such statements are untrue. I suspect that the word "stereotype" itself is prototypically used for generalizations which we aren't reasonably sure are true, and, given the harms that can result merely from emphasizing differences, are, thus, morally problematic. This is why saying "Latinos score lower on standardized tests" is not a clear instance of a stereotype, while "Latinos are less intelligent" is.

A related issue that legal theory can give us guidance on is the legitimacy of making claims about individuals based on the groups that they are members of. In a criminal trial, if a prosecutor tried to obtain a conviction in a child abuse case using little evidence other than an expert witness's claim that fathers are twice as likely to be abusers as mothers, the judge would likely disbar such evidence on the grounds that it was either irrelevant, prejudicial or both (using Federal Rules of Evidence 401 and 403). The underlying worry here is that, given that it's very easy to ignore the requirement of total evidence when doing syllogistic reasoning, it's easy to wrongly think one has good reason to believe that Jim has X, if 80 percent of Jim's group has X. In legal reasoning, the consensus seems to be that Blackstone's dictum says that we need to be especially vigilant about factors that are likely to make us judge some innocent people as guilty, so we need to be very wary of using statistical information to help us make judgments about individuals. In the everyday moral realm, I think it's reasonable for us to be similarly hesitant about using statistical information in our judgments about what to say about individuals. We should be very reluctant to claim, given no other evidence, that Mr. Hamata is probably a lousy weight lifter, if the Japanese tend to be poor weightlifters. And in general, the more negatively the trait is regarded, the more reluctant we should be to ascribe it to an individual, simply on the statistical syllogistic evidence.

If we say that it is reasonable to make it morally incumbent upon people to try to make sure their negative generalizations about groups are true beyond a reasonable doubt before saying them, how certain should "beyond reasonable doubt" be? This issue is highly unsettled in legal theory. But we would do well to pay attention to Larry Laudan's suggestion: "There is nothing nature- or God-given about the height of a standard of proof. Rather, its height reflects a collective decision on our part to place the threshold at one point rather than another. That decision may be whimsical or it might be well thought out. The practical question, of course, is how demanding to make it" (2006, 64). My view is that we should be fairly flexible with this standard. It could fluctuate based on what kinds of harms and benefits are likely to come from making such generalizations. If there's great social benefit, either to groups themselves or to other groups knowing that group members likely possess the trait considered undesirable, then we need not set the standard of reasonable doubt way above the preponderance of evidence (especially if the likely harms are not especially great). On the other hand, if making negative generalizations about a group would likely involve grave harms to group members, and there's little social benefit to anyone from believing these generalizations, then it seems not unreasonable to think speakers are morally required to have very strong evidence for such claims before making them. Working out how high we should make the burden of proof for making negative generalizations about groups in various circumstances will be an important task for anyone wanting a good systematic theory of the morality of stereotyping.[4]

I have only scratched the surface here regarding normative issues about statements about groups. But I hope to have pointed out some of the main epistemological and ethical issues people ought to have in mind when thinking about what ought and ought not be said about groups. It is important to remember that someone making an X-do-Y statement need not be holding stereotypical beliefs. But, given that people making such statements can lead others to feel negatively about groups and the people in them, we do need to carefully weigh many considerations in deciding whether and when we ought to make such statements.

The complexities regarding group generalizations pull people in many different directions simultaneously. Psychologically, we are inclined to effortlessly come to many generalizations about groups based on observing a small number of members. Psychologically, we easily come to conclusions about individual members, based on general beliefs about their groups. At the same time, people likely often feel a lot of institutional pressures from authority figures not to make generalizations about groups. They may also feel lots of pressures from local peer groups to make just these generalizations. They may feel that justice demands that people not make statements that are likely to lead to discriminatory behavior, and express revulsion at racial profiling. They may also believe that some ethnic groups are more likely to commit certain crimes, and that honestly facing this problem means that we must feel free to make explicit statements about this. I think the conflictedness people feel about these matters often makes them long for moral certainty and to have clear blanket policies regarding such derogatory generalizations about groups. Consequently you find many people insisting they should be free to say whatever they like about anyone. On the other side, you'll find many people denigrating any such statements about a group as "just a generalization." In this section I have argued that it is not easy to justify many clear blanket rules about what one ought and ought not to say about groups. What we have are lots of epistemic and moral issues, where lots of careful investigation remains to be done. We said earlier that the existence of many problems regarding the semantics of X-do-Y statements does not mean we don't sometimes have good reasons for making such statements. I suggest here that the existence of epistemic and moral problems with such statements also need not mean that we don't sometimes have good reasons for making them.

Statements about what groups do or believe are everywhere in our culture. It's hard to turn on the radio or look at a blog without hearing or seeing a comment about what red or blue states are really interested in. But prone as we are to making such statements, we are confused about how we should regard them. Are people making such statements saying something about groups as a whole or about the individuals in groups? Are they saying something about all group members or just some group members? Are they being literal, or merely entertaining? Is there something epistemically or morally wrong with such statements, or is making them a natural, acceptable, and justified way of describing what's there? In this book I've tried to help make sense of these ubiquitous but confusing statements. I've tried to sort out the different families of things that people can have in mind when they make such statements. I've looked at what kinds of arrangements of people can make it possible for a group as a whole to do things like believe and desire. I've looked at what it means for a group to have a custom or norm present within it. I've looked at ways in which we can and can't use these kinds of statements to help us explain what is going on in the social world. And I've looked at some of the main objections to these statements where it's argued that they are useless or ought not be said for various moral or epistemic reasons.

In the end, I hope to have shown what our practices illustrate that we've, perhaps implicitly, believed all along. Our typical statements about groups don't really tell us as much as we'd like them to. But it's not as if they tell us nothing at all. This is why we continue to make them all the time, but also continue to regard them with suspicion. Perhaps, by clarifying the shortcomings of our current modes of expression, one of the things this book can do is set the stage for developing new ways of talking that don't have these problems. In the meantime, we are stuck speaking and listening to the language we have. But maybe instead of having a default policy of just making these unclear statements while also being reluctant to take them very seriously, we can use the lessons of this book to draw more careful conclusions about what people really are most likely trying to say, and what is likely truly there in the social world when people make such statements. The people around us constantly speak about what the people around us are doing. We know that this is a problematic source of information, but also an invaluable one. I hope this book has helped to concretize and clarify the particular problems with statements about what others do and why they are doing it—problems that we often have only vague suspicions about. But I hope people can also use what I've said about our speaking habits and social structures to help sift through the confusing ubiquitous statements made, and use them to lead us to a greater knowledge of our social world.

NOTES

1. And even if a person does not feel actual psychic pain from other's disesteem, studies have shown that people will actually perform worse on various tasks if they are reminded of negative stereotypes people hold of the group that they belong to. (For example, women will do worse on math tests than women in control groups if they are reminded of the "girls are bad at math" stereotype before taking a test. This internalization of others' stereotypes is called "stereotype threat" (Steele, Spencer, and Aronson, 2002).

2. Few hold expressive freedom to be such a supreme value that one shouldn't even self-censor to curb harms. But there may be people who believe that truth and knowledge are such intrinsic values.

3. Another reason some may have for objecting to negative generalizations about groups is a fear that people will use such generalizations as a basis for making negative inferences about individuals within the group. Such objectors are unlikely to be mollified by the counterargument that inferences that group members must have such traits are unwarranted when the sentence doesn't say that *all* the X have Y. Given that many people will draw such inferences from the generalizations, warranted or not, the objectors reason, it is better not make the generalization at all.

It is also worth noting that even if *all* the X *were* Y, making it true that any given individual X was Y, there are still many of the same grounds for objecting to such statements that we have been making in this section. If thinking about group differences can promote intergroup hostility, the argument goes, perhaps we should refrain from making generalizations about groups in the interest of social peace.

4. So we have different ways of achieving a similar result, in this and earlier paragraphs. We might say that if a negative generalization about a group is almost certainly true, we ought to carefully weight the harms and benefits of making such a statement before deciding whether the claim is morally permissible to state. Alternatively, we could say that if a negative generalization is likely to be beneficial, then we should be less worried about how close to certain we are about it—making it more permissible to make the statement. And if negative generalizations are likely harmful, then we ought to be very reluctant to make them without a lot of proof—making them generally less permissible to say.

Bibliography

Ajzen, I., Fishbein, M., Hewsone, M., et al. 2000. Attitudes and the attitude-behavior relation: Reasoned and automatic process. In *European review of social psychology*, edited by W. Stroebe and M. Hewstone. Chichester, U.K.: Wiley.

Allport, F. H. 1924a. *Social psychology*. Boston: Houghton Mifflin.

———. 1924b. The group fallacy in relation to social science. *Journal of Abnormal and Social Psychology* 19:60–73.

Anderson, J. R. and G. H. Bower. 1973. *Human associative memory*. Washington: Winston and Sons.

Appiah, A. 2008. *Experiments in ethics: The Mary Flexner lectures*. Cambridge, Mass.: Harvard University Press.

Armstrong, D. 1980. *A theory of universals*. Cambridge, U.K.: Cambridge University Press.

Aronoff, M. 2007. Language (linguistics). *Scholarpedia* 2(5): 3175. www.scholarpedia .org/article/Language_(linguistics).

Audi, P. 2009. An argument against disjunctive properties. Paul Audi's website. www.paulaudi.net/Audi_Disjunctive_Properties.pdf.

Axelrod, R. and D. Hamilton. 1981. The evolution of cooperation. *Science* 211:1390–96.

Bach, K. 1997. The semantics-pragmatics distinction: What it is and why it matters. *Linguistische Berichte: Special Issue on Pragmatics* 8:33–50.

Bandura, A. 1977. *Social learning theory*. New York: General Learning Press.

Barkow, J., L. Cosmides, and J. Tooby. 1992. *The adapted mind: Evolutionary psychology and the generation of culture*. Oxford, U.K.: Oxford University Press.

Baron-Cohen, S. 1995. *Mindblindness*. Cambridge, Mass.: MIT Press.

Bechtel, W. and J. Mundale. 1999. Multiple realizability revisited: Linking cognitive and neural states. *Philosophy of Science* 66:175–207.

Beiderman, I. 1987. Recognition by components: A theory of human image understanding. *Psychological Review* 94 (2): 115–47.

Bennett, J. 1991. Folk psychological explanations. In *The future of folk psychology*, edited by J. Greenwood. Cambridge, U.K.: Cambridge University Press.

————. 1988. *Events and their names.* Indianapolis: Hackett.

Bicchieri, C. 2006. *The grammar of society.* Cambridge, Mass.: MIT Press.

Bierstedt, R. 1963. *The social order.* 2nd ed. New York: McGraw-Hill.

Binmore, K. G. 1998. *Just playing: Game theory and the social contract.* Cambridge, Mass.: MIT Press.

Bishop, M. and S. Stich. 1998. The flight to reference, or how not to make progress in the philosophy of science. *Philosophy of Science* 65 (1): 33–49.

Blair, J. 1995. A cognitive developmental approach to morality. *Cognition* 57 (1): 1–29.

Block, N. 1993. Troubles with functionalism. In *Readings in philosophy and cognitive science.* Edited by A. Goldman. Cambridge, Mass.: MIT Press.

Bloom, P. and C. Veres. 1999. The perceived intentionality of groups. *Cognition* 71:B1–B9.

Bogdan, R. 1997. *Interpreting minds: The evolution of a practice.* Cambridge, Mass.: MIT Press.

Bontly, T. D. 2005. Exclusion, overdetermination, and the nature of causation. *Journal of Philosophical Research* 30:261–82.

Bower, G. and A. Glass. 1976. Structural units and the reintegrative power of picture fragments. *Journal of Experimental Psychology: Human Learning and Memory* 2:456–66.

Boyd, R. and P. Richerson. 1986. *Culture and the evolutionary process.* Chicago: University of Chicago Press.

————. 2005. *The origin and evolution of cultures.* Oxford, U.K.: Oxford University Press.

Bratman, Michael. 1999. *Faces of intention.* Cambridge, U.K.: Cambridge University Press.

Brennan, E. and J. Brennan. 1981. Measurements of accent and attitude toward Mexican-American speech. *Journal of Psycholinguistic Research* 10:487–501.

Bueno de Mesquita, B. 2009. *The predictioneer's game: Using the logic of brazen self-interest to see and shape the future.* New York: Random House.

Burt, R. 1982. *Towards a structural theory of action: Network models of social structure, perception, and action.* New York: Academic Press.

Buss, D. M. 1994. *The evolution of desire: Strategies of human mating.* New York: Basic Books.

Cabaco, Ó. 2002. Convencionalidad y significado sin uso. *Theoria: Revista de Teoria, Historia y Fundamentos de la Ciencia* 17 (45): 417–34.

Carlson, G. and J. Pelletier. 2003. *The generic book.* Chicago: University of Chicago Press.

Casasanto, D. 2009. *New directions in cognitive linguistics: When is a linguistic metaphor a conceptual metaphor?* Amsterdam, The Netherlands: John Benjamins Publishing.

Cavalli-Sforza, L. L. and W. M. Feldman. 1981. *Cultural transmission and evolution: A quantitative approach.* Princeton, N.J.: Princeton University Press.

Chattabox.com. 2010. Germany thinks Greece should sell islands to reduce debt. chattahbox.com/world/2010/03/04/germany-thinks-greece-should-sell-islands-to-reduce-debt/ (accessed May 4, 2010).

Chomsky, N. 1986. *Knowledge of language: Its nature, origin, and use.* New York: Praeger.

Churchland, P. M. 1979. *Scientific realism and the plasticity of mind.* Cambridge, U.K.: Cambridge University Press.

———. 1980. Plasticity: Conceptual and neuronal. *Behavioral and Brain Sciences* 3 (1): 133–34.

———. 1988. *Matter and consciousness.* Cambridge, Mass.: MIT Press.

———. 2005. Functionalism at forty: A critical retrospective. *Journal of Philosophy* 102 (1): 33–50.

Cinyaguguma, M., Putterman, L., and Page, T. 2004. On perverse and second-order punishment in public goods experiments with decentralized sanctions. Working paper, Department of Economics, Brown University, Providence, R.I.

Clark, A. 1994. Beliefs and desires incorporated. *Journal of Philosophy* 91 (8): 404–25.

Colby, B., D. Fernandez, and D. Kronenfeld. 1981. Toward a convergence of cognitive and symbolic anthropology. *American Ethnologist* 8 (3): 422–50.

Cook, J. 1980. The fate of ordinary language philosophy. *Philosophical Investigations* 3 (2): 1–72.

Cummins, R. 1975. Functional analysis. *Journal of Philosophy* 72 (20): 741–56.

Davies, M. and T. Stone. 1995. *Mental simulation: Evaluations and applications.* Oxford, U.K.: Blackwell.

Dawkins, R. 1976. *The selfish gene.* Oxford, U.K.: Oxford University Press.

Day, P. and P. Chen. 1993. *Nonlinear dynamics and evolutionary economics.* Oxford, U.K.: Oxford University Press.

Denzau, A. and D. North. 1995. *Shared mental models: Ideologies and institutions.* Unpublished manuscript.

DePaul, M. and W. Ramsey, W. 1998. *Rethinking intuition: The psychology of intuition and its role in philosophical inquiry.* Lanham, Md.: Rowman and Littlefield.

Dennett, D. 1978. *Brainstorms: Philosophical essays on mind and psychology.* Cambridge, Mass.: MIT Press.

———. 1987. *The intentional stance.* Cambridge, Mass.: MIT Press.

———. 1995. *Darwin's dangerous idea: Evolution and the meanings of life.* New York: Simon and Schuster.

Denzau, A. and D. North. 1995. *Shared mental models: Ideologies and institutions.* Unpublished manuscript.

Diamond, J. 1997. *Guns, germs and steel: The fates of human societies.* New York: Norton.

Durkheim, E. 2001 [1923]. *The elementary forms of religious life.* Oxford, U.K.: Oxford University Press.

Ebersole, F. 1979. *Meaning and saying.* Lanham, Md.: Rowman and Littlefield.

Ehrenreich, B. 1991. *The worst years of our lives.* New York: Random House.

Emerson, R. 1962. Power-dependence relations. *American Sociological Review* 27:31–40.

Erwin, E. 1993. Philosophers on Freudianism. In *Philosophical problems of the internal and external words: Essays on the philosophy of Adolf Grunbaum,* edited by J. Earman. Pittsburg: University of Pittsburg Press.

Etzioni, A. 2001. *The monochrome society.* Princeton, N.J.: Princeton University Press.

Faison, S. 1997. China exports its own uncertainty. *New York Times*, 26 October, 4.

Farrell, W. 1993. *The myth of male power: Why men are the disposable sex*. New York: Simon and Schuster.

Feldman, A. 1994. On cultural anesthesia: From Desert Storm to Rodney King. *American Ethnologist* 21 (2): 404–18.

Fodor, J. 1968. *Psychological explanation: An introduction to the philosophy of psychology*. New York: Random House.

———. 1993. *Special sciences: The philosophy of science*. Cambridge, Mass.: MIT Press.

———. 1994. *The elm and the expert: Mentalese and its semantics*. Cambridge, Mass.: MIT Press.

Flores, T. 1990. *An American profile: Opinions and behavior, 1972–1989*. Detroit, Mich.: Galeres.

Frank, R. 1988. *Passions within reason: The strategic role of the emotions*. New York: Norton.

Frankfurt, H. 1971. Freedom of the will and the concept of a person. *Journal of Philosophy* 68:5–20.

French, Peter. 1995. *Individual and collective responsibility*. New York: Schenkman Books.

Garfinkel, A. 1981. *Forms of explanation: Rethinking the questions in social theory*. New Haven, Conn.: Yale University Press.

Geertz, C. 1973. *The interpretation of cultures: Selected essays*. New York: Basic Books.

Gibbs, J. 1965. Norms: The problem of definition and classification. *American Journal of Sociology* 70 (5): 586–94.

———. 1968. Norms. *The international encyclopedia of philosophy*. New York: MacMillan.

Gilbert, M. 1989. *On social facts*. Princeton, N.J.: Princeton University Press.

———. 1996. *Living together*. Lanham, Md.: Rowan and Littlefield.

Gilovitch, T. 1991. *How we know what isn't so*. New York: Free Press.

Goldman, A. 1993. The psychology of folk psychology. *Behavioral and Brain Sciences* 16:15–28.

Goodman, N. 1976. *Languages of art*. Indianapolis: Hackett.

Gordon, R. 1986. Folk psychology as simulation. *Mind and Language* 1:158–71.

Gould, Emily. 2008. Exposed. *New York Times Magazine,* 25 May.

Grice, H. P. 1989. *Studies in the way of words*. Cambridge, Mass.: Harvard University Press.

Grice, J. 1988. *What makes a woman very sexy?* New York: Dodd, Meade, and Co.

Grunbaum, A. 1984. *The foundations of psychoanalysis: A philosophical critique*. Berkeley: University of California Press.

Hall, N. 2008. Causation. In *The Oxford handbook of contemporary philosophy*, edited by F. Jackson and M. Smith. Oxford, U.K.: Oxford University Press.

Hamilton, D. L., P. M. Dugan, and T. K. Trolier. 1985. The formation of stereotypic beliefs: Further evidence for distinctiveness-based illusory correlations. *Journal of Personality and Social Psychology* 48:5–17.

Hansson, B. 1975. *Explanation—of what?* Unpublished manuscript.

Harford, Tim. 2008. *The logic of life: The rational economics of an irrational world.* New York: Random House.

Harris, M. 1979. *Cultural materialism.* New York: Random House.

———. 2001. *The rise of anthropological theory.* Lanham, Md.: Rowman and Littlefield.

Haugeland, J. 1978. The nature and plausibility of cognitivism. *Behavioral and Brain Sciences* 1:215–26.

———. 1990. The intentionality all stars. *Philosophical perspectives, IV: Philosophy of mind and action theory.* Atsacadero, Calif.: Ridgeview.

Hechter, M. 1994. The role of values in rational choice theory. *Rationality and Society* 6 (3): 318–33.

Hechter, M. and K. Opp 2005. *Social norms.* Russell Sage Foundation Publications.

Heider, F. and M. Simmel. 1944. An experimental study of apparent behavior. *American Journal of Psychology* 57:243–59.

Henderson, D. 2005. Norms, invariance, and explanatory relevance. *Philosophy of the Social Sciences* 35 (3): 324–38.

Hempel, K. 1965. *Aspect of scientific explanation and other essays in the philosophy of science.* New York: The Free Press.

Hodgson, G. 2007. Meanings of methodological individualism. *Journal of Economic Methodology.* 14 (2): 211–26.

Holland, J., K. Holyoak, R. Nisbett, and P. Thagard. 1986. *Induction: Processes of inference, learning, and discovery.* Cambridge, Mass.: MIT Press.

Holyoak, K. and K. Koh. 1987. Surface and structural similarity in analogical transfer. *Memory and Cognition* 15:332–40.

Hutchins, E. 1995. *Culture in the wild.* Cambridge, Mass.: MIT Press.

Jackman, H. 1999. Convention and language. *Synthese: An International Journal for Epistemology, Methodology and Philosophy of Science* 117 (3): 295–312.

Jackson, F. and P. Pettit. 1992. *Structural explanation in social theory: Reductionism, explanation, and realism.* New York, N.Y.: Oxford University Press.

Johnson-Laird, P. 1993. *Human and machine thinking.* Hillsdale, N.J.: Lawrence Earlbam and Associates.

Jones, T. 1991. *Explaining culture: Doctoral dissertation.* Ann Arbor, Mich.: University Microfilms.

———. 1996. Methodological individualism in proper perspective. *Behavior and Philosophy* 24 (2): 119–28.

———. 1997. Thick description, fat syntax, and alternative conceptual schemes. *Pragmatics and Cognition* 1:131–62.

———. 1998. Interpretive social science and the native's point of view: A closer look. *Philosophy of the Social Sciences.* 28 (1): 32–68.

———. 1998. Unification, deduction, and history: A reply to Steel. *Philosophy of Science* 65:672–81.

———. 1999. FIC descriptions and interpretive social science: Should philosophers roll their eyes? *Journal for the Theory of Social Behavior.* 29 (4): 337–69.

———. 2000a. Ethnography, belief ascription, and epistemological barriers. *Human Relations* 53 (1): 117–52.

———. 2000b. Ethnography and sister sciences: Why refuse assistance? A Reply to Weeks. *Human Relations.* 53 (3): 299–310.

———. 2001. What CBS wants: How groups can have difficult to uncover intentions. *Philosophical Forum* 32 (3): 221–52.

———. 2002. The cultural relativity of cognition. In *Proceedings of the 2002 conference of the Association for Global Business and the International Academy of Linguistics, Behavioral, and Social Sciences* 13, edited by R. Keating. Madison, Wis.: Omnipress.

———. 2003. The failure of the best arguments against social reduction and what that failure doesn't mean. *Southern Journal of Philosophy* 41 (4): 547–81.

———. 2004a. Special sciences: Still a flawed argument after all these years. *Cognitive Science* 28 (3): 409–32.

———. 2004b. Reduction and anti-reduction: Rights and wrongs. *Metaphilosophy* 25 (5); 614–47.

———. 2006. We always have a beer after the meeting: How norms, customs, conventions, and the like explain behavior. *Philosophy of the Social Sciences* 36 (3): 251–75.

———. 2007. What's done here—explaining behavior in terms of customs and norms. *Southern Journal of Philosophy* 45 (3): 363–93.

———. 2008. Unification. In *The Routledge companion to the philosophy of science*, edited by S. Psillos and M. Curd. New York: Routledge.

———. 2011. Do customs compete with conditioning? Turf battles and division of labor in social explanation." Forthcoming in *Synthese.*

Kelly, D., S. Stitch, K. J. Haley, et al. 2007. Harm, affect, and the moral/conventional distinction. *Mind and Language* 222:117–31.

Kerr, N. L. 1995. *Social Dilemmas: Perspectives on individuals and groups: Norms in social dilemmas.* Westport, Conn.: Praeger.

Kim, J. 2000. *Mind in a physical world.* Cambridge, Mass.: MIT press.

———. 2005. *Physicalism, or something near enough.* Princeton, N.J.: Princeton University Press.

Kincaid, H. 1994. Reduction, explanation, and individualism. In *Readings in the philosophy of social science*, edited by M. Martin and L. C. McIntyre. Cambridge, Mass.: MIT Press.

Kitcher, P. 1984. 1953 and all that: A tale of two sciences. *Philosophical Review* 93 (3): 335–73.

Kripke, S. 1982. *Wittgenstein on rules and private language.* Cambridge, Mass.: Harvard University Press.

Kroeber, A., and C. Kluckholm. 1952. Culture: A critical review of concepts and definitions. *Papers of the Peabody Museum of American Archeology and Ethnology* 47 (1): 1–223.

Kuper, A. 1999. *Culture: The anthropologists' account.* Cambridge, Mass.: Harvard University Press.

Kutz, K. 2000. *Complicity.* Cambridge, U.K.: Cambridge University Press.

Lakoff, G. and M. Johnson. 1980. *Metaphors we live by.* Chicago: University of Chicago Press.

Lakoff, G. 1987. *Women, fire, and dangerous things: What categories reveal about the mind.* Chicago: University of Chicago Press.

———. 1993. The contemporary theory of metaphor. In *Metaphor and thought,* edited by A. Ortony. Cambridge, U.K.: Cambridge University Press.

Lahroodi, Reza. 2007. Collective epistemic virtues. *Social Epistemology* 21 (3): 281–97.

Lambert, T., A. Kahn, and K. Apple 2003. Pluralistic ignorance and hooking up. *Journal of Sex Research* 40 (2): 129–33.

Laudan, L. 1996. *Beyond positivism and relativism.* Boulder, Colo.: Westview Press.

———. 2006. *Truth, error, and criminal law.* Cambridge, U.K.: Cambridge University Press.

Laurence, S. and E. Margolis. 2003. Concepts and conceptual analysis. *Philosophy and Phenomenological Research.* 67:253–82.

Lee, Y., L. J. Jussim, and C. R. McCauley. 1995. *Stereotype accuracy.* Washington, D.C.: American Psych Association.

Le Foch, V. and A. Somat. 2003. Norm of internality, social utility of internal explanations, and cognitive functioning. In *A sociocognitive approach to social norms,* edited by Nicole Dubois. New York: Routledge.

Leiter, B. 2007. Explaining theoretical disagreement. University of Texas Law, Public Law Research Paper No. 124. papers.ssrn.com/sol3/papers.cfm?abstract _id=1004768 (accessed August 3, 2007).

Leslie, A. 1994. ToMM, ToBY, and agency: Core architecture and domain specificity. *Mapping the mind,* edited by L. Hirchfield and S. A. Gelman. Cambridge, U.K.: Cambridge University Press.

Levi-Strauss, C. 1963. *Structural anthropology.* New York: Basic Books.

Lewis, D. 1968. *Convention: A philosophical study.* Cambridge, Mass.: Harvard University Press.

———. 1986. Events. *Philosophical papers, volume II.* Oxford, U.K.: Oxford University Press.

———. 2002. *Convention.* New York: Blackwell.

Lifton, R. 1975. *Explorations in psychohistory: The Wellfleet papers.* New York: Simon and Schuster.

Lindholm, C. 1981. Leatherworkers and love potions. *American Ethnologist* 8 (3): 512–25.

Lipset, S. 1996. *American exceptionalism: A double-edged sword.* New York: Norton.

Lord, C., L. Ross, and M. Lepper. 1979. Biased assimilation and attitude polarization: The effects of prior theories on subsequently considered evidence. *Journal of Personality and Social Psychology* 37 (11): 2098–2109.

Low Seng Guan, V. 2010. China wants U.S. to set timetable on removal of curbs on trade in high-tech products. www.bernama.com/bernama/v5/newsbusiness .php?id=500811 (accessed May 24, 2010).

Lukacs, J. 2005. *Democracy and populism: Fear and hatred.* New Haven, Conn.: Yale University Press.

Lycan, W. 1981. Toward a homuncular theory of believing. *Cognition and Brain Theory* 4:139–59.

———. 1987. *Consciousness.* Cambridge, Mass.: Bradford.

———. 1988. *Judgment and justification.* Cambridge, U.K.: Cambridge University Press.

Lyons, W. 1995. *Approaches to intentionality.* Oxford, U.K.: Oxford University Press.

Mackie, J. 1974. *The cement of the universe: A study of causation.* Oxford, U.K.: Oxford University Press.

———. 1993. Causation. In *Causes and conditions,* edited by E. Sosa and M. Tooley. New York: Oxford.

Malinowski, B. 1922. *Argonauts of the western Pacific: An account of native enterprise and adventure in the archipelagoes of Melanesian New Guinea, series no. 65.* London: Routledge and Kegan Paul.

Marr, D. and H. Nishihara. 1978. Representation and recognition of the spatial organization of three-dimensional shape. *Proceedings of the Royal Society of London B* 200:269–94.

Mathiesen, K. 2009. Groups as epistemic agents. Address to the American Philosophical Association, Eastern Division Meeting. New York City. December.

May, L. and S. Hoffman. 1991. *Collective responsibility.* Lanham, Md.: Rowman and Littlefield.

McClelland, J. L. and D. D. Rumelhart. 1986. *Parallel distributed processing: Explorations in the microstructures of cognition.* Cambridge, Mass.: MIT Press.

Mellor, D. H. 1995. *The facts of causation.* London: Routledge.

Melnyk, M. 1995. Two cheers for reductionism: Or, the dim prospects for nonreductive materialism. *Philosophy of Science* 62 (3): 370–88.

Meltzoff, A. N. 1996. The human infant as imitative generalist: A 20-year progress report on infant imitation with implications for comparative psychology. In *Social learning in animals: The roots of culture,* edited by B. Heyes and C. Galef. Salt Lake City: Academia Press.

Miller, S. 2001. *Social action: A teleological account.* Cambridge, U.K.: Cambridge University Press.

Morris, W. M., O. J. Sheldon, D. R. Ames, et al. 2007. Metaphors and the market: Consequences and preconditions of agent and object metaphors in stock market commentary. *Organizational Behavior and Human Decision Processes* 102 (2): 174–92.

Morris, T. 1994. The neural basis of learning with particular reference to the role of synaptic placticity: Where are we a century after Cajal's speculations? In *Animal learning and cognition,* edited by N. Mackintosh. San Diego: Academic Press.

Morton, A. 2002. *The importance of being understood: Folk psychology as ethics.* New York: Routledge.

Munro, M., T. Derwig, and J. E. Flege. 1999. Canadians in Alabama: A perceptual study of dialect acquisition in adults. *Journal of Phonetics* 27:385–403.

Nadelhoffer, T. and Eddy Nahmias. 2007. The past and future of experimental philosophy. *Philosophical Explorations. Philosophical Explorations* 10 (2): 123–49.

Nagel, J. 2000. Ethnicity and sexuality. *Annual Review of Sociology* 26:107–33.

Needham, P. 2002. The discovery that water is H2O. *International Studies in the Philosophy of Science* 16 (3): 205–26.

Nelson, L. 1990. *Who knows: From Quine to a feminist empiricism.* Philadelphia: Temple University Press.

Nelson, R. and S. Winter. 1982. *An evolutionary theory of economic change.* Cambridge, Mass.: Harvard University Press.

Nisbett, R. and L. Ross. 1980. *Human inference: Strategies and shortcomings of social judgment.* Englewood Cliffs, N.J: Prentice-Hall.

Nucci, L.P. 2001. *Education in the moral domain.* Cambridge, U.K.: Cambridge University Press.

Ohnuki-Tierney, E. 1984. Text, play, and story. In *Monkey performances: A multiple structure of meaning and reflexivity in Japanese culture,* edited by E. Bruner. Washington, D.C.: American Ethnological Society.

Olson, J. M., N. J. Roese, and M. P. Zanna. 1996. Expectancies. In *Social psychology: Handbook of basic principles,* edited by E. T. Higgins and A. W. Kruglanski. New York: Guilford Press.

Palmer, S. 1977. Hierarchical structure in perceptual representation. *Cognitive Psychology* 9:441–74.

Pells, R. 1997. *Not like us: How Europeans have loved, hated, and transformed American culture since World War II.* New York: Basic Books.

Penczek, A. 1997. Disjunctive properties and causal efficacy. *Philosophical Studies* 86:203–19.

Perkins, W. H., M. Haines, and R. Rice. 2005. Misperceiving the college drinking norm and related problems: A nationwide study of exposure to prevention information, perceived norms, and student alcohol misuse. *Journal of Studies on Alcohol* 66:470–78.

Pettit, P. 2002. *Rules, reasons and norms.* Oxford, U.K.: Oxford University Press.

Quine, W. 1960. *Word and object.* Cambridge, Mass.: MIT Press.

———. 1970. On the reasons for the indeterminacy of translation. *Journal of Philosophy* 67:178–83.

Ramsey, W. 2007. *Representation reconsidered.* Cambridge, U.K.: Cambridge University Press.

Reynolds, G. 1968. *A primer of operant conditioning.* Glenview, Ill.: Foresman.

Rovane, C. 1998. *The bounds of agency: An essay in revisionary metaphysics.* Princeton, N.J.: Princeton University Press.

Rommetveit, R. 1955. *Social norms and roles.* Minneapolis: University of Minnesota Press.

Rorty, R. 1991. *Essays on Heidegger and others: Philosophical papers, volume 2.* Cambridge, U.K.: Cambridge University Press.

Rosenburg, A. 1988. *Philosophy of social science.* Boulder, Colo.: Westview Press.

Salmon, M. 2001. *Introduction to logic and critical thinking.* San Diego: Harcourt Brace.

Sandomir, R. 1998 How one network's urgency spelled riches for the N.F.L. *New York Times,* 17 January, sec. A1.

Sapir, D. 1981. Leper, hyena, and blacksmith in Kujamaat Diola thought. *American Ethnologist*, 8 (3): 526–43.

Sartorio, C. 2006. Disjunctive causes. *Journal of Philosophy* 103 (10): 521–38.

Satz, D. and J. Ferejohn. 1994. Rational choice and social theory. *Journal of Philosophy* 9 (102): 71–87.

Schama, S. 1995. *Landscape and memory.* New York: Knopf.

Schneider, D. 1985. *American kinship: A cultural account.* Chicago: University of Chicago Press.

Schultz, P., J. Nolan, R. Cialdini, R. Goldstein, and V. Griskevicius. 2007. The constructive, destructive, and reconstructive power of social norms. *Psychological Science* 18 (5): 429–34.

Searle. John. 1995. *The construction of social reality.* New York: Free Press.

Seeley, T. 1989. The honey bee colony as super organism. *American Scientist* 77:546–53.

Sherif, M. 1966. *In common predicament: Social psychology of intergroup conflict and cooperation.* Boston: Houghton-Mifflin.

Shore, B. 1996. Culture in mind. Cognition, culture, and the problem of meaning. Oxford, U.K.: Oxford University Press.

Sinha, A. 2010. India wants spotlight on per capita emissions. www.indianexpress .com/news/india-wants-spotlight-on-per-capita-emissions/615777/ (accessed May 6, 2010).

Sklar, L. 1985. *Philosophy and spacetime physics.* Berkeley: University of California Press.

Snow, C. P. 1959. *The two cultures and the scientific revolution.* Cambridge, U.K.: Cambridge University Press.

Sober, E. 1999. The multiple realizability argument against reductionism. *Philosophy of Science* 66:542–64.

Sobo, Elisa Janine. 1993. *One blood: The Jamaican body.* Albany, N.Y.: State University of New York Press.

Squire, L. 1987. *Memory and brain.* Oxford, U.K.: Oxford University Press.

Sripada, Chandra and S. Stich. 2006. A framework for the psychology of norms. In *The innate mind: Culture and cognition,* edited by P. Carruthers, S. Laurence, and S. Stich. Oxford, U.K.: Oxford University Press.

Steele, C. M., S. Spencer, and J. Aronson. 2002. Contending with group image: The psychology of stereotype and social identity threat. In *Advances in experimental social psychology vol. 37,* edited by M. Zanna. Salt Lake City: Academic Press.

Stich, S. 1980. Grammar, psychology, and indeterminacy. In *Readings in philosophy of psychology, volume 2,* edited by N. Block. London: Methuen.

———. 1983. *From folk psychology to cognitive science: A case against belief.* Cambridge, Mass.: MIT Press.

———. 1998. *Deconstructing the mind.* Oxford, U.K.: Oxford University Press.

Stich, S. and I. Ravenscroft. 1994. What is folk psychology? *Cognition* 50:447–68.

Stich, S. and S. Nichols. 1997. Cognitive penetrability, rationality and restricted simulation. *Mind and Language* 12:297–326.

Sturges, G. 1972. 1000+1000=5000: Estimating crowd size. *Society* 9:42–63.

Squire, L. 1987. *Memory and brain.* Oxford, U.K.: Oxford University Press.

Surowieki, J. 2004. *The wisdom of crowds: Why the many are smarter than the few and how collective wisdom shapes business, economies, societies, and nations.* London: Little, Brown, and Co.

Swain, S., J. Alexander, and J. Weinberg. 2008. The instability of philosophical intuitions: Running hot and cold on truetemp. *Philosophy and Phenomenological Research* 76:138–55.

Tajfel, H. 1970. Experiments in intergroup discrimination. *Scientific American* 223:96–102.

Triandis, H. C. 1977. *Interpersonal behavior.* Indianapolis: Wiley.

Tuomela, R. 2002. *Philosophy of social practices: A collective acceptance view.* Cambridge, U.K.: Cambridge University Press.

Turiel, E. 1979: Distinct conceptual and developmental domains: Social convention and morality. In *Nebraska symposium on motivation, 1977: Social cognitive development,* edited by H. Howe, H. and C. Keasey. Lincoln: University of Nebraska Press.

Van Buskirk, E. 2010. Harvard-based crowdsource project seeks new diabetes answers—and questions. *Wired.* www.wired.com/epicenter/2010/02/crowdsourcing -rewires-harvard-medical-researchers-brain/#ixzz0ppqz5CxA (accessed February 3, 2010).

de Waal, F. 1997. *Good natured: The origin of right and wrong in humans and other animals.* Cambridge, Mass.: Harvard University Press.

Waller, B. 1997. What rationality adds to animal morality. *Biology and Philosophy* 12:341–56.

Wilson, D. and E. Sober. 1994. Reintroducing group selection to the human behavioral sciences. *Behavioral and Brain Sciences* 17:585–654.

Wilson, M. 1959. *Communal rituals of the Nyakyusa.* Oxford, U.K.: Oxford University Press.

Wolfson, N. 1989. *Perspectives: Sociolinguistics and TESOL.* Cambridge, Mass.: Newbury House.

Woodyard, C. 2010. *Toyota hopes to price hydrogen cars at $50,000.* content.usa today.com/communities/driveon/post/2010/05/toyota-hopes-to-price-hydrogen -cars-at-50000/1 (accessed May 10, 2010).

Wyer, S. R. and T. K. Srull. 1986. Human cognition in its social context. *Psychological Review* 93:322–59.

Index

agent: group as, xiv–xv, xxi, 49–53, 61–62, 76 , 91, 98–99, 102nn3–5, 103n6, 172, 175, 181, 186–87
Allport, Floyd H., 50, 139n13
anthropology and anthropologists, xix, 3, 108, 129
armies, 63, 65, 72

Bayesian, 5
belief/desire theory. *See* folk psychology
belief perseverance, 25–26, 188
biology, 58, 94

causal closure, 164
causal exclusion, 167–69
causation, xx, 123, 144, 153–58
Chief Executive Officers (CEOs), 102n3. *See also* corporations
cognitive science and cognitive scientists, 36, 89, 92
conditioning, 17, 99, 117–18, 123, 140, 153–54, 158, 162; and the causal exclusion principle, 167; as cause of "what's done" behaviors, 111; as part of custom or norm, 158, 165–66; operant, 104
conformity, 111–13, 117–23, 127–29, 133, 137, 153

consciousness, 83, 102n4
convention, viii, xiv, xvi–xviii, 4, 7, 11, 15, 142, 186; as distinct from other "what's done" terms, 105–7, 109–10, 119, 127, 132. *See also* linguistic conventions
corporations, xiv, 19, 51, 67, 73, 102–4, 170, 172; CEOs of, 102
countries (with beliefs or desires), xii, xv–xviii, xxi, 3–4, 51, 53, 170
culture, xii, xiv–xvi, xviii, xxiii, 11, 27, 83–84, 86, 142, 155–56, 160, 162–64, 177n5; as distinct from other "what's done" terms, 108, 119, 128–29, 133, 140n5
customs, xi–xii, xvi–xvii, xxi, 3–4, 130–31, 133, 134n1, 136n2–3, 137n3–38n7, 139n9, 140n15, 141–42, 144–45, 147, 149–53, 155–56, 158, 162–70, 176n2, 179–81, 185–86, 197; as distinct from other "what's done" terms, 105–7, 109–115, 127

Dawkins, Richard, 67
Dennett, Daniel, 54–55, 60, 73–75, 79, 96–97
disjunctive causes, 155–57, 165–66, 168–70, 177n5

211

Breinigsville, PA USA
15 October 2010
247408BV00003B/3/P